HITCHCOCK'S BRITISH FILMS

HITCHCOCK'S BRITISH FILMS

SECOND EDITION

MAURICE YACOWAR

WITH A FOREWORD BY BARRY KEITH GRANT

WAYNE STATE UNIVERSITY PRESS
DETROIT

First edition published by Shoe String Press / Archon Books 1977, © Maurice Yacowar 1977.

All photos are courtesy of the British National Film Archive.

14 13 12 11 10   5 4 3 2 1

Library of Congress Cataloging-in-Publication Data

Yacowar, Maurice.
Hitchcock's British films / Maurice Yacowar. – 2nd ed.
        p. cm. – (Contemporary approaches to film and television series)
Includes bibliographical references and index.
ISBN 978-0-8143-3494-2 (pbk. : alk. paper)
1. Hitchcock, Alfred, 1899–1980.   I. Title.
PN1998.A3H59 2010
791.43'0233'092–dc22

2010016188

Typeset by Westchester
Composed in Dante

To Ruth, with love and thanks
For happy memories

CONTENTS

Contents

FOREWORD

With the republication of Maurice Yacowar's *Hitchcock's British Films,* both traditional Hitchcocko-Hawksians and younger post-whatever turks will have cause to rejoice. This, the first book devoted to the twenty-three films directed by Alfred Hitchcock in his native England before he came to the United States at the invitation of David O. Selznick, was originally published in a limited cloth run by a small New England press more than three decades ago and has long been out of print. Since then, of course, there have been other books on this period of Hitchcock's work, notably Tom Ryall's *Alfred Hitchcock and the British Cinema* (1986) and Charles Barr's *English Hitchcock* (1999), not to mention numerous book chapters and journal articles on such individual films as *Blackmail.* But Yacowar's was there before them.

As such, it was the first book to challenge the orthodox opinion of the time that Hitchcock's "mature" period in Hollywood, from the late 1940s to the early 1960s, constituted the director's best work. In his pioneering and highly influential *Hitchcock's Films* (1965), Robin Wood flatly dismissed Hitchcock's British films as "little more than 'prentice work" and did not discuss any of them, asking, "Who wants the leaf-buds when the rose has opened?" His conclusion that "the notion that the British films are better than, or as good as, or comparable with the later Hollywood ones seems to me not worth discussion" became the prevailing view, despite Wood's retraction of this judgment more than twenty years later in *Hitchcock's Films Revisited* (1989) as "completely indefensible."

But Yacowar's *Hitchcock's British Films* is important not simply because it was the first on the subject. As a traditional auteurist analysis, it is as perceptive and as well argued as Wood's more widely known book, offering imaginative discussions of every film Hitchcock made through 1939. Rereading it after many years has given me renewed admiration for Yacowar's work. Virtually all of his readings remain illuminating, and some—on *Downhill*, *Champagne*, and *Waltzes from Vienna*—are still practically the only extended interpretations of these films. Yacowar is a critic who writes not only with insight but also with marvelous attention to textual detail and a welcome wit. Readers will particularly appreciate the chapters on both lesser films like *The Pleasure Garden*, *Downhill*, *The Ring*, and *The Manxman*, and important works such as *Murder!*, the first *The Man Who Knew Too Much*, *Secret Agent*, *The Lady Vanishes*, and *Blackmail*. Yacowar's ability to read ethical and metaphysical meanings out of some of Hitchcock's technical tours de force is both impressive and convincing, and the conclusion is one of the best overviews of Hitchcock as auteur ever published. Yacowar also is especially informative regarding Hitchcock's use of the novels and plays that were the sources of most of his screenplays.

Yacowar may have had to argue more than is necessary today that Hitchcock's films are worthy of revaluation and close attention, just as Wood felt compelled to begin his book by asking, "Why should we take Hitchcock seriously?" Such defensiveness is reflective of the time when these books were first published, but as with Wood, Yacowar's analyses admirably provide the answer. Yacowar would subsequently publish auteurist studies of the films of Woody Allen and Mel Brooks, but in my view his first book on Hitchcock was his best work. *Hitchcock's British Films* remains the most illuminating and comprehensive discussion of Hitchcock's work before he moved to California, and much of the work that has followed has extended and expanded on insights first offered in it.

BARRY KEITH GRANT
2010

PREFACE TO THE SECOND EDITION

I have mixed feelings as I reread my thirty-three-year-old book for reissue. There are bits I almost suspect someone else must have written. There my odd "Good point!" is outnumbered by "Where did he get that?"

Is it still "my" Hitchcock? Yes, because when one of these films pops up I'm riveted afresh. Though I usually see what I saw then, I'm also struck by different details and connections. The films still reward re-viewings. Of course my current readings would be deepened by the mass of intervening scholarship, especially the biographies by Donald Spoto and John Russell Taylor; Dan Auiler's work on Hitchcock's notebooks; the close individual film readings by—inter alia—Charles Barr and William Rothman; and especially Tania Modleski's, Leslie Brill's, and Robert Samuels's explorations into Hitchcock's treatment of women. I worked in a very different world then. But as I cannot redo the study, I offer this document of its time, its errors (I hope mainly) corrected, its prose smoothed, but nothing rethought.

Happily, I still find these early Hitchcocks rich enough to justify my very close reading. I am not embarrassed by my enthusiasm. Nor by my unfashionable auteurism, which even in his 1977 review the late maestro Robin Wood declared "now generally regarded as obsolete." For however vital a film's social and historic contexts, I still believe in working out the organizing intelligence behind a film. If the function of art is to communicate, to make a human connection, then the social or political influences on a work surely should not disqualify the authorial voice. However symptomatic of its time and place, a work is also somebody's story. Someone pulled together the disparate inputs, whether compositional, technical, or performative. We deny the work's humanity if we don't deal with what that motive intelligence has chosen to reveal. So long as someone tells a story—or the story is retold—the author is not dead.

Nor is auteurism, though we may have a different form. In Andrew Sarris's original import from the *Cahiers du cinema* critics, auteurism meant the tension between the dominant artist—usually the director—and the conventional material with which s/he—usually a he—worked, usually on assignment. So, for example, a Howard Hawks John Wayne differs tellingly from a John Ford John Wayne. Hitchcock's British films show him this kind of auteurist, beaming a distinctive shiver and twinkle through a surprisingly wide range of familiar genres. Through his American classics and his television series appearances, his strong persona drew him toward the later notion of auteur, a maker of such personal films he seemed unfettered by genre or narrative conventions. He became less like Hawks and Ford and more like Chaplin, Bergman, Buñuel, Fellini, Godard, Ozu, Tati—names to conjure with still. In American film today Kathryn Bigelow and Oliver Stone typify the first form of auteur, working in tension with familiar material. The more personal cinema is maintained by Woody Allen, the Coens, Hal Hartley, and Gus Van Sant in America and, for example, Michael Haneke and Lars von Trier abroad.

Like auteurism, Hitchcock is enjoying a considerable resurrection. His brand has clearly erased any Best Before . . . date. University courses are dedicated to him. (When I last taught one all my students were younger than my book. I retired.) His television series is reviving on DVD, along with the feature canon. Newsletters, conferences, and websites are harvesting Hitchcock anew. In 2001 the Montreal Museum of Fine Arts mounted a major art exhibition centered on his films. I am hardly alone in my ardor.

I am embarrassed by my errors, enough to make me feel like the Ricky Gervais of film scholarship. In explanation not excuse, I was working on the savage frontier, that is, before the pause button and rewind of the videocassette. Again, it was a very different world. My writing was necessarily based on a single viewing and—usually—the foolhardy diligence of note taking in the dark. The video revolution has enabled multiple viewings, home/office screenings, checking one's notes against the work itself, and access to supporting materials. Writing this book today, I could also access Hitchcock's American films to supplement the

British—and more works from his cohort. Digital access provides the sharpest detailing, in image and sound, that these films have ever enjoyed. This is vital for a director so punctilious that even—especially?—his apparent lapses—the miniatures in *The Lady Vanishes,* the false backdrops in *Marnie*—rather provide cogent metaphors. Mainly, I would not be as dependent on my—famously flawed—memory.

Back in the day, the 16 mm rental market offered very few of these films in Canada, so I spent my first sabbatical summer in London. I booked private screenings at the British Film Institute, where I was occasionally joined by John Russell Taylor, who was then writing Hitch's biography. He generously translated colloquialisms for me—including the extracinematic. In a Soho alley one lunchtime, a lady asked me first for a light, then if I wanted "any business." I was intrigued by her phrasing, until the worldlier Mr. Taylor explained that no (alas) she was not offering me a backup career. She expected me to pay her. That charming boyish naivete sustains me still. I supplemented the BFI screenings with a week at a Library of Congress Steenbeck (sans translator).

Long resigned to having my major goofs re-cited on my tombstone, I'm especially grateful for the present opportunity to correct them. For example, as *everybody* knows, the investigator in *Psycho* is the admirable Arbogast (Martin Balsam), not the Bogardus (Neville Brand) who snuck in from *The Tin Star* (Anthony Mann, 1957) and caught me napping at the switch. Though I diligently restored the "!" in *Murder!* I consistently misrepresented the title *Number Seventeen* as *No. 17* (shorthand run amok) and gave Hitchcock's *Secret Agent* the redundant "The" from Joseph Conrad's rhyming but irrelevant novel. Mea culpa. Where was the Internet Movie Data Base when I needed it?

As for the errors in detail and in judgment that survive here, perhaps the reader might regard them as equivalent to the defects deliberately worked into Persian carpets to preclude pride. More than anything else, rereading one's thirty-year-old text sure does ratchet up the humility.

For that, too, my warmest thanks to Wayne State University Press for resurrecting my first film book after thirty-three years. In particular I am grateful to Barry Keith Grant for his initiative and most generous words and to Annie Martin, Kristin Harpster Lawrence, Maya Rhodes, and Carissa Vardanian for their excellent work.

ACKNOWLEDGMENTS TO THE
FIRST EDITION

I wish to thank the Canada Council and Brock University for the sabbatical and research grants that enabled me to write this book. Special thanks are due to Barbara Humphreys and the staff at the Motion Picture Section of the Library of Congress, Jeremy Boulton and the staff at the National Film Archive in London, and Serge Losique at the Conservatoire d'Art Cinematographique in Montreal for their generous help. I am indebted to Ms. Jenny Gursky and her staff for their quick and reliable stenographic assistance.

Stills from the following films are reproduced by courtesy of the Rank Organization: *The Pleasure Garden, Downhill, The Man Who Knew Too Much, The 39 Steps, Secret Agent, Sabotage, Young and Innocent,* and *The Lady Vanishes.*

Stills from the following films are reproduced courtesy of EMI Film Distributors: *The Farmer's Wife, The Manxman, Blackmail, Murder!, Rich and Strange,* and *Number Seventeen.*

Introduction

Alfred Hitchcock is considered one of the world's greatest filmmakers because of his sublimely cinematic imagination, his technical and thematic experimentation, and that run of masterpieces from *Rear Window* (1954) through *The Birds* (1963).

But Hitchcock studies have centered too exclusively on his later period. In England there remains an enthusiastic preference for his classic comedy thrillers from *The Man Who Knew Too Much* (1934) through *The Lady Vanishes* (1938). Chabrol and Rohmer single out Hitchcock's silent *The Manxman* (1929), along with *Rich and Strange* (1932), *Under Capricorn* (1949), and *The Wrong Man* (1957), as "ses oeuvres les plus sinceres, ses 'films purs.' "[1] But the most common critical preference is for the period covered by Robin Wood in his seminal study from *Strangers on a Train* (1951) through *Marnie* (1964).[2] This attention to his later work elevated Hitchcock (and popular film in general) to critical respectability; but it came at the unnecessary cost of attention to his earlier work.

Apart from *The Lodger, The Ring, Blackmail,* and *Murder!* Hitchcock's earliest films are rarely shown. Kirk Bond and John Smith have written papers on the early Hitchcock,[3] and *Blackmail* has received occasional study, but otherwise little critical attention has been paid to Hitchcock's first films.

This is surprising, for the early films are a remarkably fruitful area of study for anyone interested in Hitchcock, in British film, or in aesthetics in general. Hitchcock was from the outset a brilliant experimenter in cinematic expression. Of course, he never claimed to be an artist. He has always pretended to be just an entertainer. But, as Rachael Low observes, "Hitchcock ... without bothering about pronouncements made a first sound film which suggested how the new element could be used as an integral part of film technique. Had Hitchcock been German, Russian or French, had he even presented himself as a more bohemian figure, he would almost certainly have been taken more seriously ... his flexible and inventive handling of film structure was regarded merely as ingenious continuity, and not seen for what it was, the exploration of the film's unique quality."[4] In his interviews and in his later television appearances, Hitchcock cultivated the persona of an insolent, macabre trickster. He laid no claims for himself as an artist.

Nor has he ever acted like "The Artist." He always seems more like a businessman. Visitors to the set of *Family Plot,* his fifty-third feature film, in California in 1975, reported an air of businesslike formality around the director, in his white shirt, tie, and dark business suit.[5] Even in his films, Hitchcock dressed his artists like businessmen: the murdered painter in *Blackmail,* the suicide in *Easy Virtue,* and the artist in *The Trouble with Harry.* Sir John in *Murder!,* Mr. Memory in *The 39 Steps,* and the musicians in *The Man Who Knew Too Much* confirm the discipline and rigor that Hitchcock associates with the arts, principles intrinsic to his well-known filmmaking methods, which involve meticulous preplanning and structuring. From this extremely rigorous attitude nevertheless emerges some of the liveliest film we have. The early British films show the clear beginnings of this Hitchcock spirit.

From the beginning there is Hitchcock's essential irony. His art is always that of false appearances, especially where smug security is upset by the revelation of deeper disorder. Hitchcock's heroes are consistently deprived of their security, be it their parental approval, their lover's trustworthiness, or their country's protection. Hitchcock's fascination with stairs, we shall see, is a direct expression of his preoccupation with instability, for the image of stairs immediately suggests the dangers of frightening heights or threatening basements. If the title *Vertigo* suggests this anxiety in his later work, the title of his third finished feature was *Downhill*!

For Hitchcock, irony is both a matter of technique and a style of life. He delights in presenting a public persona quite different from whatever his true self may be. And as characterizes the ironic artist, his work is less a matter of statement than a series of tests for his audience, a challenge to its independence from his sleight of hand and tricky tone. Hitchcock continually tricks his audience with against-the-grain casting; anticonventional settings and symbols; moral inconsistencies, charming villains, and culpable heroes; and a persistent subversion of the viewer's values. At the end, the viewer should find himself exposed by the film—bereft of his detachment from the work and of his independence of its maker, and committed unawares to a complex moral position by (for example) his attitude toward Norman Bates, Marnie, or Cary Grant. We go to a Hitchcock movie expecting to be tricked. The master invariably obliges. He also traps us into questionable moral commitments, having maneuvered our sentiments against our weaker morality.

Hitchcock's earliest films cover a surprising range of genres. Only three films—*The Lodger, Blackmail,* and *Murder!*—of his first seventeen features are the type of thrillers for which he is famous. Of the rest, four are dramas, four are romantic dramas, three are romantic comedies, two are musicals, and one is a parody.

And yet in whatever genre Hitchcock worked, all the films show his technical ingenuity and almost all reveal his characteristic themes: the paralleling of an innocent with a guilty; the conflict between love and duty, or selfish interest and public responsibility, or freedom and morality; and his vision of man's quavering illusion of order over an indomitable chaos. There are even early occurrences of typical Hitchcock shots: the staircases, the ladies' legs, the shadows imported from German expressionism, and even the X pattern by which the human soul is characterized as a combination of contraries. The charm of the early Hitchcock does not depend on our knowledge of his later art, however; by and large the films are enjoyable in themselves. The plots are efficiently unwound, the characters always interesting and often surprising, and the style always witty.

But the early films gain from our sense of the auteur Hitchcock behind them. We can trust our responses to their riches because we know what an artist he was to become and how little he relies on accident.

Of course, Hitchcock did not make the films by himself. Certainly large credit is due, for example, to Eliot Stannard, who wrote the screenplays for *The Pleasure Garden*, *The Mountain Eagle*, *The Lodger*, *Downhill*, *Easy Virtue*, *Champagne*, and *The Manxman*. Charles Bennett wrote *Blackmail*, the first *The Man Who Knew Too Much*, *The 39 Steps*, *Secret Agent*, *Sabotage*, and *Young and Innocent*. Hitchcock was well served by his photographers, too: Baron Ventigmilia on *The Pleasure Garden* and *The Mountain Eagle* and Hal Young on *The Lodger*. Jack Cox shot an impressive list of Hitchcock films: *The Ring*, *The Farmer's Wife*, *Champagne*, *The Manxman*, *Blackmail*, *Juno and the Paycock*, *Murder!*, *The Skin Game*, *Rich and Strange*, *Number Seventeen*, and *The Lady Vanishes*. Then there are the contributions by Alma Reville, who is credited on eighteen Hitchcock films, Ian Hay, and Ivor Montagu. But for all the others' efforts, the films remain Hitchcock's because of his control over each project and the spirit that emerges from them. As Louis Levy, one of Hitchcock's favorite musical directors, recalls, "It was obvious that he knew nothing of the notes, and tempo, orchestration, or anything of the technicalities. But he has a way of expressing himself so clearly that I always left our musical conferences with a tune written clearly in my mind, almost as though Hitchcock himself had written it."[6] So, too, the brilliance of *North by Northwest* lies in Ernest Lehman's success at writing a typical Hitchcock script. One must acknowledge the contributions of the other members of Hitchcock's team, but the films are finally his own.

The unique personality of Hitchcock's work is evident in a kind of ur-film, a story he wrote in 1919 for the first issue of the *Henley*, the social club magazine of the Henley Cable Company, for which Hitchcock worked as a young man before he worked in film:

GAS

She had never been in this part of Paris before—only reading of it in the novels of Duvain, or seeing it at the Grand Guignol. So this was the Montmartre? That horror where danger lurked under cover of night; where innocent souls perished without warning—where doom confronted the unwary—where the Apache reveled.

She moved cautiously in the shadow of the high wall, looking furtively backward for the hidden menace that might be dogging her steps. Suddenly she darted into an alley way, little heeding where it led . . . groping her way on in the inky blackness, the one thought of eluding the pursuit firmly fixed in her mind . . . on she went. . . . Oh! When would it end? . . . Then a doorway from which a light streamed lent itself to her vision. . . . In here . . . anywhere, she thought.

The door stood at the head of a flight of stairs . . . stairs that creaked with age as she endeavoured to creep down . . . then she heard the sound of drunken laughter and shuddered—surely this was—No, not that. Anything but that! She reached the foot of the stairs and saw an evil-smelling wine bar, wrecks of what were once men and women indulging in a drunken orgy . . . then they saw her, a vision of affrighted purity. Half a dozen men rushed toward her amid the encouraging shouts of the rest. She was seized. She screamed with terror . . . better had she been caught by her pursuer was her one fleeting thought as they dragged her roughly across the room. The fiends lost no time in settling her fate. They would share her belongings . . . and she . . . Why! Was this not the heart of Montmartre? She should go—the rats would feast. Then they bound her and carried her down the dark passage; up a flight of stairs to the riverside. The water rats should feast, they said. And then . . . then, swinging her bound body to and fro, dropped her with a splash into the dark, swirling waters. Down she went, down, down. Conscious only of a choking sensation, this was death . . . then . . . "It's out, Madam," said the dentist. "Half a crown, please."[7]

This vignette bears several of the trademarks of Hitchcock's film work. The "affrighted purity" beset by not just a nameless and faceless threat but by a double set of enemies—the pursuer and the threatening, false "refuge"—anticipates Hitchcock's basic pursuit thriller: Hannay hounded by police and spies, Thornhill charged with murder and fleeing spies, Norman Bates wracked by his projections of the beautiful tease on the one hand and the stern mother on the other. The image of the heroine in bondage anticipates Hitchcock's fascination with handcuffs—*The Ring, Number Seventeen, The 39 Steps, Saboteur.* France has the same threatening atmosphere for the young innocent here as in *Downhill.* The scene itself is Hitchcock's mélange of unyielding stone walls, taunting shadows, and a creaking, frightening staircase. At the end, the threat materializes as the homey dentist—as it will in the first *The Man Who Knew Too Much.* The threat is dispelled.

Or is it? The dangers that lurk in the mind, freed by ether, are so much worse than those of the actual streets.

Hitchcock tells his little story in a series of elliptical, sharp images, the kind of montage by which he would represent the fevered mind in *Downhill* and *The Ring,* where the conventional storyteller allowed himself exercises in the form of the French avant-garde. There is even Hitchcock's coy sexuality: those fiends would enjoy the damsel's . . . belongings?

The basic stance of the piece is a key to Hitchcock's later work. He sets up a fantasy of horror, tenuously attached to a normal situation, to give his audience the vicarious thrill of suffering the central figure's fear. He defines a frightening scene, only at the last pulling back to reveal its harmlessness. Of course, on a rereading the whole thing is clear; it's in the title, "Gas," but only on the second time through. Writing in a company bulletin in 1919, Hitchcock is already a bogeyman, already a tease.

Two elements in the story deserve fuller comment. First, why should the girl specify the revels of an Apache in her early dread? The name of the warlike American Indian came to be applied to a band of robbers and assassins around Paris in the early 1900s. By 1928, the term was domesticated enough to be the name of a loud hat-style. The Apache might be summoned by the rhyme between the Indian's and the dentist's headbands. That roots the fantasy in reality. Her dread of the dentist, of course, sets off her nightmare, though the gas frees it. The Apache is her projection of the dentist.

Then there is the conclusion, when her choking at the tooth's removal suggests her death by drowning. She is snapped out of her nightmare by the genial dentist. Here we have an approximation to

Hitchcock's later career. Whether to dentist or to film, the customer comes, submits to a frightening fantasy, then pays for having it "out" (the tooth, the dream, the tension), the whole macabre exchange performed by a polite and businesslike professional. The dentist may seem a savage threat to the girl, but he anticipates the filmmaker: the salutary freer of phantoms.

And so to our present study. Our objective is to provide a detailed description and analysis of each of Hitchcock's first twenty-three features, covering his first fifteen years of filmmaking. Most of the films have not been widely shown for decades, so the plot summaries may at times seem longer and more detailed than would be necessary if we were discussing *Strangers on a Train* or *Psycho*.

In a number of ways, the present approach may seem arbitrary. First, the study might have included the two wartime shorts Hitchcock filmed in England, or the features that he returned to England to make—*Under Capricorn, Stage Fright, Frenzy*—or even the oh-so-English film that marked his American debut, *Rebecca*. All are arguably films of a British stance and tone. But for purposes of convenience, the study focuses on the features that he made before moving to America. They happen to include his most neglected films.

Second, there might be some objection to my kind of analysis. But with so many approaches possible to a lively film, no analysis can pretend to comprehensiveness. I am content to leave the social and political contexts of the films to Raymond Durgnat's valuable study.[8] Instead, I analyze the way each film works within itself as a drama of themes and devices. Wherever possible, I have compared the film to the original literary work for indication of the redirections Hitchcock emphasized. Wherever possible, too, I have worked with the screenplays and dialogue sheets. If my method seems old-fashioned and literary, I have the consolation that Hitchcock could be charged with the same vices, along with a remarkable richness of verbal suggestiveness, irony, and ambiguity. Though Hitchcock is unmatched in his expressiveness, his cinematic intuition, and his sense of experiment, few other filmmakers in English have such verbal brilliance. Moreover, Hitchcock's own roots are clearly in the Edwardian melodramas and novels, so it is not inappropriate to apply literary analysis to his films, provided we remain alert to his cinematic artistry.

Introduction

This book offers a series of self-contained studies of the individual films. An appendix proposes several kinds of significance in Hitchcock's distinctive appearances in his films. Otherwise, no attempt has been made to impose either a classification on the films or a single thematic overview in their interpretation. If this deprives the study of a clear thrust in argument, one hopes it will respect each film's coherence and liveliness.

The Pleasure Garden
1925

Hitchcock's first complete feature film—*The Pleasure Garden*—was made by an already experienced hand. Hitchcock began as a title designer and writer when the American Famous Players–Lasky company opened an office in London in 1920. From his typically unpretentious remarks on this work to Truffaut, we can infer that Hitchcock's work was already expressing his personality. "Very naive" he calls one of his effects, where he used a candle burning at both ends to illustrate that "George was leading a very fast life by this time."[1] The joke may seem naive today, but in the early 1920s it must have been fresh to find a title that played its pictorials lively against the words instead of flatly repeating them or—more commonly—neglecting the title card's potential.

In 1922 Hitchcock directed a two-reeler with Clare Greet and Ernest Thesiger, *Number Thirteen*, but it was not completed. When Hugh Croise fell ill during the production of *Always Tell Your Wife*, Hitchcock finished it with the star Seymour Hicks. Then for five films directed by Graham Cutts—*Woman to Woman, The White Shadow, The Passionate Adventure, The Blackguard,* and *The Prude's Fall*—from 1922 to 1925, Hitchcock worked as writer, assistant director, and art director. He "was even sent out to turn the camera now and again."[2] Then

Michael Balcon sent him to Munich to direct an Anglo-German production based on Oliver Sandys's novel *The Pleasure Garden*.

Any suspicion—or hope—that we may be in for an Arabian Nights delight is dispelled by the credit sequence. A single spotlight shows a nightclub dancer convulsively dancing for an unseen audience. The title's Pleasure Garden is a nightclub.

The film has the glamour of the club romance but with the moral rigor we might expect of a young, working-class director. Hitchcock sharply details the moral laxity of the Pleasure Garden patrons. The men are hot, leering, lip-smacking, however elegant. The women doze. One man turns binoculars on the line of dancing legs. To focus on his favorite, he shifts to the more intimate monocle. Both visual aids detach the man from the woman.

With the Hitchcock touch, the man's leering devotion to the ladies is expressed by his ire when a passing customer steps on his foot. The dozing lady deflates the impression of hilarity that the hot faces of the men might suggest. Already there is the Hitchcock leg shot—glamorous, alluring. There is even a spiral staircase down which the girls clamber in the first shot. Hitchcock masks off the sides of the screen, as if the whole world were shrunk to that staircase. For the men of binoculars and monocles, all asteam, the world *is* that narrow.

But not for Hitchcock. He develops four contrasting settings, each with its own character and moral values: the Pleasure Garden, the showgirl's modest flat, the honeymoon setting at Lake Como, and the jungle proper. The Pleasure Garden is a false image of the jungle, as the Lake Como scenes will provide a false romantic harmony, and as the ambitious showgirl's palace is a false parallel to the modest girl's homey flat.

The plot reverses the story of the worldly city mouse and the naive country mouse. Patsy Brand (Virginia Valli) is a worldly nightclub dancer. When the monocle man tells her he has fallen in love with her blonde kiss-curl, she removes it and hands it to him. She's no blonde, but events will prove her to be both a patsy and a brand.

Patsy takes under her wing an ambitious hoofer from the country, Jill Cheyne (Carmelita Geraghty), who is robbed on her arrival in the city and is saved by Patsy from the various fates worse than death. By a kind of moral hydraulics, however, or by what Hitchcock scholars came to discuss as the transference of guilt, the contamination of innocence, or the improbability of unadulterated virtue, the sophisticated Patsy shows herself to be increasingly warm and sincere, while the supposedly innocent Jill develops airs, greed, and callousness. When Patsy rescues her from the predatory stagedoor Johnnies, Jill flashes a smile back at them. Is she a flirt or just gullible? The country mouse proves cunning. Offered a job at five pounds a week, she immediately holds out for (and gets) twenty. She throws Boss Hamilton (George Snell) that over-the-shoulder look and at tea only seems to reject his innuendo. "You shouldn't talk like that . . ." looking demurely down, "until I'm in a flat of my own."

Jill's fiancé, Hugh Fielding (John Stuart), follows her to the city before he resumes his business in the tropics. But flushed with her success, Jill gobbles the bait of Prince Ivan (Carl Falkenburg). She exploits his generosity, teases him, and repels him elegantly with her cigarette holder.[3] Jill takes her own palatial flat—"Now I am nearly a star"— and discards her mentor Patsy as "my acquaintance in the chorus."

Patsy marries Hugh's friend Levet (Miles Mander) a month before he follows Hugh to the East. The marriage bodes ill, what with Patsy's dog howling at Levet and the bride's mien far from ecstatic. The marriage begins to crumble on their honeymoon, when Levet objects to her being "sloppy and sentimental" with the villagers and discards her rose. Levet, like Jill, proves selfish and unfeeling. Hitchcock's postcard-pretty, tinted shots of the Lake Como honeymoon, what Durgnat dismisses as a "somewhat remote view of happiness," exaggerate the honeymoon mood to foreshadow Jill's disillusionment.[4] The tinted outdoor shots are undercut by the cold space in the interiors. The tinting anticipates Hitchcock's rhetoric where Anne Baxter floats slow motion down her staircase to meet her lover in *I Confess*.

In the jungle, Hugh is tormented by his separation from Jill, particularly as he hears of her association with Prince Ivan. "There are as good fish in the sea as out," counsels Levet, a line Hitchcock may have remembered from Eden Phillpotts's *The Farmer's Wife*. Levet drinks heavily with a native girl light between his legs. When Patsy arrives unannounced to nurse him through his fever, she finds the girl still between Levet's legs. Patsy refuses to stay with him for reasons both domestic (her primary virtue) and charitable:

Do you think I'd stay here now—and rob that child of her
HOME?

Patsy stays on to nurse Hugh through his fever. To win Levet's sympathy, the native girl (Nita Naldi) walks into the sea to drown. Levet
comes after her, as if to save her, but drowns her instead.

Now both men hallucinate. Hugh in his fever thinks Patsy is his
Jill, but a kiss recovers his senses. Levet from fever and guilt envisions
the dead native girl demanding he kill Patsy. As he looms over Patsy,
Levet is shot by Carruthers, the other white man at the post, sent by
Hugh to save her. Hugh and Patsy are now free to begin their life
together.

The story works as a set of fairly precise parallels. Jill and Patsy are
developed together. Hamilton defines Jill's affair with Prince Ivan:
"Cunning little minx. She'll fool him into marrying her." Then Hitchcock cuts in Levet's proposal to Patsy. Both marriages develop out of
moral and emotional vacuums. Jill is aggressive and mercenary in her
courtship. Patsy marries Levet out of numbness and loneliness, as in
his proposal: "Patsy, I'm lonely. I'm as lonely as you are." Her reply is
more resigned than passionate: "I hardly know you, yet it seems as
though I could marry you anytime you ask." Patsy marries Levet out
of numbness, as Kate will in *The Manxman*, as the girl will in *The Ring*,
as in *Blackmail* Alice will out of boredom drift into a fatal date, and as
young Charlie will summon up Uncle Charlie in *Shadow of a Doubt*.
For all these women, romance springs artificially in the absence of
lively engagement, either moral or instinctual. In contrast to Patsy's
numbness, her dog's outspoken judgments are livelier and more accurate.

Patsy is also contrasted to the native girl. As she watches Levet sail
for the East, Patsy waves him good-bye, her long, black-sleeved arm
rising from lower right to the upper left of the screen. Hitchcock dissolves into a contrary shot, the naked arm of the native girl waving
Levet welcome, her arm extending from lower left to upper right
on the screen. The juxtaposition contrasts the city girl's sleeved sophistication to the native's naked openness. This parallels the larger
opposition of true jungle to the pretend Pleasure Garden. The oppo-

site directions of the waves form an X. Levet may think he needs both women, as the X needs both contrary strokes. In the hallucination that prompts him to please the dead girl by killing Patsy, two scimitars form an X in the background, one of which he deploys. Hitchcock will use this X-editing again in *Blackmail*, when a traffic cop's hand completes an X with the dead man's hand in Alice's haunted mind, and most notably in *Strangers on a Train*.

The differences are as important as the basic similarity. In *Shadow of a Doubt*, Hitchcock's directions parallel the two Charlies (they both lie left to right on the screen) to suggest their continuity.[5] In the present image in *Pleasure Garden* and in *Strangers on a Train*, the opposing directions imply complementarity. One can read the native girl as a completion of Patsy, but Jill as the alternative to Patsy. As it happens, the X pattern so obvious in *Stranger on a Train* arises in Patricia Highsmith's novel:

> "Do you know the greatest wisdom in the world, Bruno?"
> "I know a lot of wisdoms," Bruno smirked. "Which one do you mean?"
> "That everything has its opposite close beside it."
> "Opposites attract?"
> "That's too simple. I mean—you give me ties."[6]

So Hitchcock's characteristic notion of opposites crops up in a much later source. But the idea and its visualization appear in his very first feature film.[7]

Another contrast distinguishes between jungle fever and love in terms of water. When Levet drowns the native girl, Hitchcock cuts to Patsy's hand cooling Hugh's fevered brow. The direction and camera angle are the same in both shots. The juxtaposition approximates a metaphysical conceit. The heroine brings a cool moistness to the fevered man she will eventually accept as her lover. The villain brings a cold, wet death to the lover he rejects. Moreover, Hugh's fancy that the hand is Jill's defines his love for Jill as a fevered delusion of which Patsy's kiss cures him. His wiser passion for Patsy validates her surname (Brand).

Much of the film works by way of comic deflation. When Patsy punctures Mr. Monocle's pretensions she proves the most self-aware of all the characters. She lacks only the ambition that Jill possesses in excess and that would have saved Patsy from surrendering to Levet (whose very name breathes "giving up"). Patsy tells Jill: "It's lucky for you, O Village Maiden, that you fell into the poor but honest hands of Patsy Brand." The line's playfulness detaches Patsy and Hitchcock from the serious tones of romantic melodrama.

So too the delightful image of Jill saying her prayers with Patsy's dog licking at her soles. "Already Griffith and Buñuel in the same scene!" exults Kirk Bond.[8] Jill is not as wholesome as she pretends. The dog has smoked her. When Jill kicks the dog she proves no honest supplicant. That action playfully foreshadows Jill's hypocrisy and the callous soul she will reveal toward Hugh, Patsy, Ivan—all her devotees.

Hitchcock twice deflates romantic possibilities—thrice, if one counts the landlady's announcement of Hugh: "Miss Jill's fiasco is here." One title promises something lurid—"What Every Chorus Girl Knows"—particularly as it follows Jill's come-hither smile to her boss. We see gals washing their nylon stockings in Lux. In the scene where the two girls undress for bed, Hitchcock holds on the two chairs on which they pile their clothing, while they undress off camera. He offers the sight of a girl undressing, then a second one, then coyly places the camera between them, as if uncertain which to watch, settling on neither. Hitchcock teases his audience as Jill does Prince Ivan and Patsy does Mr. Monocle.

In Hitchcock's settings, the virtuous situation is the simple flat to which Patsy brings Jill and to which Patsy returns when she leaves her husband. Jill is a social climber. The simple tea Patsy gives Hugh contrasts to the silver setting between Jill and Hamilton at her "auditions."

The film's basic irony is that the Pleasure Garden is neither a garden nor a pleasure. The real pleasure is what one finds with someone like Patsy in a flat like hers. Only illusory delights, like Patsy's detachable kiss-curl, lure clients to the Pleasure Garden. The nightclub is a sterile whirl of deceptions, teasings, dishonesties large and small.

Hamilton enjoying his cigar in front of the theater's No Smoking sign is trivial, but his indulgence shadows his subsequent introduction of Mr. Monocle to Patsy. Patsy rejects this casual immorality; Jill exploits it, wielding in real life the falsity of theater, like her cigarette holder.

The actresses try out for parts in a musical called *Passion Flowers*. But Hitchcock's backstage is a world without passion, where the girls' lives are a sequence of auditions, disappointments, and Luxed nylons, and where marriages express Jill's opportunism or Patsy's despair in place of passion. Even the final mating of Patsy and Hugh is expressed in unpromising tones:

> PATSY: We've both suffered. What has either of us to live for now?
>
> HUGH: We have one of the greatest things in life . . . Youth.

After the film's history of delusions, teasings, and disappointments, youth is scarcely a secure constant on which to build a romantic ending.

The Pleasure Garden, then, is the false playground of civilized man. For the truth about human nature and the validity of their own devotions, both men and Patsy venture out to the real garden, the jungle. There, in the form of the native girl, is a devoted passion flower. Where the fevers are truer than the nightclub torpor, the truths will out. The Pleasure Garden only plays at life and nature. It only pretends to the fertility of a garden, as lechery and greed are fake passions.

That basic contrast recognized, one can return to the title sequence of one girl dancing. Now the dance feels lonely, manic in its desperate movements, mechanical in its repetition. The dancer has neither audience nor partner, just loneliness pretending joy. That image alone should undercut the joys of civilized life in *The Pleasure Garden*. The shot can be compared to the moment in the film when the two couples meet to dine and celebrate the success of Jill's audition. Prince Ivan has not yet appeared, so both couples are at brief peace. In the floor show behind them, a couple performs in skilled harmony. If that act expresses our lovers' brief harmony, then the whole film is defined by the lonely, frantic woman dancing desperately behind the credits, both promising and pretending to a romance and a joy she does not have. The solo dance is analogous to the solitary visions (hallucinations) that are first Hugh's love for Jill, then his fever, and Levet's guilt and fever.

The settings, then, are vital metaphors in Hitchcock's first feature. Between the false Pleasure Garden and the extremity of the jungle lie, as tenable stages, the home scenes and the honeymoon scene, interludes of deceptive promise.

Hitchcock exploits another "setting" when his speech titles modify the message. Conversations in the nightclub appear against the background of a theater stage, curtains, and footlights, which impute the possibility of falseness to what is said. Conversation in Patsy's flat comes against plain, homey wallpaper. It seems to confirm the warmth in Jill's introduction of her fiancé, but the woman's tone overrides the room's. Conversation in the jungle hut appears against wooden wall slats for Levet's room and a softer backing of weave for the softer Hugh. Levet is thus associated with individual, hard boards and Hugh with soft interweaving. These backdrops establish psychological as well as physical loci. "Patsy's Wedding Day" is announced against a large question mark, which expresses not so much her doubts as ours—and her dog's—about the match. A shot of the sea backs speeches that do not take place at sea but that express the speaker's sense of the distance and isolation that the sea is causing, as in Hugh's anxieties about Jill and in Patsy's harkening for word from Levet. Caught in flagrante delicto, Levet tells Patsy, "Remember you're still my wife—and you're going to stay." Here the seascape suggests emotional detachment.

In even the incidental artwork of his first feature film, Hitchcock provides the concentrated composition that he later insisted on: "When I compose I object to air, space around figures or above their heads, because I think that's redundant . . . you are, first of all, in a two-dimensional medium. . . . You have a rectangle to fill."[9]

More importantly, even Hitchcock's first film proves he is a filmmaker of wit, moral seriousness, and lively style. In this very impressive debut the brisk entertainment has excellent design, a sense of telling character, and editing that is never flaccid.

How does man respond to the jungle in his soul? Hitchcock posits three answers. Jill and the Pleasure Garden turn to corrupt and pallid imitation. Patsy lapses into despair. Perhaps Hugh has the wisest response, a faintly idealistic resolve to begin anew to construct a personal enclave of warmth, trust, and local stability.

The Mountain Eagle

1926

Of Hitchcock's second feature film, *The Mountain Eagle,* it appears that nothing remains but the six stills in Truffaut's book. Hitchcock directed the film in 1926, again for Michael Balcon in the Emelka studios in Munich. Hitchcock again worked with Eliot Stannard on the screenplay and with Baron Ventigmilia as photographer. As in the casting of Misses Valli, Geraghty, and Naldi in *The Pleasure Garden,* Hitchcock was given an American star to ensure distribution in the United States, where the film was titled *Fear O' God.*

Beatrice (Nita Naldi) is a schoolteacher in a Kentucky mountain village. The local judge and businessman, Pettigrew (Bernard Goetzke), is jealous of her attentions to his crippled son, Edward (John Hamilton), who takes evening classes from her. Pettigrew falls in love with Beatrice and at her rejection declares her a loose woman. The villagers drive her into the hills, where she is saved by the hermit Fearogod (Malcolm Keen). To avoid scandal, Fearogod has Pettigrew marry them, promising Beatrice a divorce when she wants one. When Edward disappears, the furious Pettigrew has Fearogod arrested and charged with murder. Although no body is found, Fearogod is tried, convicted, and jailed. After a year in prison he escapes to his wife and baby. Fearogod returns to the village once to fetch a doctor for his sick child. He meets Pettigrew and they fight, but the sudden reappearance of Edward ends the feud and brings a happy ending.

The review in *Bioscope* may round out our impression of the film: "Director Alfred Hitchcock has not been particularly well served by his author, and in spite of skillful, and at times brilliant direction, the story has an air of unreality. Bernard Goetzke gives a fine performance, Malcolm Keen is admirable and Nita Naldi achieves considerable success. Many small character parts are admirably played and skillfully directed. There are some unusual lighting effects and excellent photography by Baron Ventigmilia" (October 7, 1926). Peter Noble reports that this was Hitchcock's first film to earn a reviewer's praise for "brilliant direction."[1]

The Lodger

1926

Despite the expertise of at least *The Pleasure Garden* and perhaps *The Mountain Eagle* too, it is *The Lodger* that most—including Hitchcock—consider the first characteristically Hitchcock film.[1] Certainly the director's lighting and editing effects have richened. More to the point: in *The Lodger* Hitchcock works for the first time in the suspense genre for which he grew famous.

Reportedly, Hitchcock had some problems with *The Lodger,* to the point that Ivor Montagu was given the print for polishing. Montagu recut some sequences, possibly had Hitchcock reshoot others, commissioned poster artist E. McKnight Kauffer to design the titles, and trimmed the volume of titles down to a total of eighty, low for the time. Particularly in light of Hitchcock's later development, however, one still must consider *The Lodger* a Hitchcock film. Happily, neither the critics nor the paying public shared the distributor's reservations about the film. *The Lodger* was Hitchcock's first booming success. "It is possible that this film is the finest British production ever made," enthused *Bioscope* (September 16, 1926) in a typical reaction.

The plot is based on Marie Belloc Lowndes's novel *The Lodger* about a Jack the Ripper figure, who in the novel and in the film goes about murdering blonde ladies on and off the streets and leaving a calling card as "The Avenger."[2] In the novel the mysterious lodger turns out to be the murderer, but in the film the lodger is innocent. He is the victim of the suspicions of the detective, the landlady, indeed, of the entire cinema audience. The suspense, shock, and romantic elements subserve the movie's central theme: the deceptiveness of appearances, the injustice of judging by the senses alone.

To the quiet Bloomsbury household of Mr. and Mrs. Bunting (Arthur Chesney and Marie Ault) comes the mysterious lodger, Jonathan Drew (Ivor Novello). He seems like a nice, albeit strange, fellow, but the city is in a panic over the Avenger's murders of blonde ladies, moving closer to the Buntings' neighborhood. When Drew begins to date the Bunting girl, Daisy (June), her parents' suspicions are bolstered by those of Daisy's boyfriend, policeman Joe (Malcolm Keen). Drew's hidden valise reveals a mass of incriminating material—a gun, a map, and clippings about the Avenger's murders. Joe has Drew arrested but he escapes, handcuffs and all, and meets Daisy. The police alert alarms the community, who chase Drew until they trap him by his cuffs on a picket fence. Meanwhile, Joe learns that the real Avenger has been caught red-handed elsewhere. He saves his rival, Drew, from the mob. Drew explains that he has himself been tracking down the Avenger, having promised his mother to avenge the Avenger's murder of his sister. The film closes with Drew and Daisy together in his posh quarters, the Buntings sidling off in deference and tact.

Before we meet the central characters, we get a graphic survey of the panic that the Avenger's murders have caused London. Neither novel nor film is concerned with the psychology of either the murderer or the lodger.[3] Mrs. Lowndes's novel focuses on the psychology of Mrs. Bunting, the landlady, as she drifts into a sentimental complicity with the killer, finally allowing him freedom to pursue his murders elsewhere. Hitchcock subjects his audience to the test Mrs. Bunting faced (and morally failed). He so rigs the evidence against the innocent man that the audience misjudges him and commits the double error of presuming the innocent man guilty and siding with him nonetheless.

All of Hitchcock's bravura technical devices in the film serve this function, to trick the audience into a judgment on circumstantial evidence. So the film dramatizes the variety of ways in which one's perception can mislead one's judgment. The first shot is a neon sign flashing "Tonight Golden Curls" that promises us a story about blondes, expresses the Avenger's monomania, and promises young ladies a more glamorous life. At the end of the film, Drew and Daisy kiss by the window where, just within our vision on the left, the same advertisement flashes again. What filled our vision at the beginning is now a peripheral detail. The lovers have risen above the Avenger and his victims, his obsession and their trivialities, and the camera cuts out the sign altogether by moving in on the lovers. The sign assumes a different meaning according to its altered context.

A related motif is the restriction and bias of vision. The shooting style is different from that of *Pleasure Garden,* with all its comfortable long and middle shots. Here everything is close-up, intense, restricted. We see everything so close that a sense of the whole is prevented. We read a report as it is stamped out on a typewriter one letter at a time. We read a headline—MURDER—wet from the press, so laid out that we read the word one syllable at a time, first the first, then the second, then the first. The word as a whole is a conclusion to which we leap.

The conclusion by leaping is, of course, the very error that Joe makes and that the mob more dangerously makes when they hound Drew down, intent on tearing him to pieces. Hitchcock encourages the audience to conclude that Drew is the Avenger. He later discourages their sense of him as an avenger. But first twist first.

Drew's first appearance and his every subsequent glower and gesture come from the vocabulary of the "hiding killer." They trick us into assuming his guilt. The titles appear against an expressionistic sketch of a tilted dark stranger, clearly a deranged killer. A shutter effect closes over him to reveal the story. Drew himself appears first as a shadow falling across the Bunting door (number thirteen, of course), his face swathed with a scarf. His entrance is accompanied by a power failure and an accident to Mr. Bunting, which bode ill for Drew's tenancy. When he enters his room, a passing tram sends a barrage of lit windows through the room. Averse to Mrs. Bunting's pictures of blonde ladies, Drew turns them to the wall, exposing their accusing gray backsides. He teases Daisy (heavily) with the butter knife. Playing chess with Daisy—itself suspicious, a game for the dangerous intellectual, what with its queen killing and all—he reaches for the poker, grips it, raises it, and then—as Joe enters—stokes the ashes with it instead. Drew intones the regnant morality we associate with gentleman killers, though without the biblical bent of Mrs. Lowndes's Mr. Sleuth: "Providence is concerned with sterner things than money, Mrs. Bunting."

Drew is out the night the murder is committed around the corner from the Buntings. Daisy screams but is found cowering in his arms, frightened by a mouse. Drew is caught lurking outside her bathroom, even trying the door-handle with the excuse of wanting to talk to Daisy about a dress he bought her. An overhead shot of her legs in the tub, toes twiddling securely, tempts us again to imagine a whole image on the basis of but a part.

Joe concludes that Drew is the Avenger from staring at Drew's footprint in the park. Joe does not "read" the footprint. Rather, he imposes on it images from his own experience—the lodger's somber pacing, the ominous and ambiguous phrases and sight. He wants Drew to be the Avenger, to get his romantic and professional enemies out of the way in one swoop. With that same self-interest, a newsboy exults that the murder "always happens on Tuesdays. That's my lucky day."

In the film's most famous shot, Joe and the Buntings hear Drew pacing in his room upstairs. Hitchcock shot the pace through a six-foot glass floor, one inch thick, so that the "heard" steps are seen. The striking technique makes a crucial point. The shot is an example of an audience completing on their own an impression given them only in part. This scene exaggerates the evidence in the spirit of ironic trickery, just as Drew's "guilt" is so heavily conveyed. The fact that in the ceiling shot the audience is probably jumping to the right conclusion does not alter the fact that they are jumping to a conclusion. The Buntings' "seeing" the footsteps they've heard is analogous to Joe's "seeing" in the footprint the sounds and sights for the identification he wants to make.

Hitchcock constructed a four-storied open staircase with the same double function. It visually expresses what the character hears, in this case, Mrs. Bunting in bed hearing the lodger slink out for his midnight deeds. But as well the image works as a nonrealistic projection. It does not express the fact of the lodger's leaving so much as

Mrs. Bunting's heightened state of mind, in which she omits every-thing else within her range of awareness to concentrate on the man upstairs. The shot suggests the vision of sound, true, but also the landlady's extreme predisposition.[4]

For these striking bits of film expression, Hitchcock had clear sources in the novel:

> It was intensely dark, intensely quiet—the darkest, quietest hour of the night, when suddenly Mrs. Bunting was awakened from a deep, dreamless sleep by sounds at once unexpected and familiar. She knew at once what those sounds were. They were those made by Mr. Sleuth, first coming down the stairs, and walking on tiptoe—she was sure it was on tiptoe—past her door, and fi-nally softly shutting the front door behind him.
>
> Bunting went into the sitting-room, silently followed by his wife, and then, sitting down in his nice arm-chair, he poked the little banked-up fire. It was the first time Bunting had poked the fire in many a long day, and this exertion of marital authority made him feel better.
>
> The night before, while Daisy was telling her all about the dreaded place to which Joe Chandler had taken her and her fa-ther, Mr. Bunting had heard Mr. Sleuth moving about overhead, restless, walking up and down his sitting room.[5]

In all three cases Hitchcock's poetic imagery has a literal basis in the novel, but the image demonstrates the impressionability of the senses.

The film provides some playful warnings about being deceived by what we see. A woman who saw the Avenger is frightened by a dis-torted reflection of a man clowning behind her. One chorus girl fright-ens another with a scarf and knife.

Hitchcock also distorts time. During Drew's flashback to the dance at which his sister was murdered, in close-up we see the hand lower the switch. In long shot the lights go out. But no time has elapsed be-tween the hand on the switch and our view of the darkening hall. Montagu dismisses this repetition of time: "There is here of course no poetry, no creation of a new time-scale perceived and accepted. But this repetition of time is like a liberty taken with nature and, at least at a first viewing, works effectively to heighten the melodrama instead of being perceived as nonsense."[6]

Actually, the sequence does set up an alternative time scale. Hitchcock gives a subjective record of time on two levels, in the speaker's memory and in our sight. He gives time the same stretch-and-alter that he gives space. When Drew slowly and ominously unwinds his muffler and when he slowly and ominously deploys the poker, Hitchcock plays with our perception of time. The slow or repeated motion encourages the viewer to endow a moment or a movement with more meaning than it need bear.[7]

The Lodger is a more adventurous and experimental work than the later *Suspicion*, where again Hitchcock converted a novel about a murderer into a drama about the misleading powers of—suspicion. In *Suspicion,* Hitchcock used outsized props and oratorical angling and lighting, but with nothing like his liberties with the literal image in *The Lodger.* There is one curious parallel, however. As in *Suspicion* he lit the suspicious glass of milk with a lightbulb inside, in *The Lodger* he photographed one of the blondes with her hair against a glass sheet lit from behind.[8] Both give images of innocence an inordinate glow.

Hitchcock commonly complained about the romantic softening forced by the star casting of Ivor Novello and Cary Grant. Hitchcock did not want Novello to be necessarily the murderer, though, but wanted to leave his guilt uncertain.[9] In neither film does the ending reverse the body of the film. Both films work as consistent analyses of the perceptual and paranoiac distortions by suspicion. In *The Lodger* we have no figure like Joan Fontaine's in *Suspicion* to serve as our guard. Like the mob, the original cinema audience was tempted to unjustly conclude Drew's guilt. Modern audiences face the further challenge of overcoming their facetious impatience with the film's rhetorical style.[10]

Another motif in *The Lodger* involves the contrast of circle and triangle shapes. The title art emphasizes the triangle, as the shutter effect makes a triangular flare. The Avenger's "A" signature is a bottomless triangle. The map of the Avenger's crimes traces a triangle. Drew's arrival represents the "Avenger's" intrusion into the complacent Bunting family circle, which includes Joe. His romantic tension spoils that harmony: "When I put a rope around the Avenger I'll put a ring around Daisy's finger." Meanwhile he playfully handcuffs Daisy, to Drew's foreboding stare. Drew's arrest subjects him to Joe's circles again, the handcuffs. Daisy kisses his cuffed hands, less in kinky love than to recall the romantic triangle behind his arrest/encircling by Joe.

The fashion show takes place on a stage of concentric circles with triangular windows behind Drew. As in *Vertigo,* the staircase is a rectangular coil or spiral. Ultimately, Drew is not the man of the triangle (the disturber, an agent of tension) but the man of the circle: (1) completing the Bunting family circle; and (2) trying to complete the Avenger's fate by bringing him back to the family of his first crime, bringing his career full circle to end where he began.

The discussion thus far has dealt with Hitchcock's play on Drew's ostensible "guilt," his mistaken identification with the Avenger. This leads into the final doubt about Drew's "innocence." He may not be *the* Avenger, but he aspires to be *an* avenger. The Avenger has the title but the avenger (Drew) has the killer's intention. What the Avenger may have to avenge we are not told, though we suspect it is the general sinfulness of women, particularly attractive, young blondes. Hitchcock, by giving Drew the motive of vengeance, places him in as damning a tandem with the Avenger as later he was to develop between the murderers in *Rope,* between Bruno and Guy in *Strangers on a Train,* and between Rusk and Blaney in *Frenzy.* Drew, like the Avenger, would take God's justice into his own hands. Drew is as guilty as the vigilante mob who would kill him without due process, in a film whose rhetoric demonstrates our fallibility in judgment and perception.

Joe, having selfishly hoped Drew is the Avenger, redeems himself by speeding to save him from the vigilantes. The mob's panic is nourished by the variety of press and communication shots, particularly in the opening scenes. One sequence shows police reports typed and broadcast. There are several newspaper shots, headlines, hawkers, reporters, teletypes, even radio news ("Hot over the aerial"), not to mention the neon hair-dye ad, all of which drive the public to panic. This public information parallels private perception, private misjudgment. Hitchcock himself appears as a newspaper editor deploying the reporters. He reappears in the mob that has tracked down Drew, first in the background but gradually working front and center in the mob. The director's appearance emphasizes the connection between the frantic news coverage and the vigilantes.[11]

In connecting the vicious Avenger with the virtuous avenger and then in turn with a mob of avengers, Hitchcock embarks on one of his most important themes, the guilt of an idea, a word, that may graduate into deed. In *Strangers on a Train,* Bruno acts out Guy's wish, even literally ("I could strangle her," Guy says of his wife). There is a comic version in the fairground, where a child with a balloon *says* "bang" (with instinctive animosity to Bruno) and Bruno *goes* bang with his cigarette against the balloon. At least by Jansenist theology there is no moral difference between wishing a crime and committing it. In *Saboteur* Hitchcock develops a spectrum from deed to name to symbol in the sequence of fire references: the factory blaze, the gasoline addition to the fire, the man named Fry, the extinguisher dormant in the trunk, the torch on the Statue of Liberty. The ultimate irony in *Vertigo* is that Judy's fall realizes the report or pretense of Madeleine's death-drop from the tower. In *Rope,* the moral complicity of the philosopher (James Stewart, whose words led to the murders) is made most explicit.

> You've given my words meaning I never dreamed of. . . . There's always been something deep inside me that would never have let me do that.

The philosopher is horrified to discover that the words he spoke academically were criminally realized. In *Frenzy,* in both Blaney's anger at his wife and his friendship with the bar-girl his words are followed by Rusk's murders. Hitchcock introduces this preoccupation in *The Lodger.* Mrs. Lowndes gave her Avenger the name of Sleuth. Hitchcock's lodger is given formal association not with the forces of law and order but with the avenger, either outlaw or vigilante. The Avenger is only doing what the hero, an avenger, wants to do and what we as the mob would do, given the chance.

Two virtuous characters are safe from this misjudgment. Daisy has the courage, emotional liveliness, and intuitive sense to detect her man's innocence by, like Desdemona seeing beyond her eyes, seeing her lover's visage in his mind. The other is an unnamed man in the pub when Drew is declared the Avenger. As the pub clears in a mad frenzy for a lynching, this man stays there, calm, too wise to be swept along to kill on the evidence of his senses. He stays soberly at his drink.

Another uncredited character offers an intriguing ambiguity. The girl seated next to Drew at the fashion show has been eyeing him all scene. When he leaves with Daisy, the girl heaves a visible sigh of disappointment, of frustrated availability. In the society terrified by the Avenger's threat this girl may seem foolish, one of those Hitchcock women like the new widow in *Shadow of a Doubt,* ardent for disaster. Or she may be like Daisy, with an even stronger intuition of the stranger's worth, not about to let the rampant anxiety impede her attraction. Hitchcock tells Samuels that even Daisy's attraction to Drew was based on her being "goaded by the idea that he might be Jack the Ripper."[12] This has no support in this film, though; perhaps Hitchcock took a private spring into *To Catch a Thief.* So whether we take the girl at the fashion show as a model of positive intuition or as a warning against going by first appearances may be up to us, another way in which Hitchcock's films are not just entertainments but moral tests for his audiences—and traps.

Downhill

1927

Upon the Hitchcock-Novello team's success in *The Lodger,* Hitchcock was assigned to direct the film of the play *Downhill* in which Novello starred and which Novello wrote with Constance Collier, under the pseudonym David L'Estrange. *Downhill* was released in England in 1927 and in the following year in the United States, where it carried the more cautionary title *When Boys Leave Home.*

Hitchcock was not well served by Novello, as author or star. The *Bioscope* review is fair: "It is more by the brilliant treatment of the director and the excellent acting that this film is likely to appeal to the public than by the strength of its story. But if the plot is hardly plausible, Hitchcock's treatment is of great interest. The photography is admirable" (May 26, 1927). The thirty-five-year-old Novello was difficult to accept as the quondam adolescent, experiencing his first bitter tastes of the unsheltered life.

A title proposes the focus of the plot: "Two schoolboys who made a pact of loyalty. One of them kept it—at a price." The story is told in three titled sections: "The World of Youth," "The World of Make Believe," and "The World of Lost Illusions." Roddy Berwick (Novello) and Tim Wakely (Robin Irvine) are two public (in North America: read "private") school boys, good at games and books, fast in their friendship. Roddy is at gentlemanly ease around Tim's sister (Sybil Rhoda) but shy and nervous around the sexy waitress, Mabel (Annette Benson).

Roddy dances with Mabel at the pastry shop where she works but spurns her kiss. While Tim dances with Mabel, Roddy looks after customers. Ringing up the wrong amount, he makes up the difference from his own pocket, revealing his exploitable honor. Dangerously generous, he sells an urchin a box of chocolates for a penny and makes up the difference himself. Four more urchins troop in for the same bargain!

Roddy is appointed school captain for the following year. Hitchcock pans from Roddy's school cap with its "Honour" crest to Tim's hat, perched cockily on a ravaged box from Ye Olde Bunne Shoppe, where Tim has been spending early closing time with Mabel. When she finds the proverbial bun in her oven, she takes her case to the headmaster.[1] Mabel blames Roddy, both as a woman scorned and practical ("His father's rolling in money—he's got to see me through"). Roddy shoulders the blame because he doesn't want his friend to lose his scholarship and because Berwick is better off than Wakely's clergyman father. Roddy is expelled. His first reaction is the line now taken as risible: "Can I—won't I be able to play for the Old Boys, Sir?"[2]

Roddy comes home to cold, large rooms and massive furniture. When he tries to explain his innocence, Berwick calls him a liar. At that Roddy leaves home. His progress begins with a back view of Roddy descending an escalator in the underground, sinking from view.[3]

"The World of Make Believe" finds Roddy working as a bit actor, in love with leading lady Julia (Isabel Jeans) who has an affair with the slick male lead, Archie (Ian Hunter). When Roddy is left 30,000 pounds in his godmother's will, they adopt him, giving him a sheaf of their bills to pay as an initiation fee. Roddy bites off more than he can chew, even in cigars (a joke Harold Lloyd picks up in *Feet First*). Roddy and Julia marry, but fall apart when his fortune is spent. Thrown out of their flat, Roddy descends in the elevator.

In "The World of Lost Illusions" Roddy works as a gigolo at fifty francs a dance, percentage to "Madame la patronne, expert on human nature." He is in France, in what seems to be a bright fairground at night but is a gray dancehall in the daylight.

The hero moves from the school's security and ritual through situations of diminishing formality and increasing sordidness. From playing football (and scoring), the hero moves to stage performance (and losing), thence to the role-playing of the dancehall. His game world has less and less glamour. At the dancehall, old men pay him to dance with their ladies. Lonely women come by themselves. Hitchcock gives us some fine sensual detail here. One elegant, bored man sits preoccupied with his cigarette holder while his sultry date straddles her chair, fondling her long hair.

Roddy catches—and dreads—the eye of a muscular, mustached woman (the poetess).[4] She punches her hands together in robust anticipation of his attentions for which she must pay. "You poor boy. How did you come down to this?" After he explains what a guy like him is doing in a place like that, he compliments her: "You're different somehow, among all this artificiality." But in the "searching, relentless sunlight," he rejects her invitation ("Come home with me. You'll like it.") and leaves the dancehall. "Downhill—till what was left of him was thrown to the rats on Marseilles dockside"—as in Hitchcock's dental patient's nightmare.

In his attic aerie—designed by a German expressionist merchant of cobweb, shadow, and nook—Roddy is delirious. Two blacks and a stevedore bring him down, feed him, and generously ship him back to England ("He got friends there—mebbe they give you something"). Blind instinct leads Roddy home, where his stern father welcomes him, declares that his innocence is now known, and begs his forgiveness. The film ends as it began, Roddy scoring in the Old Boys' match. The hero is back in his world of sheltered games, begrimed but no longer bewildered by the sordid realities beyond.

A simple melodrama, *Downhill* is important as Hitchcock's first confrontation with the chaos that threatens a complacent existence. It also has Hitchcock's witty visual rhymes. Early, Mabel flirtatiously nudges Roddy's foot with the toe of her shoe. In a later overhead shot, Julia nudges Roddy with her sleek, spangled leg. Roddy is now with an upper-class lady—and at the upper leg—but he still is tripped by flirts. Ivor Montagu cites Julia's leg shot as Hitchcock's ingenious attempt to "reveal the personal relationships by the contacts and avoidances of the knees" of the three people in the taxi. Admitting the idea was "excellent and, because connected by logic, not vitiated by the unusualness of the viewpoint," Montagu still rejects the shot because "the apparent distance of the knees from the spectator was so great as to jolt the spectator out of engrossment, for . . . he could not have seen what he saw unless the roof of the taxi had been removed."[5] We've seen enough God's-eye views not to be troubled by the missing roof.

Hitchcock works in some artful shadow play, from Mabel's beaded curtain, with its hints of ornamental eroticism, to the gloomy attic to which Roddy sinks. When he climbs to his room, all we see is his shadow following a black cat up the stairs. As Roddy goes up to learn of his inheritance, his shadow—the dark, gloomy projection of the man—shortens in anticipation of the good news.

Hitchcock is more modest in his title artwork here. Most of the titles have a downward weaving "road of life" cartoon. A series of shrinking numerals records the squandering of the legacy.

Hitchcock advances his scenes of memory. The waitress, in implicating Roddy, reprises their party scene in carefully selected details—her phonograph record, dancing feet, Roddy taking a pound from her, the Early Closing sign. That third detail is a lie. In showing Mabel's lie on the same literal level as the "facts," Hitchcock commits what was called a mistake in *Stage Fright,* portraying a lie as if it happened.[6]

Already Hitchcock is more interested in the psychological reality than in the physical. Kracauer commends Hitchcock for his "unrivalled flair for psycho-physical correspondences": "Nobody is so completely at home in the dim border region where inner and outer events intermingle and fuse with each other. This implies, for one thing, a perfect command of the ways in which physical data may be induced to yield their possible meanings."[7]

Hence the memory montages of Roddy's fevered conscience. The 78 record that lured Roddy into Mabel's grasp recurs in his fever but even in his cooler state is rhymed off the top of Archie's silk top hat, alerting Roddy to Julia's infidelity. Aboard the ship his mind melds memories—the record; the four women who exploited him (Mabel, la patronne, the poetess, Julia); his stern father; and the strange sights and sounds of the ship. Shots of the ship's noises root Roddy's fantasy in his physical surrounding. When he staggers ashore and home,

Hitchcock's superimposition gives the streets a phantom transparency. Roddy is the secure reality, the world around him unstable.

Much of Hitchcock's early work has a documentary feel, like the opening sequences in *The Lodger* and *Blackmail*. But everywhere Hitchcock's physical details serve his primary interest in the imagination. His delirium montages in *Downhill* and *The Ring* anticipate his strategy in *Spellbound*: "I brought in Salvador Dalí to do the dream sequences, not for publicity purposes—as Selznick thought—but because I wanted to have dreams photographed vividly. Until then, movie dreams were always blurred, always double exposures, and misty; and dreams are not like that, they're very, very vivid. What I wanted out of Dalí was that long perspective, that hard, clear, solid look."[8]

In *Downhill,* the hero's delirium montages make it clear that his primary loss is his father's favor. Berwick's coldness has contrasted to Roddy's warmth from the outset. Even before Roddy's lapse, his father scowled at the boy's chatting with Sybil Wakely. The father is immediately suspicious at Roddy's early return from school and gives his exemplary son no opportunity to explain himself. In Roddy's delirium his father's face supplants all the other figures of authority, such as the ship's captain and the London policemen. The film thus works out a kind of Oedipal tension. The son is tormented by the image of his stern, harsh father. When he turns to women, he finds only insecurity, temptation, and betrayal. From Mabel through Julia, la patronne, the poetess, his earth-mother landlady in Marseilles, young Roddy is buffeted by mean and corrupting parodies of the mother image. All are older than he is. The only woman without a motherlike power over him is Sybil, before whom he feels a boyish shame.

Hitchcock's British films in general offer harsh father figures, while in his American films the mothers threaten the hero's stability and comfort. Either parent frees a considerable anxiety. Hitchcock gives us harsh fathers in *Downhill, Champagne, The Manxman,* and *Waltzes from Vienna,* threatening father-surrogates in *The Ring* and *Jamaica Inn,* unsympathetic fathers in *Young and Innocent, The 39 Steps,* and *The Lady Vanishes.* By his age, Levet of *The Pleasure Garden* is a threatening father figure. Verloc in *Sabotage* is as treacherous a stepfather as he is a citizen.

In his American period Hitchcock gave us a gallery of formidable mother figures: Mrs. Danvers, the mother-in-law in *Notorious,* Marnie's mother, the projection of Mrs. Bates, the roost-ruler in *The Birds,* the hearty mothers of Roger Thornhill and Rusk (in *North by Northwest* and *Frenzy*). There are early strong mothers in *Juno* and *The Skin Game,* and with subordinate husbands in *The Lodger, Blackmail, Murder!, The Man Who Knew Too Much,* and *Jamaica Inn.* His American films include harsh "fathers" in *Lifeboat, Saboteur,* and *Foreign Correspondent.* Still, in his British period Hitchcock generally tended to the nightmare of the oppressive father, while in his American period he tended rather toward the dominant mother. It sometimes seems that Hitchcock cannot resist mother jokes. So in *Suspicion,* Johnny pays his train fare with a stamp and tells the conductor, "Write your mother." Even in the somber *The Wrong Man,* Hitchcock cuts from the insurance man's "I'll call to home office" to Manny saying good-bye to his mother. In the two most English American films, *Rebecca* and *Suspicion,* the threatening figures are father types, Maxim and the colonel.[9]

This tendency may invite speculation. Raymond Durgnat in another context suggests the influence of producer David Selznick: "After *Rebecca* Hitchcock's Hollywood career becomes a bifurcation between films which adapt the formulae of his English thriller (*Foreign Correspondent, Saboteur*), and smooth, sumptuous, female nightmares (*Suspicion, Notorious, Under Capricorn*)."[10] But a parent's tyranny—or a dentist—can operate as smooth female nightmare. In *Foreign Correspondent,* one father figure is abused (Van Meer) and one is the traitor (Herbert Marshall), who does not even then lose his daughter's love and support. Another possibility is remarked by Bazin: "In Hollywood films are made for women; it is toward their sentimental taste that scenarios are directed because it is they who account for the bulk of the box-office receipts. In England films are still made for men."[11] In any case, Hitchcock took an aggressive stance toward his audience by shifting from the dominant father to the dominant mother when he left England for more Momist America.

Downhill introduces another of Hitchcock's anticonventional techniques, the comic fight. Novello's fight with Hunter begins straight but dissolves into fumbling. The more extended comedy in the fight was cut out by the producers, who objected to guying matinee idol

Novello.[12] Fuller comic fights can be found in *Number Seventeen,* *Waltzes from Vienna, The Lady Vanishes,* and with poor Gromeck in *Torn Curtain.* Even in set pieces Hitchcock deflates his heroes.

Downhill is also distinguished by its use of space. Rachael Low commends Hitchcock's traveling camera in the film.[13] Mabel has a long, slow walk toward the camera to level her paternity charge against Roddy. When Roddy loses his temper, Julia cowers away from him (and the camera). Expelled, Roddy is shot high from above as he leaves the school, crossing the huge empty square alone. He is dwarfed by cold, empty space in his home and in his honeymoon suite, where the closet arches recall the school's arched doorways. Everywhere he is framed to seem a boy in a man's world. The liberty Hitchcock took with the taxi roof may also have served this function, to dwarf the hero in space and emphasize his loneliness. In contrast, his two football scores are shown in close-up; his full command fills the space. There is also some important deep focus. One shot of Roddy and Julia, seemingly alone in the background, shows a large soda bottle in the foreground, which is squirted to reveal—in a visual hiss—Archie's snaky presence.

Hitchcock uses depth to deceive his audience. "The World of Make Believe" opens with Roddy well dressed, seemingly affluent, in our first sight of him since he left home. The camera pulls back to reveal he is waiting on posh pool-side tables. Then he seems to steal a cigarette case. When the camera draws back farther, we see that he is acting the role of a waiter and picking up Julia's forgotten cigarette case to return it. A succession of appearances proves false. What in close-up seems suspect from farther back seems all right, or vice versa.

A variation on the relativity of appearance is given in the upside-down shot of Roddy entering Julia's room, as if from her perspective, with her head bent back. Dissolves between scenes also undermine the image's veracity. Julia squirts perfume at a photo of Archie, which dissolves into the man himself, the real face having lines, a wart under the cheek, and a general slickness that his photo omitted to express.

Hitchcock uses space in *Downhill* to confirm the instability of the image. *Downhill* introduces the anxiety most fully developed in *Vertigo,* his fascination with an unstable footing, which broadens into the lure of chaos beneath our normal lives.

Perhaps Roddy's concern about being banished from the Old Boys' game is not as silly as it seems. He is not just expelled but wiped from the school's record. It expresses the boy's immediate fear of having ceased to be, even as a memory. Roddy stands to lose not just the brilliant future the school had promised him but also his having been known there, with alumni rights. When his father turns on him, Roddy again realizes that a single aspersion can erase a life of honor and truthfulness. Roddy could patiently suffer the error in the headmaster's judgment. But when his father makes the same error, Roddy turns and in disillusionment and dignity walks out—and downhill.

Despite the happy ending *Downhill* remains a pessimistic work. The values, rituals, class assumptions, which the father and the school have passed down to Roddy, indeed his character and honor, are no more substantial than that wasted 30,000 pound inheritance. Indeed, like that legacy, the culture entraps Roddy in a false confidence. When Hitchcock introduced the dance-hall madam as the "specialist in human nature," he showed his hand: human nature is more sordid, more exploitative, more vulnerable, than the games and rituals of "civilization" pretend.[14]

The basic thrust of *Downhill*—like *Vertigo*—is instability, the Hitchcockian anxiety that a confident normalcy can be destroyed by an error or by a trick in fortune. Bits of comic mischief replay the theme. In the opening school scenes, a little boy with a pea-shooter hits first the fatal waitress, then Roddy's cruel father, the mischief uniting the two shapers of Roddy's misfortune. At the end that boy has matured, sports a moustache, and is himself pestered by a younger embodiment of misrule. In the pastry shop the door once opens but no one is seen. The next shot shows the little boy to have entered, too short to have been caught by the adult expectation of the camera angle. In these comic touches, uncontrollable elements ruffle the placid surface.

The school and its sport are male institutions. That Roddy's fall from grace should be caused by his father's harshness and by the charge of ungentlemanly manliness is consistent with the film's basic theme, that the securest and most traditional refuge of the securest and most traditional class can lead so directly to the skids depicted here. Melodrama though its origins might have been, Hitchcock's *Downhill* is an important, personal film.

Easy Virtue

1927

Easy Virtue is probably Hitchcock's most unfamiliar feature film. It has not enjoyed even the dismissal given *Waltzes from Vienna* and *Champagne*. In his book-length study of Hitchcock, Durgnat gives *Easy Virtue* one sentence,[1] possibly because the film was not available for screening in England and has only recently become available in America, albeit in a somewhat abbreviated print, according to William Everson.[2] Noble and Rohmer and Chabrol[3] give the film less credit than the *Bioscope* reviewer did on its initial release: "Hitchcock has done the best possible for a subject which does not lend itself readily to the medium of the screen, and he is to be congratulated on having maintained interest throughout with what proves to be very slight material" (September 1, 1927).

Larita Filton (Isabel Jeans) becomes notorious when her jealous, drunk husband divorces her. Her devoted friend, an artist (Eric Bransby-Williams), commits suicide so he can leave her his income (2,000 pounds per annum). Larita tries to make a new life under a new name (Larita Gray). "Larita could hide her scarred heart but not her magnetic charms, which soon attracted attentions she most desired to avoid." She and young John Whittaker (Robin Irvine) fall in love and marry, but his family resents her. Mrs. Whittaker (Violet Farebrother) drives John to divorce her, over the humane but passive father, Colonel Whittaker (Frank Elliot). The second divorce leaves Larita's life in ruins. The film closes on her line to the newspaper photographers who have hounded her: "Shoot, there is nothing left to kill."

The main theme is the variety of forces by which man can be divided. The lovers are separated by the Whittaker family's hidebound traditions and exclusiveness. The opening close-up of the divorce court records declare the candidates for "Division." The next shot is of the presiding magistrate's head, his wig shot from overhead to emphasize its precise division into halves. The wig shot recurs at Larita's second divorce hearing. Her first husband wears a similar parting in his hair, aligning the judge in his camp, an agent of division.

In the first trial, Hitchcock concentrates on Larita's testimony and on the questioning by her husband's lawyer. Her lawyer is not featured at all. The prosecutor and Larita often are in alternating and facing profile, faces in confrontation. The jury accepts the prosecutor's case on circumstantial evidence. A matronly juror's bias/envy foreshadows Mrs. Whittaker's rejection of Larita.

Hitchcock's lively camera separates us from Larita by distance and intervening heads. We can believe her testimony but are kept from easy identification with her. Larita's romance with John opens on a tennis court, the shot taken from behind a racquet. Again Hitchcock detaches viewer from spectacle to inhibit identification and to establish the themes of detachment, judgment, and incomplete knowledge.

In the original Noël Coward play,[4] the primary divisive agents are the Whittaker family's prejudices and neuroses. Hitchcock omits the personal problems of John's sisters to concentrate on their mother's cruelty. Where the play opens with the family awaiting the married couple, Hitchcock shows the trial scene and flashbacks for Larita's testimony. They literalize the Whittakers' impending judgment, making Larita a victim of double jeopardy. The courtroom establishes Larita's public image from which the Whittakers will not allow her private life to be free.

Hitchcock's most personal touch is making photographers the villains in Larita's life. She cowers from the paparazzi as she leaves the first trial. At the end she despairs of a fresh private life. The opening credits appear against a still camera. In the original, Larita's newspaper picture informed her in-laws of her past. The press keeps her past alive and imposes on her private life their image of what she was, forcing her to become what they claim her to be. Far from being the worst line Hitchcock ever wrote, then, the film's last line concludes the theme of public intrusion onto a personal life and the assault on love by moral prejudice.[5]

In contrast to the predatory photographers, Hitchcock's most charming scene features a switchboard operator (Bonita Hume) who eavesdrops on the conversation in which John and Larita settle their marriage plans. John has proposed. Larita has demurred but promised to phone her reply. Hitchcock holds on the switchboard operator for the duration of Larita's call. We infer the conversation from the young girl's facial changes. Clearly John has to do some coaxing. Like the photographers, the girl is an intruder but she has connected the lovers. Though she invades their privacy, she is sympathetic to them. She assumes their perspective, a rare virtue that Larita shows when she understands the Whittakers' feelings while they remain insensitive to hers.

The switchboard operator clearly prefers the real-life romance she overhears to the fiction she was reading. In contrast, the photographers force Larita to conform to their image of her. So do the Whittakers, watching so intently for Larita to drink quickly and nervously that she does. Ordering her to absent herself from the party so as not to embarrass them, they compel her embarrassing entrance. The photographers and John's own family drive the lovers apart with what they take to be Larita's past. The switchboard operator connects the lovers and warmly enjoys their sentiments. She animates the juror's suspicion that "pity is akin to love."

Between the photographers and the switchboard operator, Hitchcock introduces a concern that would occupy him most fully in *Rear Window,* the thin line between human interest and voyeurism. The photographers and the switchboard operator pull *Easy Virtue* more toward Hitchcock than to Coward's play, from whose satire Hitchcock kept only the unfair stigma of divorce.

The film abounds in witty images. When Larita and John enter an elevator together, gossips in the lobby attack. Hitchcock holds on the elevator doors as they close tight, like the gossips' minds. As if to obey his own sense of decorum, Hitchcock pulls back from the lovers' kiss to show their horse nuzzle an approaching mare. As Hitchcock pretends not to intrude into romance, he spreads its effect, from the lovers to the horses, as the phone call warms the switchboard operator. This refashions Coward's point when Larita addresses Marion's sexual frustration and repressions.

Shots of the boat's luggage compartment suggest the couple's arrival from France. In the first a French poodle perches on a case; in the second it's an English bulldog. This device contrasts the two cultures between which Larita tries to move, the French/poodle's delicacy, elegance, and possibly decadent excesses with the British/bulldog's vulgar, stubborn stolidity. For values are not so much a matter of place as of people. Creatures establish the values associated with place. Larita is not marrying into the wrong class but the wrong family. With the dogs as with the horses here, and as with the natural scenes in *The Farmer's Wife* and *The Manxman,* Hitchcock finds in nature correlatives to the human heart. If the Whittakers live in "The Moat House," it is because Mrs. Whittaker has the arrogance and exclusiveness of an isolated fortress. As Coward's Colonel Whittaker admits, "We're an insular, hidebound set."

Much of *Easy Virtue* can be taken as the Cockney Hitchcock's vision of the upper class, with the Whittakers' cavernous dining room—its massive murals of saints cold and towering—the tennis and polo games, the dull luxury of leisurely days. John emerges as a spoiled and wasted young man, indecisive, ruled by his mother, unable to sustain his redeeming love for Larita. The shallow class is easy prey to the influence of the *Tatler.* Unhappily, the real victim of the *Tatler* snoops is the warmest, liveliest, and most independent character, whom nothing in the *Tatler* could directly touch. That is the way mores work. Those lively enough to deviate suffer the stigma of "easy virtue." Of course, the really easy virtue is the Whittakers' mechanical moralizing. Larita's vulnerable warmth has nothing easy about it.

The Ring

1927

With *The Ring* Hitchcock makes a fresh start. He filmed his own story and screenplay, and for a new studio, British International Pictures. The result is a lively film with at least two points in common with the earlier work.[1] Again Hitchcock develops a pattern of circles, rectangles, and arcs. And thematically, *The Ring* deals with the basic Hitchcock situation: a man who thinks he is secure in his job and with his sweetheart loses both to an outside power. More plausibly than in *Downhill,* the hero manages to recover them.

The credits appear over a fight scene to clarify the title's "ring." "One Round" Jack Sanders (Carl Brisson) is the hero, a midway boxer challenging customers to last a round with him. Sanders demolishes a huge sailor off camera while his trainer (Gordon Harker) holds the sailor's suit for him, confident of his early—and horizontal—return. Another large challenger, egged on by his lady, trips on the rope and falls down for the count. So One Round has a good punch and luck in his corner. His sweetheart (Lilian Hall-Davis) sells tickets for him outside.

The girl attracts the Australian heavyweight champion, Bob Corby (Ian Hunter), to the tent, then to the ring, where he knocks out Sanders. Courting the girl, Corby hires Sanders as a sparring partner.

While mopping Sanders's brow, the girl stares at Corby in fascination, mussing her beau's face.

Though Sanders and the girl marry, she is still intrigued by Corby. By filling the church with the couple's carny colleagues, Hitchcock shows mismatches: Siamese twin girls arguing over which side of the church to sit on, the giant and the dwarf entering together. The carnies also establish the outsider community that a similar group has in *Saboteur,* representing the simple society that Sanders abandons for Corby's circle.

At almost exactly the midpoint of the film, Sanders's wife is assumed to be Corby's from her attentions to him after a bout. On the night Sanders wins the right to challenge Corby for the British title, his wife is out late with Corby. Sanders and his fairground friends are left alone with their flattened champagne. When she returns they quarrel; Sanders becomes violent with her and she leaves.

The climax of the film is Sanders's title fight with Corby. His wife goes to Corby's rooms and sits in his corner. The fight itself is an exciting piece of film work, because it's the first fight that Hitchcock shows in any detail. Our appetite was whetted by glimpses of the earlier fights. Hitchcock enhances the suspense by cutting away to the enthralled audience, like the tennis match in *Strangers on a Train.* For all its rhetoric, Hitchcock's fight has a more plausible choreography than some of the work of Muhammad Ali. Sanders anticipates Ali by lying on the ropes to recover his energies. Hitchcock interposes only one title—the referee's warning, "Don't hold, Corby"—to confirm the breathless pace, too fast to pause for words.[2]

Sanders freezes when he sees his wife in Corby's corner, so Corby has the first edge. Saved by the bell, Sanders recovers. He revives fully when his wife takes his hand and says, "Jack . . . I'm with you. In your corner." Jack knocks out Corby.

The three basic images in the film are the rectangle, the circle, and the arc, but the film doesn't feel that schematic. These shapes establish important contrasts in movement and value. The rectangles are modes of perception—the portals in the tent through which the girl exchanges alluring looks with either Corby or Sanders; the door and the window in the gypsy's caravan; the mirror that triggers Jack's jealous fantasy; the picture of Corby with which the girl covers her heart when Jack attacks her. The boxer's ring is, of course, a rectangle. As a mode of perception it suggests that the girl appraises her men by their performance in the fights. Jack's career and his marriage both hinge on his beating Corby.

The film abounds with ring images, either complete rings (circles) or pieces of rings (arcs). The film opens with carnival scenes—a drum beating in close-up, people going around on swings, people going back and forth in arcs on swings, the sweeping view from the swings, a close-up of a barker's drumlike mouth, a huge clown mouth in a target game. The grinning black man dunked is a comic parallel to the boxer's defeat and humiliation by downing and the general whirligig of fate.

Corby and his manager enter the fairground—and the film— between two large rings, the merry-go-rounds. The gypsy tells the girl's fortune with a ring of cards. At the wedding Corby yawns an ominous abyss at "till death us do part." The best man drops the ring and picks up a button by mistake. On the night of the Sanderses' separation the room is full of circles. The champagne goes flat in round glasses, of course, but the furniture is predominantly round, tables, chairs, except for those usually round objects of comfort, the cushions, which are rectangular, like the boxing ring. The wife enters with a round box of chocolates from Corby. The visit by Sanders's carny cronies is a circular notion too—he is back with figures from his past. Sanders tracks Corby down in a nightclub full of pointedly round tables and knocks him down in front of a huge drum.

And there are broken circles. After the wedding the gypsy is knocked down by a horseshoe, which is an arc, reminiscent of the circle of cards by which she tells fortunes. The gypsy's earrings are broken circles. Corby first proves his control over Mrs. Sanders with a wishbone.

The most important ring images are Sanders's wedding ring and the coiled bracelet that Corby buys the girl with his prize money from knocking out Sanders. She accepts the bracelet, saying it came indirectly from Jack, from his loss, but the bracelet keeps Corby between them.

Hitchcock introduces the bracelet in a shot that fades in over Jack's warm, two-handed handshake with Corby and his manager. Corby slips on the bracelet from the same position on the screen and in the same direction as the handshake, undermining Sanders's security. When Jack hugs the girl, she covers the bracelet, ashamed. She rejects Corby's handshake so as not to reveal the bracelet. When it falls in the water, Jack digs it out. In the water it makes more round ripples, a fertility of circles. He uses it as an extravagant ring when he proposes to her. The proposal image is paradoxical: Does he have to win to match the size of the man who gave her the bracelet? Does she have to grow to fill it? Or is the sentiment of a delicacy that mocks its material size?

The bracelet is a coiled serpent, an emblem of serpentine temptation and the fall from innocence. Instead of the simple embrace of the ring, it makes a reasserted grip. It is an open coil (an incomplete, unclosed circle) yet overlapped (excessive). By the absence of the bracelet from the hall table Sanders knows his wife has left him. In the last scene, Corby's second brings him the bracelet, which he found at ringside, but Corby rejects it as meaningless. The single object over which three people waged such emotional battle is at the end discarded.[3]

A trivial thing, the bracelet gains value from its associations, from the people who invest it with meaning. Anything trivial can accrue value. Boxing, ambition, achievements, a wedding ring, marriage, fate, a keepsake, a profession, a sport, a game, indeed anything with even a fugitive association with the circle here has no intrinsic worth or character but the human feeling invested in it. Any emblem or activity can fill with the importance of the heart. In the corollary, one proves one's worth by commitment—to another person, to one's profession, to a feeling, to the ring in any of its protean identities.

So the film contrasts partial commitment to total commitment, the casual to the intense, the arc to the circle. Sanders is a man of a casual, rootless, minor-league profession, until he accepts Corby's challenge. The arc swings contrast to the merry-go-rounds, the coil bracelet to the wedding ring, the open horseshoe of malevolent accident to the gypsy's circle of happy fortune. Corby is her Jack of Diamonds to be trumped by Jack, the King of Hearts. Corby wins the first battle (a temporary, arc-like triumph), but Jack wins the war(s). Both are troubled by a button: Corby can't fasten his, Jack's turns up in place of—and as a stuffed parody of—his wedding ring. Corby's hold on the girl is temporary, Jack's eternal. When Corby undermines Jack's world Sanders rises to professionalism. Corby is the intruder, an Aussie in England trying for the English title. Jack wins the title by taking command of the center of the ring and repelling Corby's attacks from the rim.

Hitchcock's best-known "touches" in *The Ring* confirm this pattern. Depicting the hero's disappointment as bubbles dying in the champagne suggests the incomplete, contrasted to pouring champagne to revive the boxers for the last round. In the first Corby-Sanders fight, the worn, dirty Round One sign is replaced by a fresh Round Two sign, signifying that Sanders is tested further than ever before. Sanders's rise in the professional ranks is recorded by a series of boxing posters, his name appearing higher each time. Where the Round Two card records his being tested beyond his usual limit, the billboards record his growing superiority over others. The card is to the billboard what the arc is to the circle, a partial anticipation.[4]

Similarly, the girl's reflection in the circles of water in the proposal scene is completed by her reflection in Jack's bucket of water during the title fight. The paradox here is that she was only half-committed to him when she accepted his proposal; her love was as unfocused as the lake. At the end her commitment is total, her love exclusively focused on Jack. The bucket becomes a circular containment, like the wedding ring.

Another scene dramatizes the overriding awareness of the circle over the arc. As Jack and his friends wait for the wife to return, as the champagne flattens, the elevator keeps bringing others home, but not his wife. First comes a noisy party, back to continue their celebrations. Then the elevator returns two women, then a lonely man, the celebrations expired. The passengers' moods show the growing lateness of the hour. To each passenger the moment is an arc, but to a higher consciousness each moment is an inflection in the larger hour beyond their awareness. So the hilarity of the first arc is redefined by the larger feeling outside, Jack's grief. And the moment of the man's loneliness is qualified by the larger sense of Jack sharing that loneliness. It is in the large commitments, the lasting sentiments, that man brings meaning to his life, relief from passing woes, and value to the minutiae of his being.

Hitchcock continued to experiment with the subjective camera. Over the face of the girl selling her tickets we see Jack winning his trial fight. We are not certain whether we see superimposed what she wishes to happen or what is actually happening. In any case the victory is an image of something possible, not yet an event. The image's uncertainty coheres with her reluctance to marry.

Hitchcock's richest delirium montage is Jack's jealous fantasy, which at the film's first screening was given an ovation. Jack begins with a small image of the girl in Corby's lap, which grows to overwhelm the image of the promoter talking to Jack. The small imposition swells to full screen. Then there is a wild mix of dancers growing distorted, piano keys twisted and runny, guitars throbbing, the nagging of a spinning 78 record, his wife kissing Corby. Jack's forehead reappears full of the guitars and record, as if he fled the kiss to the sounds of the party.

At the Sanderses' wedding, Jack's second (Harker) has a related fantasy. In his drunken stupor he "sees" Corby and Sanders square off at the wedding. As in Sanders's jealous vision, Harker sees an invisible tension as an event. The girl's vision of the fight, Sanders's vision of the infidelity, Harker's vision of the confrontation, Jack's vision of Corby's face on the punching bag, even Jack's later vision of the bracelet missing from the table, in all these subjective perspectives we share the character's more intense vision, when he slips from the ordinarily limited "arc" of his understanding to the fuller prophetic sense of the circle.

The Farmer's Wife
1928

Having proved his skill on his original *The Ring,* Hitchcock returned to adaptation for the phenomenally successful stage comedy *The Farmer's Wife* by Eden Phillpotts, based on his novel *Widecombe Fair.* Hitchcock tells Truffaut that the play ran for some 1,400 performances in the West End. It was the biggest stage success in England since the war, according to the editor of the Reader's Library edition of the novel, and was at one point performed by three touring companies in the provinces.[1]

The film may be Hitchcock's most underrated work. It is commonly dismissed as a straightforward adaptation of an obsolescent rural farce. As so often, Kirk Bond is a notable exception: *The Farmer's Wife* "in ways is his most brilliant achievement . . . a dream of filmmaking without 'high style.'" The daughter's wedding scene shows "an absolute mastery of continuity and brio." The "marvelous emotional quality" of the opening shots recalls Griffith, the party scene the Marx Brothers, and so on. A cooler, more analytical appreciation comes from John Smith, who regards the film "a higher achievement than *The Lodger*" and makes some cogent points about its import:

> *The Farmer's Wife* convincingly eschews the "permanently treacherous and ominous" universe one finds elsewhere in Hitchcock;

the film's substance is its unforced respect for its main characters' separateness from and dependence upon each other. Minta
is almost the very principle of quiet stability, and is central to the
film's structure.

. . . In *The Farmer's Wife* there is a sense of absolute submission to provided rhythms, a simple, perfect logic quietly
enacted—though the characters lose nothing of themselves in
the submission: in fact, it is the submission itself which allows
them their freedom.

Raymond Durgnat chafes at the play's period flavor and the rustic
mantle Hitchcock assumed for it, but delivers some begrudging insights: "A sense of clumsy contacts, of loneliness, infiltrates the film,
until every outgoing gesture, however clumsy, however stupid,
seems cherished. The mixture of warmth and solitudes, of pomposi-
ties and uneasiness, of imperceptiveness and apologies, of deferential but firm rebellions, catch a kind of finesse-in-oafishness which is
a pleasure to watch." Obviously, Smith's and Durgnat's political in-
ferences are poles apart. Smith sees the play expressing Hitchcock's
essential conservatism (with Minta the idealized embodiment). To
Durgnat, "Minta's cool, patient, passive style, seemingly content to
let her man go if he will, is quite as disturbing as the glamorous
teases of his later films." But Durgnat does not go further than sug-
gesting the audience's attraction to the "deferential but firm rebellions."[2]

The first thing to be said about *The Farmer's Wife* is that it remains
a funny and engaging comedy. For not many British comedies of the
period can that claim be made. The original dramatist and Hitchcock's cast deserve the credit for the continuing pleasure the film
would provide, if shown.

There is a strong, endearing performance by Jameson Thomas as
farmer Samuel Sweetland. Left lonely by the death of his wife and
the marriage of his daughter, Sweetland lists the eligible ladies and
roughly ploughs through a day of proposing to them. Finally, in a
combination of despair and illumination, he settles on his devoted
housekeeper, Araminta Dench (Minta for short, played by Lilian Hall-
Davis).

Sweetland's courtship is firmly set against the background of natural fertility and community. The opening shots are of a quiet valley, with scenes of animal peace on the farm, all plural except for the Sweetland workhorse, eating alone, an image of the master. When Sam rides out to make his first proposal, there is an extremely fine piece of landscape symbolism. In long shot Sam rides along a narrow path on a forest hillside. In the background where we would expect to see sky there is another forest. It is as if the world were entirely plush growth. The image expresses a divided unity, one forest seemingly carved into two. But it also expresses an elemental irregularity, one element dominant to the exclusion of the others. As such, the shot expresses the willfulness that will thwart Sweetland's hopes. The plushness confirms the fertility theme from the early sequences. Unfortunately Sweetland is not yet at harmony with the natural pattern, as his predatory language betrays:

> There's no need to wish me luck—Louisa Windeatt will come like a lamb to the slaughter.

> I came over like the foxes you're so fond of . . . to pick up a fat hen.

> You'll only feel the velvet glove and never know I was breaking you in.

The spirit of the rural community is expressed in the two social events that provide the peaks in the plot, the daughter's marriage and Thirza Tapper's tea party. Both events are instances of community, but both result in Sweetland's feeling alienated. The details of rural custom—ribbons on the whip and buggy to celebrate the wedding, Minta giving the ladies bags of wedding cake—express a respect for the continuity of traditions and are recorded respectfully, neither cute nor condescending. One passage of time is imaged in a homey joint roasting over the fire. A shot of the wedding banquet dissolves through the various stages of preparation, grace, feasting, and after-dinner niceties, as if the form of the event is an eternal constant through which the individual moments pass.

The irony in *The Farmer's Wife* is that Sam's intention may be in harmony with the natural and social spirit of marriage, but his willfulness violates the community peace. The beribboned horse and buggy is still a plain old horse and buggy underneath. Sweetland begins each proposal by announcing that he is going to be married. His proposals are rough and unflattering, sometimes even insulting. And the matches he tries to make before settling his eye on Minta are unfitting for him.

He courts the ladies in reverse alphabetical order—orderly, but wrongheaded. The first four candidates are neatly contrasted. The first is too self-sufficient for him. The second is independent but too nervous for marriage. The third is too girlish and the fourth too mannish. If such terms may be applied to ladies in fiction, the first and fourth are too hard and the middle two too soft.

Each time he is rejected Sweetland loses his temper and refuses to continue his friendship with the woman. The rejections progress in anger and indecorum. The proposal to Louisa Windeatt (Louise Poynds) ends so:

> Don't think that I shall come up your damned hill again.

> And you haven't treated me in a very lady-like spirit over this job. . . . You ain't nice-minded.

That "damned hill," of course, is the plush, full forest divided in itself and admitting no alternatives.

To propose to Thirza Tapper (Maud Gill), Sweetland arrives half an hour too early for her tea party, catching her undressed, in the bathroom, soaping herself. After much stumbling, his proposal—"Now some men look for a bit of fat on a female"—is fortunately interrupted by the maid's entrance with a plate of quivering aspic, which both expresses and increases the hostess's nervousness. However shaky, Thirza too pleads independence: "But I shall never seek the shelter of a man's arms, not even yours." Sweetland's rage reduces her to tears, at which point the maid returns with an emblem and amplifier of her mistress's mood, a plate of spilling ices. "How was I to know the ices would melt if I left them near the fire?" she cries. The proposal ends with the man yelling, both women crying, and ices and jelly slopping about.

At this point Hitchcock leaves Sweetland in order to concentrate on the party, the quirks of the guests, the general comedy of a community event exercising its loose control over individual eccentricities. "I ain't the party, George," says Ash, but he does embody the idea of the party as he tries manfully to submit his personal style to the occasion's demands. Hence his struggle to keep up his pants, from an ill-fitting borrowed livery, particularly when he wheels about the parson's aged mother. When the party adjourns to the garden, Ash can be himself: throw a spoon at Thirza's maid, drink his tea from a saucer, and wolf the cakes three at a time.

It is significant that Ash should be the focus of attention when Sweetland is off. Gordon Harker's misogynist handyman is a foil to his more civilized master. Ash is Sweetland's alter ego, the full expression of the antisocial, arrogant, and incorrigible aspects of Sweetland's character, which he controls by film's end. Ash's misfitting livery and clumsy fumblings are a fair image of Sweetland's romantic quest. Early in the film there is a very touching exchange between Ash in the farmyard and Sweetland up in the mistress's bedroom. Without a word Ash looks up and Sweetland sadly shakes his head, signifying the hopelessness of his wife's condition. Ash has little to do with Sweetland for the remainder of the film, dealing mainly with Araminta, but he remains a comic expansion of Sweetland's social maladroitness.

When Samuel proposes to postmistress Mary Hearne (Olga Slade), all pretense of decorum is abandoned. Mary laughs at his proposal: "You? At your age?" It is as if Ash's spree has caused the social reins to drop:

SAM: Have you got the face to call yourself a girl?

MARY: What the mischief should I call myself, then?

SAM: (stooping, so that they are nose to nose) Full blown and a bit over. . . . That's what I call you. The trouble with you is, you are too fond of dressing your mutton lamb fashion.

MARY: Is this a nightmare?

SAM: Your hat is.

MARY: You old sheep . . . to come to a woman in all her prime and beauty . . .

SAM: Don't think you were the first, cause you wasn't.

The proposal ends with Mary in hysterics and the entire community trying to soothe her and wondering what Sam did to her. Thirza pats Mary's hand, steps back but continues the patting movement, and faints into Ash's arms, imperiling again his hold on his pants.

We don't see the fourth proposal, but we can infer its tenor from the barmaid's hearty character. Where Phillpotts's Mercy Bassett (Ruth Maitland) is a delicate flower-lover who spends time over her decision ("too weak and floppy," observes Sweetland in the play), Hitchcock's fourth candidate is a robust, hearty woman who physically drags Sam over to return the flower he gave her. Hitchcock's women grow in strength. The first two are flattered by the proposals, but the second two are insulted. Instead of showing us Mercy's rejecting Sweetland, Hitchcock shifts to the romantic rivalry and pique of Mary and Thirza, in other words, the spreading dissension caused by Sweetland's courtship.

Part of the film's pleasure derives from the homey humor of the original play. Hitchcock respects the colloquial aphorisms of the original. So from Ash comes misogynist humor:

> Holy matrimony's a proper steam-roller for flattening the hope out of a man and the joy out of a woman.

> Beer drinking don't do 'alf the 'arm of love-making. If I were the Government, I'd give the drunkards a rest and look after the lovers.

Out of modesty or reticence Hitchcock omits Phillpotts's logic between the sentences in the latter example: "For why? Drink's a matter between a man and himself. Love's a matter between a man and a woman and that means the next generation."[3] Ash is cynical about Sweetland's revived ardor, in keeping with his antisocial function:

To see an old man in love be worse than seeing him with the whooping cough.

They do say that the next best thing to no wife be a good one.

The latter respects Minta's promotion.

Hitchcock keeps Minta's witty reactions to Sweetland's list of possibilities. So of Louisa Windeatt:

> SAM: I don't mind the pillowy women . . . so long as they be pillowy in the right places.
>
> MINTA: A woman that's a pillow at thirty be often a feather bed at forty.

The film is Hitchcock's wordiest silent film but the humor has its own various rewards: as humor; as country atmosphere, the Devon dialect consistent with the setting and the manners; as moments of social connection in the characters' lives; and as significant characterization. Minta, for example, shows a solid, independent mind and a generosity of spirit in the way she helps her master plot his campaign with no thought for herself. Far from being the passive lover Durgnat describes, Minta is simply unaware of her feelings for her master. The film delicately traces the growth both of her feelings and her awareness of them.

As usual—and despite the film's wordiness—Hitchcock exploits physical objects for their emotional associations. This also keeps Sweetland's quest for a wife domestic, however coarse his manner. So he first mentions his decision to remarry: "There's a female or two be floating around my mind like the smell of a Sunday dinner." His appetite is gentle and domestic. Two pieces of confetti on Sweetland's hair as he waves his married daughter off emphasize his desolation. Mrs. Sweetland's deathbed instructions to Minta are "And don't forget to air your master's pants" (a bowdlerized version of the original, "See master's pants be put to the fire"). A series of shots show Sam's underwear being washed or hung to dry, revealing Minta's faithful service, their intimacy, and the master's loneliness. On his large marriage bed, now with but a single pillow, his underwear suggests an absent body.

Some sentimental play evolves around the fireside chair that Sweetland's wife used to occupy. After Sweetland sees his daughter off, the foreground of empty furniture expresses his loneliness. The fireside chair expresses his particular missing of his wife. When he stares at it somberly during his daughter's wedding, it shadows the celebration. The camera pan suggests his glance moves from the left chair, his wife's, to the empty chair on the right, his own. Her void has left one in his place too.

As Sam and Minta "run over the possibles and impossibles," he visualizes each candidate in turn in his wife's chair. They reappear to taunt him with their rejections. When Sam returns from his third debacle and is preoccupied with the fourth hope, Minta sits casually in the wife's chair. Only then, when she waves him off to Mercy Bassett and as if her late mistress's chair has prompted her, does Minta recognize her own feeling for Sweetland. She returns inside and caresses the chair's back, which elegantly fits her shape.

When Sam returns defeated, Minta is nervous. She fumbles with a button then retreats behind the chair. She caresses it for comfort when Sweetland in his anger glares at her. For the first time she expresses her regard for him: "I won't hear a strong, sensible man talk like that." That calms him enough to settle into his chair. Minta steps in front of the wife's chair and is more outspoken: "What be women made of nowadays? 'Tis enough to weaken your faith in the whole pack of us." While Sam in his fantasy relives his shame by the other women, Minta eases into the wife's chair. As she still does not see herself as a possible wife to Sweetland she enumerates other "possibles." But seeing her in the chair drives out his other visions. When Thirza and Mary return, having decided to marry Sam, Mary seats herself in the wife's chair. Sam curtly calls her over to the kitchen table instead, leaving it for Minta.

By comparison, the bracelet in *The Ring* was an obtrusive symbol, drawing from outside the work its associations with Eden, for example, and being imposed on the plot. The chair in *The Farmer's Wife* fits so naturally into the action and the setting that it does not register as a symbol at all, and its emotional effects pass unremarked but felt.

Sam's proposal to Minta differs in two ways from the earlier ones. With the others his catch-line was "I am a man that a little child can lead but a regiment of soldiers couldn't drive." With Minta his pride and stubbornness are gone: "I'm offering myself so humble as a worm. Hope's gone, but I'd like to mention one thing in my favour. . . . A little child can lead me." Sam is softened by overhearing Ash remark that his master will throw a tantrum if Mercy Bassett rejects him too. Seeing himself from outside his own ego, Sweetland checks both his ire and his willfulness: "I be tamed to hearing no," he prefaces his proposal to Minta.

Second, for the first time God figures in Sam's courtship:

> The Lord works the same as lightning and don't give warning. . . . If you repent this bit of work, then may I lose my salvation.

Sweetland's humility shades into a religious spirit. This proposal is a matter of sentiment and sacrament both, where in earlier proposals Sam attempts to impose his will.

The political implications of *The Farmer's Wife* lie somewhere between Smith's and Durgnat's positions, perhaps closer to Durgnat. The film is affectionate toward the traditions of life, granted. But its primary energy is that embodied by Ash and purged from Sweetland. The comedy in Sweetland's courtship and Ash's wilder comedy represent the antisocial spirit's resistance to manners and decorum.

There is a deal of emotional impact in the fine performance of Minta, in the images of loneliness, and in Sweetland's gradual discovery of his proper wife. But the life of the film lies in its satiric vision of decorum on the brink of disaster, where courtship breeds dissension, confidence humiliation, and the hero's earnest attempts to connect, alienation. The film does not trace the usual comedic progress from chaos to order, but the dissolution of community into chaos. What order is ultimately achieved is due to Minta's wisdom and grace. At the end, both Mary's and Thirza's orderly lives, self-control, and self-respect have been shivered. Mercy's warm camaraderie has been found shallow. For Ash there is no hope of socialization.

Faithful though Hitchcock was to the play, it remains a Hitchcock film. Its fragile civility anticipates those blacker visions in *The 39 Steps, Saboteur, Psycho, North by Northwest, To Catch a Thief, Notorious, Rebecca,*

Topaz, The Birds, and *Family Plot,* where society's security and decorum are undermined by lurking forces of chaos.

The Farmer's Wife provides, finally, a revealing demonstration of Hitchcock's work as adapter. With few exceptions, after all, Hitchcock based his films on others' work. Here he trims the text to sharpen its focus. He omits one Sweetland daughter completely and with her the romantic tangle of two courtships, two suitors, a legacy, and much community gossip thereon. Where the play works up to the daughter's marriage, Hitchcock quickly passes over the wife's death and the daughter's marriage to focus on the aftermath. Eventually a marriage does reassert the community spirit. Hitchcock focuses on Sweetland, for whom the daughter's marriage is a celebration not unmixed with grief. The single marriage planned at the end of Hitchcock's version lacks the festive resonance of Phillpotts's conclusion.

By moving the melting ices from the beginning of the Thirza scene to the end, Hitchcock shows a shrewder sense of timing, but also makes that scene a microcosm of dissolution, climaxing in catastrophe, not reconciliation. Hitchcock's Sam comes earlier to Thirza's party than Phillpotts's, not just interrupting her plans, but proving agent of her exposure. Hitchcock also delays the discovery of Minta's feelings for Sam.

Most important is Hitchcock's alteration of the Churdles Ash character, the film's unaccommodated antisocial spirit. His comic business with the ill-fitting livery, the falling pants, the wayward wheelchair—none are in the play. Hitchcock's Ash both embodies and is victim of antisocietal chaos. Hitchcock drops the political radicalism Phillpotts gave Ash:

ASH: To hell with the men that can't shave their own chins and lace their own boots—that's what I say.

THIRZA: I'm afraid you're a terrible socialist, Mr. Ash.

We ain't put into the world to imitate our fathers. Life ban't writing in a copy-book. Go your own way and make history, I told Smerdon not a week agone.

Let them follow as can't lead, I said; and if you can't break away from your dead father's ideas and your live mother's apron-strings at your age—then there's no hope you'll ever set the sieve afire.

Waste! Wicked waste, I call it. This sort of wanton feeding everywhere; and if a table like this could be seen by the men in that monkey-
house they call Parliament, no doubt something would be done. But
our turn will come. They laugh loudest that laugh last; and the work-
ers will laugh last.[4]

If Hitchcock were the conservative that Smith contends, he would
have kept these speeches by his comic butt. But he is not. Hitchcock's
art does not bring order to chaos, but exposes the chaos underlying
the delusion of order. He strips Ash of his politics because the disorder
Hitchcock saw as early as 1928, as early as *Downhill* in 1927 or *The
Lodger* in 1926, lies beyond politics. Its roots are in man himself, in his
willfulness, in his deluding perception, in the tricks of fate to which
he is prey, in his shallow claim to be rational and civilized.

Champagne

1928

Hard upon the brilliance of *The Ring* and *The Farmer's Wife*, and but a year before *The Manxman* and *Blackmail*, Hitchcock produced what may be his worst feature film, *Champagne*. *Bioscope* gave it brief praise, perhaps grateful for Hitchcock's enlivening the British film scene: "This is bright entertainment, due mainly to the performance of the volatile Betty Balfour. The photography is excellent" (August 28, 1928).

But for once we can agree with Hitchcock's modest claims: *Champagne* "was probably the lowest ebb in my output," he tells Truffaut, "there is no story." Truffaut disagrees: "I enjoyed it. Some of the scenes have the lively quality of the Griffith comedies."[1] To Bogdanovich, Hitchcock explains that the original plan for the film was scrapped as not entertaining, "So we ended up with a hodge-podge of a story that was written as we went through the film and I thought it was dreadful."[2]

Millionaire Gordon Harker is opposed to his daughter Betty's (Betty Balfour) engagement to "a boulevard sheik," the Boy (Jean Bradin), and to her wasteful living. So he pretends to have been wiped out on the stock market. Unknown to all, including us, the father has hired an old friend (Theo von Alten) to pretend to be a Vile Seducer, in order to keep an eye on Betty. Betty and the Boy and the father are reconciled at the end.

Now, the film Hitchcock originally planned to make: "My idea was to show a girl, working in Reims, whose job is to nail down the crates of champagne. And always, the champagne is put on the train. She never drinks any—just looks at it. But eventually she would go to the city herself, and she would follow the route of the champagne—the nightclubs, the parties. And naturally she would get to drink some. In the end, thoroughly disillusioned, she would return to her old job at Reims, by then hating champagne. I dropped the whole idea—probably because of the moralising aspect."[3] To Bogdanovich, Hitchcock recalls the last line the film would have had when the girl returned, broken and miserable, to her job. For each new shipment she was sending off she would say, "Well, that's going to cause some trouble for somebody."[4]

That is a touching story. Hitchcock's planned fable might have ramified into issues of responsibility for others' downfall. But then he catches himself. His story is too moralistic; it suggests he might think champagne is evil. The big city, 13,000-pound-a-year director is revealing a trace of Cockney Puritanism, so the film is spun around.[5] Instead of a poor, virtuous country girl's introduction to the corrupting luxuries of city life, a spoiled rich girl is reduced to the hard life. Nothing survives this inversion.

Entertainment values this romantic melodrama certainly has: the vicarious delights of the posh life, some good bits of comedy. There is even Hitchcock's usual flair with expressive devices. Von Alten kisses Betty's hand and joins her table in the ship's dining room in one of those pre-Resnaisian time tricks, first in long shot, then in middle, to make their meeting portentous. Betty's memory of the New Year's Eve dance on the ship freezes to a still in a travel agent's window, the deprived Betty standing cold outside in front of a taunting Bureau de Change sign. The "change" does double service. Hitchcock plays an extended sequence in the conditional tense, like Richard Todd's lie in *Stage Fright* and Mabel's in *Downhill:* Betty imagines the horrible danger that von Alten warns can befall a girl. The danger seems to be happening to her, until the scene snaps back to the conversation.

Reminiscent of the solitary, manic dancer in the credit sequence of *The Pleasure Garden,* a lady dances wild and alone in the floor show behind Betty, the Boy, and the Vile Seducer. The dance suggests the Boy's sordid suspicion and Betty's flutter at her embarrassment of riches, two opposed perspectives at once. The solo dancer is replaced by a rather sloppy couple. Betty, left alone with the Boy in her club, starts to dance by herself in her seat when she senses that their harmony has been broken. Again a solo dance shows false hilarity. Behind them several couples provide images of mismatch—two women dancing joylessly together, a tall, thin woman dancing with a too-short fat man. They amplify the desperation in Betty's dance, but the Boy misunderstands her and stomps off, abandoning his love to the loose life he assumes she is enjoying.

The film cracks from this double moral perspective. On the one hand, the girl, her society, and the champagne are held up to be value-less. On the other, no dangers materialize and no moral alternative is presented. What results is a mix of the artful (as the details above) and the clumsy (the improbable newspaper headlines that advance the plot).

In *Champagne* the comedy of the seasick suitor seems imposed to no purpose. It will work better in *Rich and Strange,* a romantic comedy where Hitchcock's ironic undertow is more clearly formed, where the seasickness is one of a number of diseases and lassitudes, from boredom through fatigue, through seasickness, *l'amour fou,* digestive nausea, and finally, the gray sickness of domestica. In *Champagne* the situation serves only to give the Vile Seducer an advantage in sophistication over the Boy, which the plot does not support.

Hitchcock told Truffaut that his favorite gag in the film was the drunkard who sways when the ship is steady but walks a perfectly straight line when everyone else struggles to keep an even keel.[6] The joke is a parable of solipsism. The film's larger movement is reflected in this man whose competence and confidence stem from his own vision, independent of the real world.

This relates to the technical high spot in *Champagne.* The opening shot shows a champagne bottle aimed at the audience (like a gun), popped, and poured. Through the flat ring at the bottom of the glass, we first see the luxury life aboard the SS *Aquitania.* The last shot is again through the tilted champagne glass, the Vile Seducer toasting the young couple. This frame summarizes Hitchcock's film and its characters as frothy and insubstantial as a champagne bubble.

In a posh restaurant, four waiters shape air in their hands to convey the father's order of dessert, in contrast to the girl's similar movements when she rolls and kneads real dough to bake bread. The upper class's insubstantiality contrasts to the substance with which the poor must grapple. In a related sequence, a plate of junk originates in the kitchen, is fondled, dropped, rolled, replaced by a multitude of dirty fingers, until it finally appears as an elegant plate in an expensive restaurant. The high-society image proves seamy.

The champagne glass frame anticipates the shot in *Spellbound*, where the audience is given Gregory Peck's perspective through a glass of drugged milk. It in turn sets up the shot where we look down the gun barrel with which Leo G. Carroll is about to kill himself. Hitchcock eschews gimmickry for its own sake: "Trying to make . . . cinema, some new directors find odd angles to shoot from, but they still only produce what I call 'photographs of people talking.'" And he explains his *Spellbound* milk shot: "I was playing with white there, in preparation for the denouement, which had to do with snow. Throughout the film, I wanted to make a sort of leitmotiv of that color."[7]

The through-the-glass shot, with Peck's vision of the world drowned out by the drugged milk, puts us into the position of the man who is uncertain of his own responsibility for a murder, of his own identity, and of his own memory. Hitchcock's gimmick is rich in its implications and interplay with the audience. The two subjective shots shift our identification from the possibly guilty Peck to the guilty Carroll. The *Champagne* "frame" feels artificial because it's unrelated to the film's themes.

The film could have been Hitchcock's harshest vision of the upper class and its luxuries, at least until *To Catch a Thief*, but the champagne life is not consistently evil. We find no justification for the father's attack on Betty's nightclub job: "How dare you, a daughter of mine, disgrace yourself like this?" Not when his lie drove her to seek employment. The father loses all sympathy when he pounds his intercom in anger, drawing a crowd of office staff for no reason; smoking a huge cigar in bed while Betty goes to pawn her jewels (and is robbed of them); idly doing push-ups while she struggles to make the bed; and opposing her marriage to the Boy, clearly their moral superior. Betty is supposed to learn a lesson from a reprehensible, pleasure-loving tyrant.

Betty herself flounders in Hitchcock's uncertainty. In her heyday, she mocks her maid by donning her humble shawl. But even in her reform she feels her own nose in proud contrast to a secretary's hooked one. What is Hitchcock's point? That we should be proud of our unearned advantages over the less fortunate? Hitchcock also ridicules Betty's attempts at practicality. Her cooking sends her father to a ritzy restaurant; whose home cooking would keep him from it? Her fiancé's confidence that "You'll make a mess of it [her job] like you make a mess of everything you lay your hands on" is confirmed by her two flour handprints on his jacket. That is a joke in search of a butt. Is the girl wrong to try to bake or the man for considering her hopeless? The Boy's line justifies the uselessness of the rich. Rare in Hitchcock, points are made without direction or consistency. *Champagne* lacks Hitchcock's coherence. It's more like pins in a pincushion, pointing every which way.

The pincushion does seem to be the upper class, though, by Hitchcock's original impetus. But the film is not consistent. Betty shows a satiric strength when she goes for a job in the nightclub:

—Can't you see I'm the maitre d'hotel?
—I'm sorry. I thought you were a gentleman.

On the job, she gives carnations to the boys in the band instead of just to the customers in formal suits. She seems victimized by snobbery, but did she make a mistake or was she being playful?

Champagne remains an emblem of the wastefulness of the upper class (a prejudice overcome in *The Ring*). In Paris, Betty brags to her beau about her new friends, new cocktail, and new gowns. He replies coldly to all three: "I've always understood that simplicity is the keynote to good taste." Even as a reformed working girl, she pauses to ask the bartender about the new drink she is about to serve the Vile Seducer. "A Maiden's Prayer" neatly combines the supposedly Vile Seducer's utility with the hint that he too is an innocent. Yet her priggish boyfriend frequents the expensive club where she works. The moral perspective is inconsistent.

Perhaps *Champagne* would make more sense if it were titled *False Alarm*. It exercises the false alarm (expressing the complacency of the upper class) more than it warns of the dangers of champagne (a complacency of the lower class). For *Champagne* is not like *Downhill*. Betty suffers nothing like Roddy's parental neglect and social skid. After all, she stays in her posh world, trying for a job as a fashion model, then working in a nightclub she used to frequent, where she is expected to party with the customers.

Among *Champagne*'s several false alarms, a tango act is interrupted when everyone rushes out of the ballroom as if for some disaster (whether to witness or to avert). But no, the rich girl has only splash landed her daddy's plane to join her fiancé. The primary false alarm is the father's bankruptcy claim. His indictment of cutthroat capitalists ("Wall Street took advantage of my absence") is just a false alarm too; they're too nice a lot ever to do that! The audience and the Boy are alarmed at the Vile Seducer's apparent success but, not to worry, he's just protecting Betty from men like him. The Boy seems to abandon her, to her and our (false) alarm. Later he finds her in the Vile Seducer's flat (but she *hasn't*) and she brains the Boy, thinking he's the Seducer (false alarm). A woman leaps from a balcony as if to kill herself but that too is a false alarm; the jump is into her partner's arms for their nightclub dance. This act has two morals: (1) it takes one to take a dive but two to tango; and (2) relax, don't worry, everything is all right, have a good time. The warning against various vices and extravagances (of which champagne is emblematic) concludes that those dangers are exaggerated. For perhaps the only time, Hitchcock's accommodation of his moral vision to his responsibilities as an entertainer rendered his film incoherent.

Champagne ends as it began, the world reduced to the bottom of a champagne glass. The high life is such a dreg. The last scene is not just reassuring, however. As Betty throws the Vile Seducer another suspicious glance, he flashes a sinister smile. The father blesses the match, but the lovers have not really improved their understanding of each other. They quarrel over who should take the initiative on the wedding arrangements. And their marriage still depends on the security of her wealth. There may be a fine, black-lined film trying to get out here, but it's trapped in the bubbles.

The Manxman

1929

If *Champagne* suffers from the unresolved tension between the moralist and the light romantic, *The Manxman* explores the tension between the moralist and the passionate romantic. Hitchcock frames the film with the moral he took from the title page of his source, Hall Caine's extremely popular novel: "What shall it profit a man if he gain the whole world and lose his own soul?"[1] But in the film the romantic holds sway. The result is a film with brilliant characterization, camera work, and evocative use of landscape, but to which the drawn moral seems irrelevant.

The Manxman is perhaps not a total success like *The Farmer's Wife*, but it is as unfairly neglected. The *Bioscope* reviewer recognized the triumph of Hitchcock's style over his source material: "Only a skilful director like Hitchcock could have devised from a story of this kind a picture of such remarkable power and gripping interest" (January 23, 1929). John Russell Taylor admits there are "excellent things" in the film (unenumerated) and praises Hitchcock for the "admirable, restrained, and severe fashion" in which he dealt with the melodramatic Caine novel.[2] Most commentators on Hitchcock ignore *The Manxman* altogether. John Smith's study is weakened by his omission of this film and *Downhill* ("Individualism: A Selection of English Hitchcock"), for in no Hitchcock film (except *The Skin Game*) does Hitchcock deal more clearly with the individual's duty to break with the traditions of his class.

Rohmer and Chabrol rate it with *The Ring* as Hitchcock's best silent work. Unlike *Champagne*, *The Manxman* "est un film tres ambitieux et sans aucune concession":

> Pour la première fois, Hitchcock pénétrait dans un domaine qui lui est devenu cher, celui du vertigineux. La situation de *The Manxman* est sublime parce qu'elle est inextricable et refuse l'artifice. Elle est inextricable parce qu'elle ne s'appuie pas sur la malignité des personnages, ni sur l'archarnement du sort. Hitchcock s'est plu à décrire minutieusement, complètement et sans faux-ruyant, le confit moral opposant trois etres dont les actions sont practiquement irreprochables. La faute est la faute du genre humain. La morale ordinaire est impuissante à résoudre leurs problèmes. Chacun est obligé d'assumer ses propres responsabilités, de se forger une ethique . . . La mise en scene est deliberement axee sur les visages, sur les regards. La péripétie est repoussée a l'arriere-plan. Cette purete que l'on se doit de louer, ne va pas d'ailleurs sans son revers: le trait hitchcockien, dont *The Ring* avait déjà prouve l'efficacité, est ici presque totalement absent.

Perhaps *Downhill* bears the seeds that Chabrol and Rohmer find here in full flower.[3]

The powers at British International Pictures thought so little of *The Manxman* that it was shelved for some months and was only released after the success of Hitchcock's brilliant sound debut, *Blackmail*. By then this classical silent film had had its day.

Hitchcock did not like *The Manxman*. "The only point of interest about that movie is that it was my last silent one," he tells Truffaut, "it was a very banal picture." He denies Truffaut's sense that Hitchcock "believed in this film": "It's not a matter of conviction, but the picture was the adaptation of a very well-known book by Sir Hall Caine. The novel had quite a reputation and it belonged to a tradition. We had to respect that reputation and that tradition. It was not a Hitchcock movie, whereas *Blackmail* . . ."[4] To Bogdanovich, Hitchcock even gives an erroneous plot summary: "A kind of old-fashioned story. An assignment, more or less. It was a domestic melodrama, you know, the illegitimate child and the brother and the judge—one of those things full of coincidences—the brother happens to be a lawyer and the poor girl gets involved with a fisherman and so on."[5]

There are no brothers in the film and in the novel there are only half brothers, the noble fisherman and the wastrel gentleman, the lawyer being a cousin. "Romantic and novelettish" is how Peter Noble dismisses both *Champagne* and *The Manxman*.[6] Unfortunately, those terms have stuck. Even the sympathetic Kirk Bond dismisses it as "on the whole conventional and old-fashioned. . . . There are a few nice shots, but little else."[7]

The film opens with a ship's flag waving the triskeles, three-legged emblem of the Isle of Man. Lawyer Phillip Christian (Malcolm Keen) and fisherman Pete Quilliam (Carl Brisson) grew up as bosom friends. The lawyer helps the fisherman fight the encroachment of steam trawlers against the herring boats. Both men are attracted to the innkeeper's daughter, Kate Cregeen (Anny Ondra). When Pete speaks for her first Phillip gives way, though she clearly prefers Phillip. The girl's father, Caesar Cregeen (Randle Ayrton), rejects Pete as "a penniless lout." Entrusting Phillip with Kate's care, Pete goes off to the African gold mines to make his fortune.

In Kate's diary "Mr. Christian" soon becomes "Phillip." They fall in love but remain within the limits set by Phillip's pledge to Pete. Then word arrives that Pete is dead. This frees the love between Phillip and Kate, but Phillip expects to follow his forefathers into the position of deemster (judge). Marriage beneath his station might spoil his chances. Pete suddenly returns, alive and wealthy, and claims his Kate. Phillip won't let Kate break Pete's heart by either revealing or continuing their affair. Pete and Kate marry, and they have a daughter. She is Phillip's.

Unable to bear the strain, Kate leaves Pete and rushes to Phillip. First he urges her to return home, then he relents and gives her shelter. Pete protects Kate's name by telling everyone she is on holiday in London. He is overjoyed when she returns, but crestfallen when he finds she has come to retrieve her baby. When Kate tries to drown herself, she is saved and brought before Deemster Phillip Christian for sentencing.

After Pete pleads for her, the judge releases Kate to her husband. But Caesar Cregeen accuses the judge of having alienated his daughter's affections. Phillip resigns the post of deemster and amid a hissing, gawking crowd (that anticipates Father Logan's release in *I Confess*) strides out to a new life with Kate. The lovers walk up a dark country hillside under glowering clouds. The last image is of lonely Pete, bleary-eyed on his boat in the community of boats fishing in the night.

The opening triskeles prepares the allegory of the ternary nature of man. The blissful community of Pete (body), Phillip (mind), and Kate (soul) is disrupted by Pete's willful insensitivity and Phillip's failure to subordinate his rational ambition and friendship to his passion for Kate. To the credit of Hitchcock and his actors, nowhere do they seem to be playing types or ideas. The story is one of Hitchcock's richest in terms of the revelation of human nature and sorrows of the heart.

As in *The Ring,* Brisson is a tough-spirited but ingenuous lover. Miss Ondra may seem too shallow to be the prototype of Hitchcock's cool blonde—like the volcanic glaciers Ingrid Bergman, Eva Marie Saint, and Grace Kelly—but she earns the title upon hearing of Pete's supposed death.[8] In the deep center background, amid shadowy inn patrons, at Phillip's arrival she wheels around with a glowing and intense "Phillip—we're free."

In the novel, Kate reacts to that news with conventional tears (85) and to Pete's return with numbness (132). Hitchcock's Kate is numb at the first news of the death, then renewed by her joyful love. To Pete's return she responds with tears and is numbed when Phillip resigns her to Pete. In the novel a physical fever numbs her for the wedding, with Caesar's complicity (156), but in the film her numbness is emotional. She is completely passive: the veil is dropped on her, the ring slowly slipped on, a man's arm reaches out for her to take. Her only lively motion is her manic laugh when at the wedding feast her husband corrects her father's gloom with "Hey, Caesar, this is a funeral, not a wedding." It is.

Nor is her unwanted husband the usual unfeeling boor. Pete has only acted lovingly, if exuberantly. The romantic tragedy is deepened by how lovingly he fondles "his" daughter. When Kate comes to take the baby, Pete struggles to restrain himself from caressing, even touching, the woman he loves. His tentative reaches and checks express his gentleness, his feeling, but also a sensitivity that he lacked as a young man, which caused the tragic mismatch.

Simply, Pete leaps to the conclusion that Kate will marry him and that Phillip has no interest in her. Pete coaxes Phillip into speaking to Caesar on his behalf, then hoisting him on his shoulders to say good-bye to Kate (Hitchcock's addition to the novel, where Phillip waits for him under an apple tree). From her side-glances and gestures it is clear that Kate frolics with Pete but reserves her highest and deepest regard for Phillip. Pete wrings her commitment in a moment of playfulness, and he does not hear her attempt to correct his misimpression.

Kate responds to Pete as a girl to a boy, but to Phillip as a woman to a man. The fisherman (felicitously) tells her at one point, "Aw, Kate, hold your capers—be serious awhile, darlin'." The playful girl grows into a passionate woman, as Caine states in the novel (e.g., 76, 133). At such great costs, Pete learns to be sensitive to others' unexpressed emotions.

Nor are Phillip's motivations simple. He has Roddy's noble ethic in *Downhill*: the more affluent of two loyal friends should accede to the less fortunate. So he puts Pete's case to Caesar, not his own. Hitchcock's lovers don't consummate their affair until Pete is thought dead, though Caine's do earlier, from Kate's aggressive ardor (103, 115–17), which Caine does not condemn. In turning Kate back to Pete, Phillip is driven by his oath to his friend, his fear of breaking his friend's heart, and his own knowledge that his father lost his deemster's post, fame, and fortune by marrying beneath his station. In remaining a close friend of the new family, Phillip pays dearly for this decision—and often.

At all three points of this love triangle there is a complex of emotions and motives. The simplest exchange accrues irony and emotion, as when the doctor comes down from the daughter's birth, finds Pete and Phillip waiting, and asks Phillip, "Which of you is the father?" Had he known Kate was carrying his child, Phillip avers, he would not have put his other concerns above their love.

As the action setting is the Isle of Man, enislement is a basic theme: people are isolated by their own will (Pete), by their principles (Caesar,

Phillip), and even by their own connections to others (Pete to Phillip, Kate and Phillip to each other, the young Christian to his deemster forefathers). Hitchcock depicts this isolation by shooting important scenes from outside a barred window, with the most important character often outside, cut off from the determination of his fate, or ceding us his perspective. Thus Pete watches Phillip plead Pete's case with Caesar. The shot is reversed on Pete's return, when Phillip is on the outside, reluctant to enter to greet his friend. Pete bids Kate good-bye from outside and below the window. Thought dead, Pete writes his letters home against the glass on similar windows, the outsider about to return, having met the conditions to cross Caesar's threshold. When Phillip and Kate finally leave Pete's cottage with the baby, the whole town is outside, pressing their shocked faces against the windows. Hitchcock's lovers are trapped in windowed boxes. Their love achieved, they are trapped outside the boxes, together but bereft of community.

The courtroom is a maze of boxes of people. This anticipates the inner office where the mother is interviewed at the start of the 1934 *The Man Who Knew Too Much,* the screen in *The Paradine Case,* and the miniature boxes/windows/screens behind which people live their secret lives in *Rear Window.* The lovers' refuge in the telephone booth in *Blackmail* anticipates the couple quarreling in the record-store booth in *Strangers on a Train.* Boxed victims are a Hitchcock motif.

Here even status isolates. Phillip's outdoor romps with Kate contrast to the artificiality of the floral mural, lampshade, and sofa cover in his aunt's living room, where Mrs. Christian warns him that marriage to the innkeeper's daughter would cost him his deemstership.[9] Kate meets Phillip in the flowers, Pete on the rocks. The cold, neat, blank panels in Phillip's office contrast to the detailed homey furnishings of Kate and Pete's cottage, with lively textures of plaster and rough wood, full of mementoes of ostensible sentiment and shared experience. These differences catch the cost of Phillip's honor.

When Kate tries to drown herself, Hitchcock dissolves from the close-up of the water, the ripples, her air bubbles, to a close-up of another dark pool, the inkwell into which Deemster Christian dips his pen to write a sentence. The dissolve anticipates the one to Janet Leigh's eye from the bath drain in *Psycho.* The pool that has all but overwhelmed the girl and can yet doom her to a life more miserable than

The Manxman *(1929). Pete (Carl Brisson) and Kate (Anny Ondra) pose in their rocky love.*

death is under Phillip's control both as judge and as lover. As judge, Christian can sentence Kate to imprisonment, either in jail or with her husband. As lover, he can again reject her or embrace her. Plunging his pen into the ink is both sexual and jurisprudent. The girl's water is dark because Phillip became judge. He gave her up for the profession of inkwells and verdicts.

By shooting Deemster Christian from the inkwell up, Hitchcock emphasizes his remoteness from the people to whom he was once so close. Pete's fumbling language bridges the gap, as he addresses Phillip alternately as judge and as friend: "Beg pardon, sir, but as you know she's my wife. . . . I'll take her back, sir. Please let her go, Phillip." After the deemster sets her "free to go to her husband," that is, acts as sympathetic judge (but as unsympathetic lover), Pete reverses the order: "Dear old Phil. Er—thank you, sir." The symmetry of Pete's rhetoric pivots on the judge's verdict.

One brilliant detail catches the friends' isolation by their concern for Kate. Waiting for the birth of the baby, Pete and Phillip play checkers, but dumbly. Phillip makes a foolish move, but Pete doesn't notice the free jumps it gives him. As a rule, of course, a chess or checkers game in a film doesn't even have the pieces on the right squares. But Hitchcock is in the details. His checkers players are preoccupied, alone even as they play together. Neither friend tries to win.

Hitchcock also makes his best use yet of settings. Kate and Phillip consummate their love in an empty mill. Phillip stands back in the middle of the room, surrounded by space except for an ominous tangle of rope at his feet. The mill has the idyllic associations but without the sinister omen of the mill in *Foreign Correspondent*. Kate is excited by the mill wheels, but the image—wheels turning wheels turning wheels—reflects their own lives run by forces beyond their control. Pete's mechanical assumption of Kate's love and Phillip's mechanical obedience to his friend and to his family tradition also lurk in the image of the mill wheels. As a slight force sets the wheels moving for a long time, they signify the extensive consequences of a human action—Pete's casual promise, the love between Phillip and Kate, Kate's suicide attempt and subsequent trial. "The mills of God grind slowly," the hypocrite Caesar observes at the wedding feast, which is held where Kate and Phillip consummated their love. The romantic tragedy unwinds from those remote impersonal cogs.

In his brilliant use of landscape, two shots anticipate Antonioni, as Hitchcock isolates and dwarfs the human figure in stone and shadow. Going to meet Phillip, Kate leaves the restrictive inn, passes a web of boats, then takes a long walk along a high horizon under a thickly clouded sky. She comes into what to her would seem to be a clearance, but what we see—wheel beyond wheel, circle beyond arc—is a small space heavily framed by dark rock. The next shot is of Phillip, even lower on the frame, under an even heavier complex of rock frame and burden. Their embrace is shot from farther away and from a dark cave, as if their freedom is already threatened by shadowy observation. In a seven-shot sequence, the lovers are overwhelmed by the rock formations, hard and sterile, where they cower in small pockets of space.[10]

After all the emotional impact of the plot, the characterization, and this evocative imagery, the moral rings false: "What shall it profit a man if he gain the whole world and lose his own soul?" The moral

The Manxman *(1929). Phillip (Malcolm Keen) is dwarfed by a rock formation that anticipates the landscape symbolism of Antonioni.*

does not gibe with the characters, the film, or the romantic-tragic mood. Phillip gained high office but at the cost of a happy marriage. The moral does not fit him because his ardor was checked more by his friendship to Pete than by ambition. Nor can he be called a lost soul, given his atonement.

Neither does Pete prove that lesson, as he would have lost Kate to Phillip even had he not gone to Africa to make his fortune. The moral doesn't suit Kate either, even though one title describes her as "an adored, unhappy wife whose misery brought death unto her soul." It is hard to blame Kate for anything other than love. She urged Phillip to marry her despite Pete's return: "I'm glad Pete's alive but it makes no difference. I don't love him. . . . Yes, I promised myself to him, but I've given myself to you." Kate certainly does not sacrifice her soul for some worldly ambition. Indeed, Hall Caine seems to approve her seduction of Phillip, the man she loves, and Hitchcock's Kate is less calculating.

The only character to which the moral does apply is Caesar Cregeen, but he is a bit player. Caesar is the most malicious, craven, unattractive character, a lost soul if there ever was one. His materialism results in the friends' tension. With rare honesty he welcomes Pete back, "hearty and flush o' money." His greed undercuts him: "See, Kate. You waited for him, and the Lord's spared him for you." "Marriage be a mighty reverent thing," he says, but Cregeen presides over a blasphemy, a marriage that separates lovers instead of uniting them. If Hitchcock sees Cregeen's hypocrisy, he must prefer that Kate marry Phillip. But such a minor figure can hardly bear the moral of the film.

The framing moral coheres with the tentative religious structure. Phillip Christian vies with his friend/disciple, the saintly Peter, for the soul possessed by the savage, earring-wearing Caesar. But it does not cohere with the emotional thrust and values. Perhaps this moral tag dignifies what Caine, then Hitchcock, may have feared would otherwise be taken as an empty—or sordid—romance.

Hitchcock closes on a different tone. To Caine there is a glory in Phillip's promotion and a triumph in his resignation to walk in shame with the woman he loved but abused. His shame is glorious:

> "My father's aspirations were not the call of a stern vocation, they were mere poetic ambition. As a poet he might have been a great man, but as a Deemster he must have been a mockery, a hypocrite, an imposter, and a sham." (121)

> The higher he rose, the lower he had to fall. Truly the steps of his Calvary were steep. Would he ever ascend it? (357)

> "In conquering the impulse to go without confessing, I conquered the desire to go at all. Here, where my old life has fallen to ruin, my new life must be built up. That is the only security. It is also the only justice. On this island, where my fall is known, my uprising may come—as is most right—only with bitter struggle and sorrow and tears. . . . And, meantime, she who was worthy of my highest honour will share my lowest degradation. That is the way of all woman."
>
> The exaltation of his tones infected everybody. (376–77)

> Under the weight of so many eyes, her head was held down but those who were near enough to see her face knew that shame was swallowed up in happiness and her fear in love. Phillip was like a man transfigured. The extreme pallor of his cheeks was gone, his step was firm, and his face was radiant. This was the hour of his triumph: this, when his sin was confessed, when conscience had no power to appall him, when the world and the pride of the world were beneath his feet, and he was going forth from a prison cell, hand in hand with the fallen woman by his side. (377–78)

This is heady, soggy stuff, but quite more romantic and exhilarating than the caution to which Hitchcock turns his story. He keeps Caine's moral but gives his lovers an ignominious departure up the dark hill. To Hall Caine the story of Phillip and Kate would be "The World Well Lost," but to Hitchcock there is a rueful "All for Love" instead.

Paradoxically, for the body of the story Caine's version limps on moralizing prose and Hitchcock's takes poetic wing. Hitchcock's lovers are more sinned against than sinning, bound apart by trivial codes. By the poetic thrust of the film, Phillip sins not by loving but by subordinating his love to his friendship, to his ambition, or to both.

This is psychologically convincing too. So is Hitchcock's change on Caine's Pete. Hitchcock's Pete is furious to learn his friend has loved his wife, where Caine's nurses Phillip back to health, warmly wishes them both well, and gives his wife a convenient divorce. "Pete, we too have suffered," Hitchcock's Kate says to still his ire. Her line has more honor and wisdom than Phillip's resignation speech:

> I stand before you—a man who has broken faith with his best friend and taken away a woman's honour. . . . You gave me your trust which I am unworthy to bear. I am not fit to sit in judgment on my fellows, I have sinned against God and man. . . . I resign this—the dignity I have strove for, that I may devote myself to righting the wrong I have done.

Hitchcock makes Phillip and Kate great tortured lovers who find the courage to shuck the obstacles to their love. But he kept the simplistic moral. This division between the artist's conscious morality and the

74

poetry of his work explain why, for both Caine and Hitchcock, the moral does not fit.

In terms of Hitchcock's development, *The Manxman* is a minor gem. It has his richest text up to that point, the most touching characterization, and some of the strongest imagery. Hobbled by a tangential morality, the film is still a fuller realization of human nature than his subsequent thrillers.[11]

Blackmail

1929

The irresolution in *The Manxman* between the moral conclusion and the film's romantic spirit is overcome in *Blackmail*. Indeed,
from *Champagne* through *The Manxman* to *Blackmail* Hitchcock moves
away from adherence to conventional tenets and toward the subversive spirit for which he is known.

Blackmail is Hitchcock's first essentially subversive film. It is as if
he made *The Farmer's Wife* but drew Sweetland at Ash's level or made
Roddy of *Downhill* prefer his life on the Marseilles docksides over "The
Land of Make-Believe" of his public school days. But such plot rewrites
can be left to Raymond Durgnat.[1]

Hitchcock modestly describes the film as an exercise on the traditional conflict between love and duty. The film begins—and, he claims,
was to end—with a straightforward, documentary-style record of the
arrest, fingerprinting, booking, and jailing of a criminal.[2] This demonstrates the policeman's duty and daily business.

That would have framed the personal story of Detective Frank
Webber (Johnny Longden). After work he meets his girlfriend, Alice
White (Anny Ondra), and they go off for dinner together. They squab-
ble and he stomps off. When he relents and goes back for her, he sees
her leaving with another man. This man is a smooth, cultured, sym-

pathetic artist, Crewe (Cyril Ritchard), who takes Alice to his room, prevails on her (without much trouble) to change clothes, and tries to seduce her. When the seduction becomes rape, Alice grabs a bread knife and kills him.

Assigned to investigate the case, Frank finds one of Alice's gloves in the murdered man's studio and hides it to protect her. A blackmailer, Tracy (Donald Calthrop), has the other glove and threatens to turn in Alice and Frank. But the artist's landlady saw the victim talk with Tracy the night he was murdered, so the blackmailer becomes the chief suspect. Frank bullies Tracy into a panic. Fleeing Scotland Yard along the roof of the British Museum, Tracy falls through a skylight to his death. The Yard considers the case closed. Alice decides to confess to the murder but the police chief passes her on to Frank, who persuades her to remain silent. The lovers live on, the blackmailer punished with death, the murderess and the compromised detective free, and all with the amoral approval of the audience.

Hitchcock claims that his producers would not let him make the film he wanted in which the police would have tracked Alice down and, finding Frank with her, assume he is making the arrest. He would then put her through the cold booking procedures with which the film opened, then walk out with his superior, who would say, "Going out with your girl tonight?" Frank would end the film with "No, not tonight."

Where duty triumphed in Hitchcock's original draft of the film, love or selfishness triumph in what the producers took to be a more upbeat ending. The producers unwittingly chose the more radical ending because it "looked" more conventional, a romantic happy ending. The censors who gave Buñuel his marvelously subversive conclusion to *Viridiana* made the same happy error. If the producers did force the present ending on the film, then Hitchcock was compelled to the subversion he repressed in his previous two films. In any case, the imposed ending stands as an integrated ironic whole.

Not until *Shadow of a Doubt* and *Strangers on a Train* did Hitchcock again reach such intense cohesion and irony. So, for example, the Whites' gossipy neighbor tosses off a line that seems casual: "But I don't think the police are what they're worth." The line works in her catty characterization. As an expression of the popular antipathy toward law and order, it recalls the stone thrown at the police in the first reel. Moreover, the verbal ambiguity challenges Frank's integrity. The line can mean: (1) the police are not worth their salary—the neighbor's likely intention; (2) the character of the police is not what it seems to be—the cynical public view, which Frank will prove; (3) the individual policeman does not live up to the traditions of the Yard, that is, the honor of the force; or (4) the Yard as a continuing institution is worth more than the sum of its individual parts. These various meanings are carried by but don't weigh down the line of sparky characterization.

The detectives' second conversation parodies the main plot:

> DET. 2: So the next time I went to another tailor and found out that it was no better than the first.
>
> DET. 1: Ha ha ha
>
> DET. 2: But I thought as it was on the expense account I'd keep to it.
>
> DET. 1: Ha ha ha
>
> DET. 2: You should see the mess he made of it. I told him I wouldn't pay for the thing, but the trouble is, he's got my material . . . (speech gets lost in surrounding noises). (1)[3]

In order, Detective 2 parallels Alice's bored "tryout" of another beau, her feelings of freed irresponsibility and Frank's of police privilege, and their control by someone who has their "material" (as the blackmailer with Alice's glove).

The subversive irony in *Blackmail* may slip by undetected. For one thing, the film was initially received with tremendous acclaim as Britain's first sound film and a masterpiece.[4] It remains a landmark in the history of the sound film, although it has become fashionable to sneer at it.[5]

The film's technical effects make it a pivot point between the silent and sound film. Hitchcock filmed *Blackmail* as a silent thriller, but the studio was building its sound stages in order to follow on the success of *The Jazz Singer*. There were already experiments in part talkies, even in England.[6] The plan was for the bulk of the film to be shot silent and the last reel to be done with sound, but Hitchcock anticipated studio pressure to convert the film to sound: "When producing the film in silent form, I was imagining all the time that it was a talkie. I was using talkie technique, but without sound."[7] The Czech actress Anny Ondra was not fluent in English, so Joan Barry crouched off camera to recite her lines while Miss Ondra mouthed them phonetically. Phyllis Konstam's stage engagement required her being dubbed by Phyllis Monkham for other sound retakes. The British censor's certificate declares "Blackmail (synchronized)."

The first reel of *Blackmail,* the documentary record of the police alarm and the arrest of the petty criminal, works like a silent film. There are six sound effects in the opening reel: a van door shuts, a stone is thrown through a window, car horns sound, a cell door snaps shut, some men chat, and there is unsynchronized dialogue at the end. Otherwise the opening reel could be a silent film with a recorded score.[8]

The technical tricks and devices can distract us from a critical analysis of the film. Most writers on *Blackmail* have oohed or yawned at the technical bravado of the film but have not proceeded to a definition of what the film is doing. The exceptions to this in English are Raymond Durgnat and Beverle Houston and Marsha Kinder to whom much of my argument is indebted.[9]

If the film's place in the history of sound film has obscured its ironic import, that documentary opening has as well. As Durgnat suggests, "Very few spectators seem to register its anarchistic side, perhaps because the opening sequence is so strong, firm and self-contained that its image of the police survives the ironies which follow. . . . It encapsulates any indulgence of disorder within a strong general affirmation, at least for those spectators for whom law and order is sacred."[10] It is assuring to see Scotland Yard get their man so efficiently in that opening sequence. It is refreshing to have the impersonality of that initial police process leavened by the touch of human love in Frank's treatment of Alice later. For the criminal's dissolve of face into fingerprint is a bit cold and heartless. It is reassuring to find Detective Webber preserving Miss White's face from that reduction.

Or is it? It is if one is Miss White. But if one is not, as indeed the vast majority of the film's audience over the years has not been, then the real terror derives from the combination of the police efficiency in the first part and the selfish detective's subversion of the law in the second. The petty gunman of the opening sequence, the genteel rapist, and the seedy little blackmailer are nothing like the threat to our social order and security that a self-serving policeman is.

Blackmail may have begun as a standard love versus duty story: "This idea was the origin of my first talkie, *Blackmail*. The hazy pattern one saw beforehand was duty—love—love versus duty—and finally either duty or love, one or the other."[11] But the film shifted its emphasis, whether because of the producers' pressure or because of its redirection to sound. Instead of the sentimental consolation of love conquering all, we have the frightening prospect of a social order subverted—by a policeman. Nor does Webber ultimately serve his girlfriend that well. Admitting she had accidentally killed to defend her honor would have been easier than bearing the additional guilt of Tracy's death and Frank's corruption.

The film is also a brilliant examination of the limits and problems of human communication. The film is not just *in* sound; it is *about* sound. As usual, where Hitchcock's technique is most arresting, his technique is most meaningful.

The film demonstrates the difficulties in human speech at the same time as it exults in its new power to present it. The first dialogue we hear is the flying squad getting its directions garbled over the radio. For the information to be conveyed clearly, it must be written and passed along as a note (to be read, like old movie titles). Still, as visual analogues for the way sound can connect people across distances, by radio or by phone, the next shots show arches—men standing under a large bridge; children playing under narrower arches. As the transparent ceiling and open staircase in *The Lodger* were visual substitutes for the sound experience, these bridges, by reaching across space, embody the aural connection.

The landlady's phone call to the police demonstrates communication through speech, but it more dramatically demonstrates the breakdown of understanding if one has only words to go on. The split screen shows the policeman taking the call with his back to the caller:

POLICE: Who did you say it was?

LANDLADY: Mr. Crewe.

POLICE: Who?

LADY: No—Crewe. I tell you, it's 'orrible.

POLICE: All right, don't you worry, I'll send round straight away. What number did you say, seven or eleven?

LADY: Thirty-one.

POLICE: Thirty-one?

LADY: What?

POLICE: Thirty-one I said.

LADY: No no. Thirty-one. (7)

Even where there is agreement and understanding, words leave confusion. Frank has trouble on the phone later: "What? Who?" We don't hear his message.

The conversations tend to be banal. "I'd better go," says Alice; "I see," says Crewe. But she is undressed and he plans to steal her dress to facilitate his seduction. The characters' words belie the intensity of their situation.[12] The friction between Alice and Frank, aggravated by the noise of the restaurant, is independent of what they say to each other. Words don't handle her restlessness or his impatience. So they have to act out their moods, she by accepting the artist's invitation to a change and Frank by walking out on her. When words fail Crewe's landlady, she resorts to gesture to describe Tracy: "When he spoke to you he went like this."

Of course, the police inspector goes "like this" too, has precisely the hand-rubbing mannerism that nails Tracy. So the gesture is not unique like a fingerprint. Nor is language as clear and precise an identification of meaning either. The dialogue ripples with puns, once we attend to the dramatic presence of the new sound and the theme of language: "Heard of," "It's still my word against hers," "Our word is as good as, or better than, that of a jailbird." The tension between the detective and the blackmailer is a clash of "words." The film's title is significant in this respect. It does not focus on the murder or the rape but on the threat of the report of the deed. The word is greater than the thing itself or at least more frightening to the principals. As a covering (gloves) is the clue and the incrimination, the cover-up is greater than the crime. Webber is a corrupt policeman because he subordinates his duty to uncover the criminal to his desire to conceal her. Concealing her from the law exposes her to him, leaving her in his thrall.

Language that fails to express can be used to conceal. Hence Webber's verbal fencing with Tracy. Language delays Alice's confession. With her verbose windup, she doesn't get out her pitch before the phone interrupts:

> What I was going to say was this—if I didn't say what I have to say now. . . . I'd rather not wait. What I wanted to say was . . . (The telephone rings) I was the one who . . . (13)

As she delays her confession, Hitchcock draws us into hoping she will not get it out. The audience identifies with the criminal through her prolonged words here. With the sinking car in *Psycho* and the deaf cleaning lady in *Marnie,* Hitchcock achieves the same effect with space.

Words failing, the character may retreat to noise—like the landlady's scream at discovering the corpse. Idle noise expresses the confidence before the fall: Crewe singing in expectation of an easy seduction; Frank whistling before he finds the shocking glove; Tracy humming and whistling before his victims slip his trap. Or to silence: Alice's nervous tension, for example, and the quiet exchange of glances by which Frank reads Alice's guilt and she senses that he knows.

Hitchcock also uses dramatic sound effects. Indeed, noise works like language. Or language does not work any better than noise. While the film demonstrates the failure of the legal system to escape personal manipulation, it also demonstrates our inadequate communication system.

The restaurant noises aggravate the lovers. The doorbell jangles in Alice's head the morning after, at Tracy's, at Frank's, a nerve-wracking reminder of the outside world's inevitable intrusion into one's personal area. After Alice's sleepless night, her canary's shrill gaiety evokes the heartless nature in Thomas Hardy.

The famous sequence where the neighbor's speech is reduced to a murmur from which Alice can only pick out the word "knife" works as noise as well. Ten times the word recalls the murder. But the word by itself is no more language than the doorbell is music. It is only a sound that plays on her guilt and anxiety by her personal associations. It fails to do what language should do—connect to someone. Instead it isolates Alice from the breakfast company. Her guilt corrupts the function of "knife" in social language, as Frank's personal twist will corrupt the social function of justice later.[13]

As the "knife" scene distorts what she hears, Alice's guilt affects what she sees in her long walk after the murder. She only sees the exposed arm of the mannequin, which recalls the corpse's outstretched hand. She sees only the wino's hand. On the Good Cocktail sign the neon hand and shaker becomes a hand with a knife. The traffic cop's hand forms an X with the dead man's, Hitchcock's familiar junction of law and outlaw. But all the limp, exposed, and accusing hands are chosen by Alice's guilt.

As well as reminding her of the dead man, the hands express Alice's vulnerability. Her cartoon began with a dot that accidentally slipped from her hand. More to the point: she is incriminated by her gloves. One is in the blackmailer's possession and one is at the scene of the murder. Neither cover her. The glove with holes is an emblem of at first concealment, then exposure, and finally the combination: exposure by/for concealment. So the dead open hands are images of Alice's exposure. Frank's hands work in the contrary way: they close over to conceal Alice's glove; they cover her hands to console her. In contrast we have the pointing finger of the laughing clown in Crewe's painting.

The telephone booth in the store helps the lovers hide from the world not connect to it. Alice retreats to the booth to escape the neighbor's gossip. She and Frank are trapped by Tracy there: "Detectives in glass houses shouldn't wave clues." Recalling the stone thrown at the police in the opening sequence, we see that Detective Webber is protecting the woman he should be arresting.

The White house offers only temporary refuge. The staircase gets Alice away from the bird song. The front door shuts out the street noise. But there is no real escape. Alice goes from the bird song to the gossip to the street noise. As reality inevitably seeps in, Tracy insinuates himself into the store, into the phone booth, into the kitchen, and into Mr. White's favorite chair.

The film's third kind of failed communication is "body language." As in *The Lodger*, Hitchcock dramatizes the deceptiveness of appearances. Gestures can be as ambiguous as words. The quick movement of the first criminal's shadow toward his gun is a brisk warning; the thrown stone is the community's comment on the police. Those statements are clear.

In the artist's flat, however, the gestures are less certain. Alice's actions may encourage the seducer. She comes to his flat, traipses around, and removes her dress. Conversely, the artist's brief remorse when his first kiss is rejected suggests that he may be a greater gentleman than his later force suggests. He may be as impulsive as Alice.

At one point the shadow from the chandelier falls across his face, giving him the appearance of the traditional stage villain.[14] The image is ambiguous. It tempts us to draw Alice's conclusion, that the gentleman is a villain. Or we might take it as Hitchcock's playful reminder that things often are not what they seem to be; the shadow is but a shadow and we would be sharing her paranoia to characterize him by it. In a later parallel, Alice writes Frank that she has decided to give herself up to the police. As she rises from her chair, her head slips into the shadow of a noose. Again, this (planned) accident in lighting expresses Alice's paranoia, hanging being an unlikely sentence for the chaste maiden. Perhaps Alice's noose neutralizes Crewe's mustache.[15]

From that noose Hitchcock cuts to the brass nameplate outside the new Scotland Yard, bright and shimmering, with passing pedestrians appearing distorted, as if in a fun-house mirror. The shot reiterates the subjective bias of the shadow shots and the more general theme of visual distortion. This sign appears straightforward in *The 39 Steps*.

Objects can be as ambiguous as gestures. The first thing we see are spinning discs, but we don't know what they are until the camera pulls back to show they are the hubs on the wheels of the police van. We don't know how large the statue of the god is in the British Museum until Tracy slides down the rope behind it, providing a sense of scale. Otherwise it could be the size of the analogous mask hanging in Crewe's studio. The nature of objects also depends on their context. Tracy does not immediately recognize what the cigar lighter is.

And from a single object, who knows what can develop as the context shifts? Alice drops but a dot on Crewe's canvas. That defilement leads her to draw a comic head, which prompts the artist to guide her hand to complete a nude body in sensuous detail:

Blackmail (1929). The artist (Cyril Ritchard) wears an evil shadow moustache as Alice White (Anny Ondra) undresses to pose for him.

> I'll hold your hand—steady—now the legs, then down here, not too thick, down along there, down like this leg . . . good . . . along here . . . let's see . . . right . . . here we are, back again, that's the ankle—now there—there . . . there. (5)

That routine is a comic miniature of the studio scene, the girl having come for some playful headwork, conversation, but (artists being what they are) finding the body soon forced into play. Though embarrassed at the nude shape, Alice still signs the picture, as later she will try to admit responsibility for the murder.

There is almost nothing in this film, not a phrase, term, character, mood, object, situation, or moral value, that remains a constant. All is in flux; all meaning depends on context. As Durgnat points out, Frank's portrait in uniform on Alice's dresser is boring compared to her movie stars, reassuring when she's lonely or insecure, but threatening when she sees it the morning after the murder. Though the helmeted policeman Alice sees outside Crewe's studio "is at once an ironic reminder of the boy-friend whom she may yet be seduced into betraying, he is too far away to save her from rape if the artist turns ugly, yet he is near enough to be a threat once she has become a murderess and has to sneak her way out."[16] The instability of the film's basic referents provides the true anarchism and irony of *Blackmail*, making it Hitchcock's blackest vision before *Psycho*.[17]

The most protean symbol is Crewe's painting of the clown. At first it's the artist's full-bodied work, massively superior to the amateur Alice's. The clown's heartiness emphasizes her nude's fragility. The clown image itself assumes various expressions. Upon Alice's arrival in the studio, it promises gaiety. It leers at her when the atmosphere turns erotic. When the same face accuses her after she kills Crewe, she slashes at its harsh laughter. The clown later catches the furtive Frank's concealment of the glove and taunts him. At the end the painting is carried past Frank and Alice into the heart of the Yard, where it will point its accusing finger at the duped police force.[18]

The clown painting works as one of three kinds of art in the film. The clown is the spirit of corrective comedy, like the fool's manic wisdom in *King Lear*. By that clown painting, art persists despite the mortality of artist and the insensitivity of audience. Art survives, reflecting but impervious to the tragedies of individual lives. Walking home from the murder, Alice passes a theater advertising a new comedy. The happy neon signs advertising Gordon's gin for purity, the nightclub scenes, her own cartoon, even the detective's opening conversation about the tailor, all set Hitchcock's tragedy of boredom, attempted rape, murder, and the evasion of justice against the backdrop of a comic world. The painting, like its dapper artist, works as a test of the people it meets. It is the very spirit of irony, seeming innocent but a tricky test of its viewer's moral alertness.

The second kind of art is film itself. As one might expect of a film heralding a new era, Hitchcock's *Blackmail* is extremely aware of itself as a sound film. The themes of speech, noise, and silence relate directly to the fact that this was England's first sound feature film. The insulation of the telephone booth may allude to the bulky soundproof booths in which the cameras were kept.

Hitchcock playfully undersells his medium. "What's your hurry?" Frank asks Alice, "We're only going to the pictures." Her boredom—

she's seen everything that's on anyway—reflects the thirst for mere novelty that the sound fad seemed to the silent masters. The laughing clown does not need sound for all its tones and kinds of laughter.

In the dialogue sheets the conversation between Alice and Frank on the movies is even fuller. To Alice's "I've seen everything worth seeing," Frank responds, "You haven't seen 'Fingerprints'—I'd like to see that . . . er, you see a bit about Scotland Yard, it might be amusing, they're bound to get all the details wrong." "I don't see why," Alice replies, quarrelsome: "I did hear they'd got a real criminal to vet it so as to be on the safe side" (2). This exchange is an unfortunate loss. The outlaw knowing the inner workings of the police force anticipates Frank's final character. It also makes parodic reference to *Blackmail* itself, which begins with the arrest and fingerprinting and develops a considerable body of finger imagery. *Blackmail* could have been called *Fingerprints,* if Hitchcock had stressed the identification instead of words and concealment. Hitchcock's credits identify the actor playing the detective sergeant as "Ex. Det. Segt. Bishop (Late C.I.D. Scotland Yard)," which authenticates *Blackmail* like the putative *Fingerprints.* Finally, "the safe side" is the police side, particularly for a self-serving criminal. Again Frank is imaged in the film-within-the-film, but so playfully is Hitchcock covering his bets with a hired authority and himself another accusing jester.

The third kind of art is represented by the British Museum through which the police hound Tracy to death. The British Museum is the repository of old culture, inherited values and traditions, analogous to Scotland Yard.[19] The British Museum is large, dwarfing the people who rush through it. The detectives' chase of the blackmailer violates the museum, particularly as its massive godheads exude the dignity of a temple. The closing drama there profanes the noble British Museum as the noble Yard is contaminated by Frank's self-service.

As that chase and fall involve the museum's Reading Room, reading is the violated tradition here, as the sound film prefers listening to reading. This point would not stand up as a response to the museum scene alone, of course, but it is supported by the fully developed themes discussed earlier: the failure of speech to communicate, the preference of physical expression over verbal, writing over speaking, gesture over words. The museum scene in turn adds point to Hitchcock's

Blackmail *(1929). The maker Hitchcock, trying to read on the underground, is disturbed by the obstreperous young. On the right, Frank (Johnny Longden) and Alice (Anny Ondra) seem ominously uneasy on their date.*

signature appearance in the film. On the underground, Hitchcock tries silently to read a book but is pestered by a noisy boy who covers Hitchcock's eyes. The man of traditional film/culture is bothered by the upstart's noise.

The museum expresses the dignity of classical art, while the comic clown expresses its subversive charge. The museum's massive godheads express the divinity beyond human power and man's reach through art to understand or even to imagine. But the stone god is impervious to the petty people rushing to their doom. As the canary's glee is maddeningly insensitive to Alice's anxiety, the museum gods offer no help to suffering man. The artistic and religious values for which the British Museum stands here fail to make human contact, to respond to human suffering, or to give direction for our needs. In these respects the high art is less effective than the laughing clown that variously engages its audience. Preferring the clown's lively cheekiness over the frozen museum gods, Hitchcock valorizes the ironic, subversive potential in the popular arts of which *Blackmail* is a brilliant example.

Hitchcock probably didn't regret having to work with sound. With sound, color, 3-D, he would always relish *using* a new technology, not just exercising it. But when Hitchcock opens his story against the detectives' raucous laughter and ends on the compromised couple's nervous titter, the clown's unheard laughter is all the more eloquent.

Elstree Calling
1930

From *Blackmail* Hitchcock went to work on the first British musical, *Elstree Calling,* directed by Adrian Brunel. The film is an undistinguished series of music-hall acts, featuring such stars as Jack Hulbert, Cicely Courtneidge, Anna May Wong, Jameson Thomas, Donald Calthrop, Tommy Handley, John Longden, and a particularly offensive comedian, "Little" Teddy Brown (e.g., "Here is the Hebrew parade: To the bank, to the bank").

In Hitchcock's running gag Gordon Harker struggles to repair a small television set, as if to receive in his living room the variety acts that the cinema audience is privileged to see. Hitchcock again has fun with a newfangled technology. As he played with the awkwardness of language and sound communication in *Blackmail,* he dramatizes the awkwardness of the machinery here. His attitude toward the new technology recalls the Elizabethan dramatists' toward language: exulting at its flexibility, but with distrust for its capacity for honest clarity.

As he looks back on the innovation of sound, Hitchcock tells Bogdanovich, "I think what sound brought of value to the cinema was to complete the realism of the image on the screen."[1] But his first work with sound in *Blackmail* was hardly naturalistic. To Truffaut, Hitchcock takes a more plausible position: "Well, the silent pictures were the purest form of cinema; the only thing they lacked was the sound of people talking and the noises. But this slight imperfection did not warrant the major changes that sound brought in. In other words, since all that was missing was simple natural sound, there was no need to go to the other extreme and completely abandon the technique of the pure motion picture, the way they did when sound came in."[2] In *Blackmail* Hitchcock certainly retained useful conventions of the "pure motion picture."

Something of Hitchcock's detachment from the industry's unmixed enthusiasm for sound emerges from a rare piece of film in the archives of the British Film Institute. In a test take from the set of *Blackmail,* Hitchcock teases Anny Ondra:

HITCHCOCK: Now, Miss Ondra, you asked me to let you hear your voice on the talking pictures.

ONDRA: (laughs) But Hitch, you mustn't do that.

H: Why not?

O: Well, because I can't speak well.

H: Do you realize that the squad van will be here any moment?

O: No, oh my god, I'm terribly frightened.

H: Why, have you been A Bad Woman or something?

O: Well, not just bad but, uh . . .

H: But you've slept with men!

O: Oh no! (Shocked, giggles and turns her back toward camera)

H: You have not. Come here. Stand in your place, otherwise it will not come out right, as the girl said to the soldier.

O: (Turns away, laughing)

H: That's enough.

Hitchcock says "talking pictures" with distaste.

Elstree Calling was released on September 29, 1930, one week after the release of Hitchcock's new feature *Juno and the Paycock.*

Juno and the Paycock

1930

The lazy, strutting braggart, "Captain" Boyle (Edward Chapman), would rather drink with his lying, thieving buddy, Joxer Daly (Sidney Morgan), than work or attend to the needs of his family, which responsibilities fall on his wife, Juno (Sara Allgood). Lawyer Charles Bentham (John Longden) brings news that the peacock Boyle stands to inherit 1,500 pounds from a distant relative. Bentham woos the Boyle girl, Mary (Kathleen O'Regan), away from her simple suitor, Jerry Devine (Dave Morris). Anticipating the legacy, the Boyles overextend themselves buying luxuries. But an error in Bentham's wording of the will costs them the inheritance. Having made Mary pregnant, Bentham goes off to America. Devine is willing to take Mary back until he learns she is pregnant. Meanwhile, the Boyles's son, Johnny (John Laurie), who lost an arm in his struggle for Ireland and who lives in fear for having informed on another young rebel, is taken off and executed. Juno bewails their dashed hopes, shamed daughter, lost son, and shattered life in the shadows of their repossessed flat.

Hitchcock's film of Sean O'Casey's play was received with real enthusiasm. James Agate, in the *Tatler* of March 5, 1930, reports that "the audience audibly revelled in the film's humours, and was audibly moved by its heart-rending close." Agate himself calls the film "very nearly a masterpiece." Though a "photographed play," it "completely justifies the talkies. . . . A magnificent British picture."[1] For a film to justify the talkies was no small feat. Agate had called *Elstree Calling* "unmitigated footle, which would have bored an infants' school."[2]

Hitchcock dismisses the film as "just a photograph of a stage play":[3] "I must say that I didn't feel like making the picture because, although I read the play over and over again, I could see no way of narrating it in cinematic form. . . . I photographed the play as imaginatively as possible, but from a creative viewpoint it was not a pleasant experience."[4] As to its rave reviews, "I was actually ashamed, because it had nothing to do with cinema. The critics praised the picture, and I had the feeling I was dishonest, that I had stolen something."[5] Still, Sean O'Casey was pleased with the film, for which he wrote the additional dialogue. O'Casey proposed he and Hitchcock do another film together, based on incidents in Hyde Park, but the story turned into the play *Within the Gates*.[6]

Hitchcock and Agate are correct. The film was one of Hitchcock's most conservative treatments of a text. He may have been awed by the excellence of his cast, mainly Abbey Theatre players, including Sara Allgood, the original stage Juno, with the addition of two unknown actors who came up trumps. The Scot John Laurie played the haggard Johnny Boyle. The demanding role of the paycock went to an Englishman, Edward Chapman, as the original actor, Arthur Sinclair, was on tour.

Hitchcock makes some small changes in the text, including the ending. O'Casey ends with the paycock returning home drunk and ignorant of his son's death and his family's dispossession. Hitchcock ends on Juno's solitary grief, a simpler but more moving note than O'Casey's dying strain. "Perhaps Mr. Hitchcock was right," remarks Agate. "Irony is a kittle thing to submit to a film audience, and probably this admirable film producer has chosen wisely in ending on a safe note."[7]

O'Casey opens with Mary and Juno and ends with Boyle and Joxer. Hitchcock opens with a new street scene then goes to Boyle, Joxer, and Mrs. Madigan in a pub. The street scene, as well as "opening the play out for the film," approaches the Boyle family by way of the social background. Hitchcock moves from the public to the private. This counters both Juno and the paycock's desire to stay uninvolved in public matters. The Boyles find the troubles reaching into their home.

The opening addition also establishes community as an important theme in the film. The orator's speech, delivered by Barry Fitzgerald, runs as follows, until it is interrupted by gunfire:

> Fellow countrymen, continuously and courageously we have fought and struggled for the national salvation of Ireland. When we have thought together and fought together we have always won. Remember that. When we have thought together and fought together we have always won. When we have been divided in thought and opposite in action we have always lost. Now the way out of this anxiety, and out of this self-destruction, and out of this distress, is for us all to form up formally together again and to stand not for this party or that party, not for the Die-hard Republican or for Free Stater, but for an ordered, wide-awake Ireland. Broad-shouldered—tested—hardy-hearted men, in face of wounds, in spite of death, we must get between our enemies who strive to kill each other, we must blame them, we must keep them from one another and unite them once more in the bonds of unity, peace. . . .

At the reference to broad-shouldered men, we get a close-up of thin Joxer twitching heartily. The speech gives the political background Hitchcock may have felt a film audience needed. As the speech prescribes nonpartisan unity, Joxer's villainy is to breed dissension. He is a wedge between Juno and her paycock, between Boyle and his family responsibilities, and (comically) between Boyle and the tailor.

Hitchcock makes two significant deletions from O'Casey's text. He drops the quips against the Catholic clergy: Boyle's remarks about Father Farrell in act 1, scene 1; his claim to have defended the patriotism of the priests in act 2, scene 2; and his remarks on the "passin' away" of religions in act 2, scene 2. This may have been a sop to cinema's wider, less-sophisticated audience or Hitchcock's own reluctance to offend Catholicism. O'Casey's ecclesiastical satire might have discouraged the community unity. Hitchcock similarly omits a juror's anti-Catholic prejudice in *Murder!*[8] Perhaps consistent with his own Catholicism, in *Juno* Hitchcock converts O'Casey's nondescript tailor, Nugent, into a stereotyped Jewish tailor, Kelly. Where Nugent teaches the Boyles a lesson in funeral decorum, Kelly teaches commercial trickery.

Hitchcock's more serious omission is of all reference to Mary's strike, indeed, of any sense of her as a well-read, free-thinking individual. She is plain, without the blossoming independence and forcefulness O'Casey gave her. As a result the dissension in the Boyle family is not a matter of generations gapping or of new education and new values challenging the old ways but of a family shattered by lapses in traditional morals.

Hitchcock gives Boyle Joxer's last line:

> Children at home don't give a damn now. Still, I suppose it's the same everywhere. The whole world is in a terrible state—of chassis.

In Hitchcock's film Boyle is impatient with Johnny sitting in front of the fire, leaving no room for Boyle. In O'Casey's scene the observation bore a larger irony, as Boyle had not yet heard how terrible his own "chassis" is or how damned for not giving a damn he is. O'Casey's cosmic irony is reduced to domestic frustration. Hitchcock's Mary mutely accepts Devine's "Are you fallen as low as that?" where O'Casey's made an elegant, biting, poignant quotation from Devine's own socialist lecture:

> Then we saw our globe of beauty
> Was an ugly thing as well,
> A hymn divine whose chorus
> Was an agonizin' yell;
> Like the story of a demon,
> That an angel had to tell.
> (act 3, scene 3)

Hitchcock keeps Devine's unwitting pun—"With Labour, Mary, humanity is above everything"—but generally saps O'Casey's Mary of all wit, intelligence, and spirit. This simplification is worse than Hitchcock's failing to rethink the play as cinema.

Hitchcock gives Mary one touching moment. In O'Casey, Mary waits at Juno's sister's while Juno tells Boyle about her pregnancy.

Hitchcock sets her outside her home, without comfort or company, so that Boyle can throw her his frostiest look when he and Joxer go drinking. With Mary in the foreground, the shot gives her our pity, but not the respect that O'Casey's Mary commands.

Elsewhere Hitchcock steps up the comedy. He gives Mrs. Madigan a song about adultery instead of O'Casey's song of fidelity. He finds comedy in Boyle's miserly reactions to his cousin's charitable requests. Boyle's philosophizing—"What is the stars? . . . What is the moon?"—is comically undercut by his ravenous attack on his sausage. He takes his feet off the new sofa but empties his pipe on it.

Hitchcock also steps up the pathos. In the last shot, in the room stripped of family and furniture, Juno's apostrophe to her dead son is spoken to an empty chair with a broken back, the chair Johnny sat in for his first appearance and in which he huddled before the fire.

For the most part, Hitchcock's camera work is unobtrusive. He gives his fine actors their stage and usually keeps to a stationary middle-distance shot of their conversation. He lowers his camera to sniff the floor for a clue when Boyle paces about before pouncing on the frying pan and sausage he had rejected. It follows Mrs. Madigan's eye to the sideboard as she declines offers of tea, then stout, holding out for the whiskey she has espied.

Hitchcock holds on the pretentious Boyle during Bentham's explanation of theosophy, so as to catch both the ideas of the speech and Boyle's impenetrable smugness. The last scene between Mary and Devine is a tight two-shot, but when he has left her the camera draws back to show her alone in the cold, unsympathetic world.

The camera movement focuses on Johnny at key ironic moments. He slips into the frame when Bentham raises the matter of ghosts. The haunted Johnny lurks in the background when the characters speculate about death but is there for the camera to dolly in on when Boyle will toast the happy times ahead. Johnny stands behind Juno for her line, "If Mary goes, I go," even though he shares Boyle's righteous shame. For all his bluster, Johnny is still his mother's frightened little boy in need of protection. Hitchcock's one excess is in ending each act with Johnny's visions of the rainy window and the sound of a round of gunfire (well, men off camera hitting leather with canes, but that connoted gunfire).[9]

Hitchcock's favorite scene was a technical challenge. In the living room sing-along, Captain Boyle offers to play the new phonograph instead of taking his turn to sing. Hitchcock emphasizes the community feeling of O'Casey's choice of song ("If you're Irish, come into the parlor") by showing the friends and family singing warmly together. Johnny does not sing but is occasionally cut in alone. He is in close-up when the record is joined on the sound track by the dirge of the passing funeral procession, and the singers stop to hear the procession described. The corpse is the boy Johnny betrayed. The others leave to join the procession. The dirge continues in the background when Johnny goes to look at the Madonna but finds the mobilizer there with his fatal summons.

For this crucial scene, Hitchcock had the "record" sung off camera with an orchestra. A prop man sang the lead, holding his nose to provide the tinny sound. The cast sang along on camera. At the other side of the studio, Hitchcock had a full choir singing a funeral hymn. The scene was difficult to set up, but it provides the film's most dramatic moment. Here the Boyle family is at once most warmly together—and most poignantly separated from their son. Here the film registers the impossibility of celebrating a joy secure from the outside world. This is a brilliant moment in an otherwise conservative adaptation.

Murder!

1930

Hitchcock's third sound feature, *Murder!,* has suffered not so much neglect as misrepresentation. For one thing, a surprising number of commentators call the murderer the heroine's "fiancé." He is a friend, his passion unreciprocated. Indeed when the hero asks if she loves the man she is sheltering, she replies, "That's impossible. Why, the man's a half-caste." She loves her detective.[1] Raymond Durgnat has the heroine murdering her fiancé but on the next page sheltering him out of love.[2] The film is also misrepresented as either a satire on the hero's effete snobbishness or as an exercise in Hitchcock's snobbery, neither reading—as we shall see—being accurate.

Even the title is usually misrepresented. To my knowledge, only Kirk Bond refers to the film correctly as *Murder!*[3] Everyone else calls it *Murder.* Sans exclamation mark, they miss the title's histrionic tone and its warning that another murder, of a convicted innocent, is about to be committed.

Nor is it commonly recognized what a rare film this is for Hitchcock. *Murder!* is Hitchcock's first whodunit, and he made few others: *Stage Fright, The Trouble with Harry,* and *Psycho,* films where the audience accompanies the quest to determine who committed a murder.[4] Hitchcock's preference for suspense over mystery is well known, as in his early identification of the murderers in *Vertigo, Frenzy,* and *Family Plot.*[5]

A jury finds actress Diana Baring (Norah Baring, no relation) guilty of the murder of her company's leading actress, Edna Druce. But one juror, the famous actor-manager Sir John Manier (Herbert Marshall), remains unconvinced of her guilt. While Diana awaits execution, Sir John investigates the crime, aided by the stage manager in Diana's company, Ted Markham (Edward Chapman), and his actress wife, Doucie (Phyllis Konstam). Sir John deduces that the murderer was the actor Handel Fane (Esme Percy). Sir John tries to trap Fane by auditioning him for a new play, which he modeled after the Druce murder (compare with *Hamlet*). Fane escapes confession there but later, when Sir John attends Fane's high-wire female impersonation circus act, Fane writes out his confession and leaps into a noose. Freed, Diana becomes Sir John's new romantic lead, at least onstage and perhaps off as well.

Murder! is more thoughtful and ingenious than Hitchcock's later exercise in the theater of life, *Stage Fright. Murder!* also stands as Hitchcock's fullest statement on the function of art in life.[6] Several portentous remarks aim the film at Pirandellian abysses without letting its feet off the ground. "I should like to remind you," says the judge, as if he had any choice, "that truth is often stranger than fiction." "It's absurd," remarks Diana of her verdict; in the shooting script the term was originally "ridiculous." While the "theater of the absurd" was a genre yet to be defined, "absurd" often referred to art that depicted the illogicality of life. That is James Agate's usage in his review of *Juno and the Paycock.*[7] The change from "ridiculous" to "absurd" expresses Diana's sense of her situation as an image from theater, rather than as a life moment. There are several theater-type settings: the palpably false street scene, the jury room, the bathroom singer's "stage," the drawing room, the scene of the crime, the play-within-a-play, the circus, and, of course, the theater itself. Sir John's apartment and Norah's prison look like stage settings. The murder setting has several proscenium arches.

Hitchcock goes well beyond the reassertion that "All the world's a stage." He demonstrates the danger of framing off life as if it were art. The problem is where to center one's vision to determine what is the stage and what the wings. Here the drama usually happens in the

Murder! (1930). *The mirror in the back shows us the discovered corpse of Edna Druce. The framing beams make even the actors' real world seem a stage.*

wings, as when the police inspector haltingly interviews the performers between their stage appearances. We glimpse their coming to fuller—but irrelevant—life in their roles onstage. Diana makes this error when she refuses to tell the court, then Sir John, the subject of her argument with the murdered woman that fateful night. Diana is convinced it is irrelevant: "He has no connection with the case." The ladies were discussing the man who—it turns out—was the murderer.

Hitchcock does this kind of framing himself. To start the investigation, he shoots the stage farce from the wings. Once his—and Sir John's—indirections have found direction out, he closes on a frontal shot of the proscenium stage. As the theater approach has grown from the askew perspective to the normal frontal, the play onstage has changed from a chaotic farce—the characters change costumes several times—to a romance in which the hero, his girl, and his aides play images of themselves. At the end, when we first see the new couple together in a living room, we assume it is their real romance. Only when the camera alters its framing by pulling back do we see that it is a stage performance. Still, we hopefully infer a romance.[8]

Hitchcock minimizes the trial scene, focusing instead on the jury debate, where the miscarriage of justice and the livelier theater are happening. The trial opens with a theatrical title—"Rex v. Diana Baring"—in a flourish of trumpets, over the official coat of arms of the Calendar for Assize.[9] In the trial our frontal view of the jury makes them seem like characters in a play facing us for inspection. Their heads turn in unison with the testimony, as in the tennis game in *Strangers on Train*. Here the point is not the jurors' concentration but their malleability. They swing with each argument, like the weather vane evoked by Fane's changes of role or identity. The swaying jury contrasts to the intense audience at Fane's circus act. The art (circus) achieves an involvement beyond life (the trial).

The jury room scene is more theatrical than the trial. The jurors drift from individuation to an even choral conformity. It begins when the three little old ladies nod as one that they would like to sit together, not so much out of modesty, it would seem, as out of respect for some invisible stage designer's purpose.

The jurors seem more intent on revealing themselves than on reaching the truth about someone else. One lady considers Diana innocent because of her good family origins, while another is suspicious of the "brazen" women of the upper class. Such subjective judgment tells us more about the judge than the judged. Mrs. Ward flaunts her crumbs of psychology. The timid Matthews wonders how the psychological explanation of "daytime sleepwalking" could pertain to a nighttime murder. Shackleton takes a firm line, then dissolves:

> I think the whole business is hateful. There's too much responsibility placed on our shoulders. . . . The world's a reeking pit of sentiment. . . . Guilty, I suppose.

In the novel this man was named Smith. Hitchcock's name suggests his firmness and evokes shackles, either as his argument will imprison Diana or as it imprisons him as he argues himself into despair. From Shackleton's too-general concerns Hitchcock goes to the too-narrow concerns of Daniels. He intuits (accurately) Diana's innocence on the strength of her appearance but is attacked for his bias and cajoled into voting guilty too. Indeed, the three who doubt the case against Diana are won over not by argument or evidence but by browbeating. All the jurors have their bias. They can't frame themselves out of their perspective on the case. Even before he has called for the first vote, the jury foreman has been practicing his fancy capital G on his blotter. The jurors center on themselves rather than on the case.[10]

In another askew framing, Hitchcock keeps the camera on the vacated jury room while the verdict is pronounced in court—the stage now. Continuing the jurors' self-centeredness, the court clerk enters, dusts, picks up a useful cigar butt, and hears the verdict from the outside.[11]

Sir John is saved from the other jurors' confidence by his background in theater. He is experienced in framing and roles. The jury scene turns expressionistic when Sir John's arguments against the other jurors are beaten back with increasingly loud, increasingly quick replies: "Any answer to that, Sir John?" Finally he is overwhelmed by their choral "Any answer, any answer, any answer to that, Sir John?" The veer from dialogue to chant puts the audience into Sir John's beleaguered position.

The jurors' chorus may sound like theater, but it is only vehement complacency. Sir John describes what he wants to do:

> I have trained myself to—how shall I put it—apply the technique of life to the problems of my art.

Now, "I find myself applying the technique of my art to a problem in real life." From his theater experience, Sir John will try to grasp someone else's experience. Both as actor and detective, he will project beyond his own experience to understand someone else. Having projected himself into Diana's situation, he has lost the other jurors' certainty. They reduced her to their own impressions. He reaches out to understand her. This reading derives from the novel: "The jurors looked at each other. Each one of the twelve knew the verdict he would have given as an individual, but did not care to make public the mental processes whereby the verdict had been reached. The habit of the majority was to leap to conclusions and cling to them" (106). Where the other jurors dissociate themselves from the accused ("like a father" is how Daniels puts his regard for her, most kindly), Sir John takes kinship with her as his starting point.

Of course, putting one's self into another personality is what actors do and what Sir John alone of the jurors can do, without Shackleton's crumbling crust of sympathy. Hitchcock three times refers to understudying, by which an actor is prepared to assume someone else's role. Understudies replace Druce and Baring after the murder and Sir John has his understudy summoned when he leaves his play to perform as detective. In the novel Sir John was between productions and the Druce-Baring play was canceled immediately. Hitchcock clearly wanted the understudy motif. Sir John engages an expert understudy, Doucie Markham, when her husband comes to work for him as stage manager offstage and on.

In hiring Markham, Sir John rewords his art-life plan: "We use life to create art and we use art to—how shall I put it—to criticize life." He warns against being so preoccupied with art as to ignore life. The "criticism" Sir John gives life is not judging it but explicating it like a text. He seeks to understand the ambiguous events leading up to the discovery of the corpse, with the dazed Baring neither admitting nor denying her guilt, but pleading loss of memory. His clues: an empty brandy bottle, an unidentified policeman passing the murder scene, blood on the cigarette case, a broken sink in the dressing room of Ion Stewart and Handell Fane, who wore police suits in the farce. The dramatist-detective solves the case by using all these props, by casting the missing role, by understudying and thus understanding first the accused and then the murderer, by staging the play-within-a-play, and finally by completing the story.

The dramatist also knows that reality differs according to our perspective of it. As he tells Markham, "If we approach the case from another angle we may arrive at a different result." As in framing, something may seem different according to what our vision isolates. Or something can be misrepresented or disguised. In the opening sequence Hitchcock pans past a row of apartment windows. Through the blind over the third window we see the shadow of what appears to be a thin young girl, slowly and elegantly slipping into her gown. When she raises the blind, we see she is a rather haggard creature, rushed and disheveled. The blind blinds. Lest this seem my subjective judgment, here's Hitchcock's shooting script: "A glimpse of a silhouette of a beautiful figure and profile on blind. As the latter goes up we find to our disappointment that it is the angry face of a not very attractive woman" (3). The wise theatrical can keep his grip on the difference between the apparent and the real, the actual and the plausible, but the unwise either can't or chooses not to.

Two parallel food fantasies confirm this point. When Sir John invites the Markhams to lunch, Doucie puts on her usual airs. Her demure "little tid-bit" is undercut by a quick shot of her Guinness and cheese (in the book, as they say, it's liver-and-bacon and stout). She later calls "my negligee" the bloomers we saw her struggling to get into. Her food shot is paralleled by the sumptuous feast that flashes through Sir John's mind when he considers spending the night at the Red Lion Inn instead of at the constable's noisy home. Both cut-in food shots intrude into the narrative. Sir John's tells the truth for the artist (the meal he could have) while the other exposes an impostor (Doucie pretending elegance). The artist controls his fancy toward the projection of the truth. The impostor—Doucie here on a small scale; the female impersonator Fane working under an assumed name later—uses image to deceive. Markham is more honest than Doucie, so his cut-in of Sir John's thick carpets is a subjective hyperbole, neither a lie nor a pretense.

As an actor, Sir John controls his emphasis, his sense of proportion. So he can pluck a minute piece of significance out of seeming chaos, for example, the clues that emerge from the noise and tumble of the policeman's five children and cat and the chatter of Mrs. Mitcham and Doucie. So, too, pointed lines and images of performance emerge from the chaos in the wings. Hitchcock holds on the mad shadows on the tent, against the carny noise, when Sir John reads Fane's confession. Of course, Sir John can also assume false identities, such as Mrs. Mitcham's maid or Fane's ostensible employer. But the actor plays roles to arrive at the truth, not to deceive. The chaos of life can be brought to order by an artist's clear, humble, and balanced vision (as Markham's false teeth can bring his mumbles to words).[12]

So Sir John is not "nonchalantly uninvolved" in the case, as Durgnat claims. His apparent detachment is the actor's cool analysis, in con-

trast to the jurors' fervid egos. There is no doubting Sir John's commitment to the case. The one uncertainty is his romantic interest in
Diana. In the novel Sir John has clearly fallen in love with her. But in
the film this is not definite. He claims some responsibility for her,
having once auditioned her and advised her to tour the provinces. He
is touched to find his portrait on her dresser. When he enters "Diana"
in his appointment book, the detective might—or might not—be slipping into the role of lover. At the end he joins her with a professional
euphemism: "You must save those tears. They'll be very, very useful
in my new play." But we don't know they will be lovers. Hitchcock's
last shot is a salon scene. In the shooting script the setting is less intimate: Diana in outdoor clothes hands footman Markham a jewel case.
Hitchcock's romantic close suggests but does not ensure a romance
for the two leads. This should acquit Sir John of charges of self-interest
in his crusade. He tries to save the girl from an unjust hanging for
justice not (yet) for love.

Hitchcock's Sir John is better than writers on *Murder!* suggest. Comparing his hero to the source may clarify Hitchcock's intentions. By
simplifying his name from Sir John Saumarez to Menier (and "Martella" to "Diana"), Hitchcock eases viewer identification. He changes
"Novello" to "Markham," out of loyalty to his old star, Ivor. "Foulkes" he
changes to "Bennett," out of either simplicity or decorum. In changing
the name of the other suspect, Ion Marion, to Ion Stewart, Hitchcock
omits the lexical image of narcissism, self-containment, even self-attack
performed in "Ion Marion."

More importantly, Hitchcock omits all the novel's jabs at Sir John's
vanity and selfishness:

> He did not want Martella to hang: he wanted to take her back to
> the Sheridan in triumph, his new find, his new and magnificently
> advertised star, bound to him by fantastic ties of pure gratitude.
> (217)

> That would be notoriety, a very different thing. It would not do
> for his theatre. (288)

> The author of *Griselda's Garter* had made a profound study of Sir
> John Saumarez. He knew that any part written for that great

man must contain, if it were to do him justice, opportunities for tender humour, casual strength, wit, wistfulness, and his smile. (298)

None of this is in the movie, nor does Hitchcock include Druce and Markham's irreverent parodies of Sir John in the novel.

Indeed, the Sir John of the novel is a narcissist, his mirror an emblem of his self-love. A critic, for example, writes

that if Sir John Saumarez would occasionally go out into the highways and hedges of real life for a model, instead of depending entirely on his shaving-glass, he would cease to be the extremest example of narcissism since Louis XIV. (123–24)

His growing love for Martella (Diana) intrudes on his self-love:

"It wasn't as if I were in love with her," said Sir John to his shaving-glass next morning, angrily, and instantly cut himself rather badly under the left ear. (127)

Except in the looking-glass he had never seen anything so expressive as her smile. (314)

Hitchcock's bathroom mirror scene is the technically most accomplished scene in the film and the pivotal point both in plot and thematic movement. Far from proving Sir John's self-concern, it involves him in Diana's case.

The bathroom scene has two striking pieces of technique. A thirty-piece orchestra off camera plays the overture from Wagner's *Tristan and Isolde,* as if from Sir John's radio. Sir John delivers a soliloquy voice-over, all while he stands before his mirror, shaving.[13]

While Sir John studies his face the Wagner (art) draws him out of self-concern. Then a police bulletin interrupts the music to request help from the public. The music and the call for help remind him of Baring. When his man brings him a brandy, Sir John remembers that Diana doesn't drink brandy but the brandy had all been drunk. This Sir John, far from the novel's narcissist, is concerned with others' problems, particularly when affected by art. The film's shaving scene inverts the meaning of the mirror in the novel, improves the character of Sir John, and shows how art can serve life.

With Sir John using his art to save a life, the film hardly attacks the English class system. Hitchcock neither disdains nor admires any class here. Sir John's high social status reflects his status in the profession, which he turns to address someone else's life problem. The film is about art, not about the class system.

Far from condescending, this Sir John is kindly to Mrs. Mitcham, and befuddled but patient with the constable's children. In the film Sir John is even nicer than in the shooting script and far nicer than the novel. Hitchcock dropped Sir John's habit of keeping visitors waiting (75–76), among the other Great Man airs. A change in the lunch scene with the Markhams confirms his generosity. In the shooting script Doucie goes at her soup with the teaspoon, then, embarrassed by Sir John's proper choice, switches to the soupspoon (87–88). However, in the film when Doucie takes the wrong spoon, Sir John follows her example, and is followed in turn by Markham, rather than embarrass her. Again the artist assumes someone else's position.

On this point the critics shared the bias of Diana Baring's jury. So O. B. Hardison: "The class theme emerges first in *Murder*. The hero is titled and is played by Herbert Marshall, whose public image has always been that of an aristocrat . . . there is considerable undercutting of the image. Marshall plays an actor (a hint of self-parody), and in two scenes he wantonly insults lower-class characters. The treatment reveals a mixture of admiration and hostility and doubtless reflects attitudes toward his betters that young Alfred took with him from the grocer's shop."[14] Hardison's claim would read better for *Downhill* and *Champagne*. To *Murder!* it has no relevance whatever. Durgnat is as far off: "Hitchcock criticises the dilettante streak in the gentlemanly detective."[15] Where? Not if one compares the film to the novel. Not even if one does not, for the gentleman solves the case and saves a life. An actress, but a life.

From John Grierson came a more significant attack on *Murder!* Granting that "Hitchcock is the best director, the slickest craftsman, the sharpest observer and finest master of detail in all England," Grierson gives a facetious summary of *Murder!* and concludes that its "excellences are incidental excellences. They dress out the banal issue so that the separate scenes hold you as they would not, under a lesser director, come near to doing. But the issue pokes its empty face at you, at every turn." Grierson commits the reviewer's occupational hazard, an interpretation based on the first impact of the film for which it is then dismissed. So he finds Hitchcock snobbish toward the English poor: "He finds it more a matter of regret that they have no dinner jackets than that they have no dinners." The film uses the thriller format to insist on art's service to needy humanity. If Hitchcock in this film left the great Grierson behind, no wonder other critics seem to be on about another film altogether.[16]

The final issue in *Murder!* involves the villain Fane's transvestitism. Ernest Betts makes an extreme claim: "More interesting than any technical gimmicks is Hitchcock's awareness of dissolving ethical standards, of the whole atmosphere of moral and psychological change. He confronts homosexual and other issues in a manner considered bold at the time."[17] Durgnat rewrites the film: "It leaves us, sophisticates of 1970, in little doubt that 'half-caste' means 'left-handed,' which means bisexual or homosexual."[18] To Truffaut *Murder!* "in essence is a thinly disguised story about homosexuality."[19] Well, if it is, it is more than "thinly disguised." The film is neither "about" nor does it "confront" homosexuality. It explores neither the psychology of a homosexual nor the psychology of others' responses to the man's homosexuality.

In the novel Fane is "half-caste," which provokes Miss Baring, who had been raised in India, to a deeper aversion than the English company members hold toward him. Diana's Indian background was dropped in Hitchcock's shift from the trial room to the jury room. He kept her aversion rather than invent another motive.

With that background, the "half-caste" need not denote homosexuality. Nor does the transvestitism, given the British farce tradition of male performers in drag. The policeman thinks Mrs. Drewitt is coming off but as Markham informs him, "No, it's Mr. Fane. One hundred percent He-woman." As the "woman" switches into a policeman's uniform, his voice drops from female to male. Suspect Ion Stewart changes from a uniform to a dress, then hops onstage, tied. "I assure you, Inspector," says Fane gallantly, "I am not the other woman in the case." He is, of course, the other man and the killer. Where the novel has Fane leaping through hoops, doors, and skylights, Hitchcock has him leaping into one fatal noose. Perhaps he deliberately eschewed the spectacular; or he felt the image of Fane leaping through rings was a too-sexual image. In any case, where the novel has Fane in a clown disguise at the end, Hitchcock has him as a female impersonator. Fane's profession clearly includes dressing in drag. He also wears a bobby's suit, which does not make him a detective. That he loves Diana should rebut the charge that he is homosexual.

Fane's epicene image is another of a man playing roles. Where Sir John acts as other people to find the truth, Fane projects multiple images to conceal his truth. Here theater harbors genuine artists and impostors. An individual mixes selves and appearances. Fane's shifting image evokes Diana's lawyer's defense of her client: "Is there anything so hardy as the behaviour of sheer innocence?" One reason Diana is convicted is because she has refused to play the role of the innocent damsel. She is innocent even if she prefers not to project conventional innocence. Sir John is a responsible citizen despite being an aristocratic actor. Fane can be straight even if his job puts him in drag. That could be what "one hundred percent He-woman" means.

Fane and Sir John form a romantic triangle with Diana, with several points of tension. Diana can have Fane but dreams about Sir John. Fane loves Diana but will leave her to die in his stead, while Sir John, who hardly knows her, devotes himself to saving her. Fane hides behind false images but is doomed to stay himself. Sir John deploys a fertility of selves, as a slight wording change in the shooting script reveals. When Sir John finds his photo on Diana's dressing table, her landlady remarks, "Why, why, it's of yourself, sir" (97). Hitchcock preferred a more ambiguous wording: "That's one of you" (one of your selves/images; a picture of you).

Whether or not Sir John marries Diana after the film is irrelevant. By his acting Sir John is already potent and creative. Handell Fane and Sir John are both elegant men, Hitchcock having dropped Fane's coarse negroid features from the novel. In discovering Fane's guilt, Sir John does not discover an aspect of himself (as Bruno can be called an aspect of Guy's self, and Uncle Charlie of Charlie's), but what but for the grace of God (and the grease of social custom) Sir John might have been.

This may be Hitchcock's reflection on the class system. Sir John was born into the top of society and Fane into the bottom. For no cause of their own, that is, Fane was doomed to the futility of self-concealment, in his theater and in his life, while Sir John had opportunities to fulfill himself and proceed to understanding others. From the shaving scene on, Sir John accepts those responsibilities.

The Skin Game

1931

As in *Juno and the Paycock,* Hitchcock's adaptation stays generally close to Galsworthy's *The Skin Game.* Only close comparison reveals changes and shifts of emphasis.[1]

The plot pits the progressive, vulgar industrialist, Hornblower (stage star Edmund Gwenn), against the traditionalist gentry, the Hillcrists (C. V. France and Helen Haye), who have luxuriated in their estate "since Elizabeth." The cast credits define the social hierarchy, listing the family groups, first the Hillcrists, then the Hornblowers, then Dawker, the peasant Jackmans—down the great chain of being. Of course, one of the Hornblower sons, Rolfe (Frank Lawton), is courting the Hillcrist girl, Jill (Jill Esmond).

The Hillcrists reject Hornblower's offer of friendship, then publicly snub his daughter-in-law, Chloe (Phyllis Konstam). Lady Hillcrist deploys their shady steward, Dawker (Edward Chapman), to thwart Hornblower's plans to buy the Centry, a neighboring farm with which his factories would encircle the Hillcrist estate. Dawker reveals that Chloe before her marriage had been a professional divorce correspondent. To conceal this shame Hornblower surrenders the Centry to the Hillcrists. But Dawker discloses the secret to Chloe's husband, Charles (John Longden), who leaves her. The pregnant Chloe tries to drown herself in the Hillcrist pond. She is pulled out, too late to save the child and perhaps herself as well. Hillcrist apologizes to Hornblower who, noble in his grief, refuses to be consoled as he bears off the girl's body.

Durgnat makes a cogent point about the characters' names, though he gets them wrong: *"The Skin Game* shows Hillcrest the gentlemanly landowner at bay against Hornblow the coarse pushing industrialist. The names couldn't be more appropriate: lyrical rolling countryside, essentially modest—hills not mountains, versus the clamorous and militant bragging of own-trumpet-blowing."[2] Of course, it's Hornblower, a more active name with a pedigree in C. S. Forester. And instead of the rolling, graceful peak in Hillcrest there is a holding back, a tightness in Hillcrist. But this is Galsworthy's music, not Hitchcock's.

Hitchcock makes two important omissions. He keeps Hillcrist out of his wife's vile plans, half-aware but uninvolved. Thus, where Mrs. Hillcrist represents the destructive opposition to the new, Hillcrist represents those too passive to defend their honor. Hillcrist does not appear in the living room immediately after Hornblower's submission, as he does in the play (act 3, scene 1). The film cuts Hillcrist's self-defense before Jill: "We *had* to fight for our home. I should have felt like a traitor if I hadn't" (act 3, scene 2).

The other major omission improves Hornblower. Hitchcock drops his abuse of the exposed Chloe (act 3, scene 1). Here's Galsworthy: "So that was your manner of life! So that's what ye got out of by marryin' into my family! Shame on ye, ye Godless thing!" And Hitchcock: "Ay; ye look a strange, wild woman, as I see ye." This Hornblower gently shelters his daughter-in-law and is free from the snobbishness that characterizes the Hillcrists. Hitchcock moves Mrs. Hillcrist's snub of Chloe from the Hillcrist home to the public auction to magnify the insult and grounds for Hornblower's indignation.

The Hitchcock/Gwenn Hornblower is the liveliest force in the film. He is introduced by name and voice before he is shown. The opening pastoral montage (Hillcrist country) is disturbed by a traffic jam with raucous blowing of horns on a (Hornblower) pottery truck. We hear Hornblower evicting the cottagers in the shadows on the left, but all we see is his chauffeur pacing nervously on the right, as if he is ashamed of being an accomplice. Hornblower's negative aspect precedes him.

But Hornblower gains our sympathy when the Hillcrists rebuff his articulate case for friendship. He asks Mrs. Hillcrist, "Am I lucky to have no past, mum? Just the . . . future?" "Oh, I've got the future all right," he says, looking down at the coins he has been jingling. His coins are visibly inferior to the wealth behind the Hillcrist poise, but that lacks Hornblower's substance. His scenes with Chloe both before and after her exposure give him a warmth beyond anyone else's in the film.

Although the Hillcrists think they are contaminating themselves with Hornblower's methods, Hornblower draws on them for his evil. When the decorous Northerner pronounces the charge against Chloe ("Were a woman that went with men, to get them their divorce"), Hornblower stares at Lady Hillcrist, perhaps to avoid Chloe's eyes, perhaps to draw from Lady Hillcrist the vile will to say that. This dramatizes Hillcrist's earlier euphuism: "Who touches pitch shall be defiled" (act 2, scene 1). The man without heritage can't exploit the past as Mrs. Hillcrist can.

But the Hillcrists are clearly fighting a losing battle. The question is whether they will lose as the gentlemen they claim to have been or will debase their ancestors' name. Jill calls her dad Dodo, he being of a breed soon extinct and a cowardly dimwit. At the auction Mrs. Hillcrist is jarred when a colleague appreciates the town's recent improvements and the prospect of electric lights, all Hornblower's doing.

Ultimately, both the Hillcrists and the Hornblowers are debased by trying each other's methods. Hillcrist uses Dawker to bid against Hornblower in the Centry auction but embarrasses himself with his own shrill bid. He feels cheapened by this open contest. Hornblower, however, wins by using Hillcrist's device, getting someone else (the duke's agent) to bid on his behalf. Both sides are diminished by their ploys.[3]

Neither class can live in the other's style with honor. Mrs. Hillcrist firmly puts Dawker in his place ("Get up, Dawker") when he presumes to sit next to her at the auction. He accepts her insult. As Hillcrist tells Jill, Chloe "committed her real crime when she married young Hornblower" without divulging her past, her unworthiness of even that name.

Hitchcock makes a number of minor changes. Chloe's maid Anna does not have the spying role Galsworthy gave her, so the question of whether Chloe is persecuted or paranoid does not arise in the film. Chloe is saved the demeaning job of firing her maid on suspicion. Hitchcock reduces Jill's cheeky talk in her first scene with Hillcrist, in her falling out with her mother, and in her scene with Hornblower and Hillcrist. He gives Hillcrist the title phrase of the film—the skin game referring to the unscrupulous wheeling-dealing by which Hornblower has been expanding his fortune and the Hillcrists defending theirs—where Galsworthy had Jill use that slang. Hitchcock makes Jill more sensible and makes more disappointing the lovers' failure to bridge the families.

Hitchcock's lovers try less than the play's to end the feud. Even love retreats before the forces of greed and arrogance. In the first scene the lovers are carried along by their respective family forces. Hitchcock's Rolfe does not oppose his father's evictions (as in act 1, scene 1: "You haven't been doing that, father? . . . I hate it!"). The film absents Rolfe from Hornblower's scene with the three Hillcrists. In the play Hornblower accuses Jill of turning Rolfe against him, but in the film the lovers do not even challenge the feud. In their first appearance the lovers travel on family emblems: Jill is on-screen right on a horse, eating an apple from the family grove; Rolfe is in an automobile on the left, lower than the rider but more progressive. In the ensuing traffic jam, the dialectic between car and horse shifts to car versus sheep, from the Hillcrist perspective to Hornblower's.

Jill's clothing deflates the possibility of romance dissolving the tension between the families. Despite her antipathy toward Dawker— "He's so common," "pugnacious"—her jodhpurs are closer to Dawker's leggings than to any dress of a Juliet. Rolfe's original line, "Suppose we joined, couldn't we stop it?" becomes an almost romantic proposal in Hitchcock: "Couldn't we join together?" This scene is set in the romantic garden in Hitchcock, against the family living room in Galsworthy. Hitchcock's romantic possibilities fade before the feud.

With the lovers falling in behind their family positions, Hitchcock diverts from his usual pattern, where love conquers duty (*Pleasure Garden, The Lodger, The Ring, Champagne, The Manxman, Blackmail, Waltzes from Vienna, Sabotage, Young and Innocent,* and on through the

American films *Torn Curtain* and *Topaz*). Still, it is clear that the lovers *should* overcome their destructive family loyalties.

Hitchcock even softens Dawker's characterization. By calling Chloe Mrs. Clay, he cites her past name without further disrespect. Her name connotes vulnerability. Galsworthy's "You're a pawn in the game and I'm going to use you" is softened in Hitchcock: "You're only a small fry and I've got to use you." As Chloe and Dawker are both small fry, Dawker is not in a position to play her. The will in "I'm going to" softens into the resignation of "I've got to." Both are driven to use what they can to survive. The Hillcrists thus preserve in Dawker the shadiness they exploit in Chloe. Hitchcock omits Chloe's sexual offer to Dawker, as he alters Dawker's "Keep your pecker up" to "Keep your spirits up," our knowledge of Gilbert and Sullivan not being what it might these days. Similarly, Dawker's "If there's a screw loose anywhere" becomes "If there's a weak point anywhere."

Hitchcock's first shot is the Hillcrist grove, which three men enter to chop down a tree. The last image is of a huge tree being toppled, as old nobility gives way to a new functionalism. The lovers' first conversation centered on clearing the family grove. But they do nothing to prevent either the chopping of the tree or the unbalanced fighting over it. The final, chopped tree would stand for the Hillcrist family and their class in the Galsworthy play. But in the Hitchcock film, given the sympathetic inflections to Dawker, Chloe, and mainly to Hornblower, the tree stands for both families, for family feelings, for the love that binds families and should bind families into larger communities.

For all Jill's sympathy for Chloe, only after Hillcrist's apology and Hornblower's dignified withdrawal does Jill step forward to take Rolfe's arm. By then the division between the families has gone too long, too far, too deep. More than a simple gesture is needed to bridge the abyss. Rolfe had just run from the lifeless Chloe to stop the foolish fight of the living (Dawker and Hornblower) over the land. Lovers must fight fighting, here as in *Secret Agent* and *Torn Curtain*.

The Skin Game is a balanced, moving performance by Hitchcock. Compared with *Murder!* it may not be very exciting, but it was still one of the best films of its year. Unfortunately a four-film slump—or incubation period—preceded his golden age thrillers.

Rich and Strange

1932

After his three adaptations of well-known properties (*Juno, Murder!, The Skin Game*), Hitchcock took an extremely personal tangent with *Rich and Strange,* from a screenplay by Alma Reville and Val Valentine, based on a story by Dale Collins. Though unlike anything else in Hitchcock, it anticipates the cynicism of his great American period. As the disjointed tones and incidents expose the lead's smugness, this film leads directly to the Cary Grant films, particularly *To Catch a Thief* and *North by Northwest.* For its time, however, the film was more strange than rich so it was rejected by the critics and the public. "This is definitely not Hitchcock at his best," quoth the usually adulatory *Picturegoer* (June 11, 1932).

John Grierson's attack was more fundamental:

In trying new material Hitchcock has found himself outside both his experience and his imagination . . . his mind does not quite appreciate the wonders of the world he is trying to use. . . . His sense of space, time, and the other elements of barbarian religion, is almost nil. . . . We have waited patiently for the swing of event (preferably of great event) to come into his films, something that would associate him more profoundly with the dramatic wants of common people. Something serious, I am afraid, will have to happen to Hitchcock before we get it.[1]

Grierson only attacks Hitchcock for not being Grierson. John Russell Taylor responds to the film without predispositions:

> It is interesting as one of his most immediately personal, "felt" films; one suspects that in it, unselfconsciously and even perhaps a trifle naively, the young Hitchcock was wearing his heart on his sleeve, and when the reaction of critics and public was thoroughly unfavourable he decided to set up securer defences the next time. Hence, perhaps, his . . . thrillers . . . films in which ideas close to his heart could be touched on more safely, under the guise of popular entertainment, than when left to speak out for themselves in films like *Rich and Strange*.[2]

The film is not as didactic as Taylor suggests—or as Grierson desired. The later thrillers will accommodate Hitchcock's themes of guilt, chaos, and obsession, shifting better than this romantic comedy.

Then, too, before Hitchcock got around to *The Man Who Knew Too Much* he worked through two even lighter genres, the burlesque in *Number Seventeen* and the musical in *Waltzes from Vienna*. *Rich and Strange* was Hitchcock's last grave film before *Secret Agent* and *Sabotage*. It owes less to the light comedies that follow than to its sober precedents in *Juno and the Paycock*, *Murder!*, and *The Skin Game*.

Fred Hill (Henry Kendall) is a bored accountant who yearns for the adventurous life represented by the ship painting on his wall. A relative leaves him some money ("to experience all the life you want by travelling everywhere") so Fred and his wife Emily (Joan Barry) sail around the world. Fred is seduced and robbed by a bogus princess (Betty Amann), which drives Emily to the gallant Commander Gordon (Percy Marmont). But even when Fred leaves Emily she refuses to run off with Gordon, particularly when he tells her that Fred's "princess" is a fake and an adventuress. As Fred and Emily are reconciled and sailing home broke on a steamer, they are shipwrecked. Chinese looters save them. They watch one die while his mates stare on unperturbed. Their meal turns out to be the cat they fondled earlier. A

117

baby is born on the junk. Fred and Em return to the humdrum security of their old routine.

The plot segments have very disparate tones. A kind of silent comedy sequence details the pesky bothers in Fred's life—his Dickensian office, his intractable umbrella amid a horde of efficients, the crammed underground, teasing ads. "I want life," he tells Emily. "You want some liver pills and some fruit salts," she replies, not so arch as prescient.

The second section opens with the title's quote from *The Tempest*:

> Nothing of him that doth fade
> But doth suffer a sea-change
> Into something rich and strange.
> (*act 1, scene 2, 399–401*)

Thus Ariel describes Ferdinand's drowned father. The marine metamorphosis of a corpse is a harsh but not inappropriate summary of Fred and his adventures. The film was released in America, sans Shakespeare, as *East of Shanghai*.

As the location footage was shot silent, only about one-fifth of the film has dialogue. Hitchcock plays up this discrepancy with occasional titles, as in silent film. The Hills' voyage is like a family album with facetious captions. Our hero's seasickness is introduced with "To get to France you have *to cross the channel*." "To get to the Folies Bergere you have to cross Paris" introduces a montage of overly familiar sights, sounds, and pinches.[3] Hitchcock emphasizes the tedium and exhaustion of travel over its romance. The section ends with a close-up of Emily's transparent nightie through which the camera seems to move. The shot dissolves to one of her in it, but any lurid expectations are frustrated by the next title: "Marseilles—and the big ship bound for the Far East."

The third section presents the couple's estrangement on their voyage. Emily is extremely attractive for her warmth and candor. "It's a good thing we're not in love," Gordon tells her, when she claims her Fred is more clever than he is; but Gordon grows enchanted with her. "Love is a very difficult thing," she deflects. "It doesn't make people brave, like you read in books. It makes people timid. . . . Everything becomes magnified by two. Sickness. Death. The future. It all means so much more." She feels more blessed by her marriage than Gordon does by his happy bachelorhood.

The shipboard events seem trivial beside the weight of Emily's sentiments. Again there are album captions: "Fred," "Port Said," "The Princess," "Suez Canal," "Carnival." "Fred had met a princess" comes between two close-ups of Emily beaming at his pleasure and success.

Fred completes his seduction of/by the "princess" at the carnival. The costumes set up a range of innocence and experience. Fred sees himself as a sheik, to the "princess's" siren, but before their tryst he must escape a long dance with Miss Emery (Elsie Randolph), who is dressed as Little Bo Peep. The sheik is a sheep in wolf's clothing.

The Hills separate but seem destined to reunite. They keep meeting. In a traffic jam Fred and Emily in separate rickshaws are jammed together, jostling but not speaking. Once reunited, Emily insists that their marriage has been strengthened by their experiences. Their separation has stripped them of their illusions. She loves him for (i.e., despite) what he is, no longer blindly.

But the couple is still at sea. They huddle together in the night, sure that they are about to drown in the shipwreck, while just outside their porthole is a ladder to safety. Their despair delays their rescue.[4] The next morning, Fred returns to his sharpness: "The silly things you ask." When she asks to use the men's washroom ("ours is under water"), he is priggishly liberal: "Yes. No sense in being suburban." Earlier he scolded her for taking her camera ashore. He even scolded the strange woman before he was told she was a princess. His near escape from a broken marriage and even death has not tempered him. "Those are dummies, aren't they?" he says of the Chinese who save and feed them.

When Emily wants to go to help deliver the baby, Fred holds her back: "These dumb Chinese breed like rabbits." Fred remains smug and superior:

EMILY: That woman's had her baby.

FRED: How could she?

EMILY: Well, anyway, she has.

Rich and Strange *(1932). At the costume ball on the ship. Foreground left to right: Fred Hill (Henry Kendall), the ersatz princess (Betty Amann), and Emily Hill (Joan Barry).*

When Emily cries maternally at the sight, Fred mistakes her mood completely: "We'll be all right. We've got each other." At the start of the film Fred is laughable, a comic strip husband. In his adventure with the princess he is a vain fool. But after the shipwreck, far from having learned from experience, he is mean.

The coda shows them back home, enjoying the steak and kidney of which he had earlier complained, the family cat safe on the kitchen table, the hearth a glowing reassurance against the storm warning on the radio. But the marriage is no better off than before. Fred and Emily quarrel over whether his new job warrants their buying a new house. And Fred's new job involves traveling. His disasters, temptations, failures, and foolishness will continue, particularly without Emily there to help him. Their restored security is false.

Fred fails to recover his lost dignity. Emily remains naive and obedient. Hitchcock's homey heroes can't handle anything outside their most mundane experience. They cannot escape their dullness. Early in their travels, Fred totters atop a high trunk to do the budget tally, recalling the position he left behind. You can take the hick out of the tedium, but you can't take the tedium out of the hick.

Each situation exposes Fred's incompetence, self-righteous arrogance, and vanity. In his ludicrous affair, he fumbles with the princess's veil, gets caught with Bo Peep, barges into the wrong cabin then seems totally wasted by the foray. No one else has his unwarranted confidence. Even the abrasive Miss Emery is smarter, as she chooses an oriental rug by rubbing her shoes clean on it. Her balance of the exotic new and the practical habits of the old is quite beyond Fred's grasp.

Fred has nothing like Emily's generosity. Having left her, he is indignant about her affair with Gordon: "How far has this thing gone?" Both romantic temptations are different kinds of selfishness. For the princess, "If a woman can't hold her man, there is no reason why he should take the blame." For Gordon, "You can't save the Freds of this world." Fred subscribes to that irresponsibility, but Emily clings to her duty.

What Fred thinks is wrong with his life is what is wrong with himself. In the underground he sneers at the life above his own—"Clothe your wife at Carridges"—and at the life beneath—a traveler wolfing down a messy sandwich. The film develops the distinction between place and self. So one title reads "Colombo—but it was people not places that mattered to Emily now." The confusion between place and person animates this joke:

EMILY: Someone's just pinched me.

FRED: Where? (looking about)

EMILY: You know where.

As Fred is concerned with the place, not the self, he thinks travel will end his miseries. With comical dislocation, he drunkenly sets his watch by the elevator dial.

So where you are is not as important as what you are. Repeated foot shots define the points where man articulates to his place. Hitchcock cuts from the Follies leg line to a close-up of Emily's feet, her toes curling, shoes kicked off for comfort. The provincial intimacy of Emily's feet plays warmly against the dancers' professional glamour.

Paris is identified by a shot of feet around a pissoir (it's a Hitchcock family album).

Gordon's courtship of Emily is played out in parallel foot shots. They stride across the night deck, she in a trailing gown, he in his naval slacks. As they glide over chains, over a coiled rope, their romance crosses formal bonds. Sailors are partying around a romantic accordion ditty in the background. In a fit of dizziness Emily falls into Gordon's arms and they kiss. That changes everything. The accordion strikes a discordant note, the sailors fall to quarreling, and the lovers stride more deliberately back across the rope and chains, past a regiment of gossips. The innocence of their attraction has been disturbed, their calm shivered, and the images of bond and discipline reasserted. Emily returns to Fred's sickbed, where he still complains about the steak and kidney pudding. The monotony is in Fred, not his situation. The chains and coil are only objects, unless one chooses them as an excuse.

Rich and Strange has no hero, only degrees of selfishness, naivety, and vanity. It also has nastiness. Some is the characters'. The princess knowingly refers to Emily as the waiter so Fred will enter dishabille to meet her. Some of the nastiness is Hitchcock's. The cat is fed to the heroes, but Hitchcock also shows us its skin stretched to dry. The Chinese looter's death by drowning is prolonged as he is dipped down into the water, trapped by a rope around his ankle. This is not the stuff of comedy. Like *The Tempest,* Hitchcock uses a storm and the characters' isolation to test the achievement of their vain desires.

Ariel there is none, but for Hitchcock's black, puckish spirit. Nor is Commander Gordon, the lonely gallant, a fit Prospero. Our heroes are barely above the level of Trinculo and Stephano. The metamorphosis brought on by the sea is not an enrichening but a deadening. Our hero is set yet deeper into his delusions of adequacy. He remains at odds with his world but also comes to odds with his wife. Their false assurance and petty bickering seem their last means to conceal his hollowness.

Fred in his arrogance and Emily in her servility lead not so much a dull life as a selfish one. The glamour of all the world cannot brighten the vision of such narrow souls. This theme connects *Rich and Strange* to the center of Hitchcock's moral ethos. Perhaps there is a touch of personal confession. As he tells Truffaut, unlike *Champagne,* here he may confront his own provincialism, his own inexperience and naivety.[5] From now on, perhaps scorched by his critics, he would develop more adequate heroes.

The Hills are close to the center of Hitchcock's work. Fred's hunger for excitement foreshadows young Charlie lying bored on her bed, feeling a pointless and unacted-on pity for her mother and craving the thrill of a visit from Uncle Charlie. Fred anticipates the James Stewart figure's sickly romanticism in *Vertigo* and the heroes' smug complacency in *North by Northwest, To Catch a Thief, The Birds,* and *Torn Curtain.* In these later films Hitchcock was better served both in script and in casting, but *Rich and Strange* is an intriguing augur of his later concerns.[6]

Number Seventeen
1932

Hitchcock's next three efforts were seriously marred by his studio's financial difficulties. He directed *Number Seventeen* for the failing British International Pictures, then worked as producer for *Lord Camber's Ladies,* a quota quickie, "a poison thing. I gave it to Benn Levy to direct."[1] Hitchcock's musical, *Waltzes from Vienna,* for Gaumont-British, he calls "my lowest ebb. A musical, and they really couldn't afford the music."[2] All three films have their occasional charms but none is a success.

Number Seventeen makes the strongest impact, for two reasons. It has a remarkable chase sequence, with jewel thieves and detectives scampering from car to car as the train hurtles through the night, finally colliding with a ferryboat. The film also has a comedy that shifts between the burlesque and the surreal.

The film is based on a comic thriller that J. Jefferson Farjeon wrote for the well-known actor Leon Lion. Lion produced the play and starred in it. It was such a stage success that Farjeon novelized it as well.

In the film Lion again plays Ben, a hobo formerly of the merchant marine, who is found in the deserted house (number seventeen) by a detective (John Stuart) who is tracking down some jewel thieves. Together they find a disappearing corpse; a plucky young girl, Miss

Ayckroyd (Ann Casson), trying to find her father; and a gang of jewel thieves plotting to escape on a freight train that runs underneath (!) the old house. The detective hijacks a Green Line bus to catch up with the train. His romantic sympathies shift to an ostensibly mute girl (Anne Grey) in the gang. He ends up with the thieves under arrest and the girl (talking now), while old Ben saves the jewels.

The deserted house and the train are two traditional settings for such adventure films. Hitchcock jams them together to guy both types. Of course, if a train can run under a house, then a bus can chase a train and a train can collide with a ferryboat. This all happens in *Number Seventeen,* with Hitchcock's tongue even farther in his cheek than usual. *"Number Seventeen* reflected a careless approach to my work," he tells Truffaut.[3] To Durgnat, "That train, coach, ferry and all are clearly models doesn't spoil things in the least, our natural preference for large-scale and genuine catastrophes being compensated for by nostalgic references to Hornby Trains and Dinky Toys, all taking on the curious artificiality of a dream, like a Trinka puppet film."[4] The toys still generate suspense. Twice the bus and train seem to be converging until a sudden bridge slips the bus under the speeding train. Hitchcock intercuts the bus-train race with shots of the slow ferry approaching its collision. Hitchcock contrasts rhythms, speeds, tones, as well as modes of transport. But he balances his fine control over tempo with a sense of the ridiculousness of his material. He gives the bus model human habitation by cutting in shots of the tumbled, indignant passengers, and such careful details as the "Stop Here for Dainty Teas" sign the bus hurtles past.

Certain passages are surreal, like Ben's description of the contents of his pockets:

> There you are, a handkerchief. I used that to gag him with. A piece of string. I stabbed him with that. Sausage: that's what I hit him on the head with.

In the novel instead of sausage it's a "pencil. Real lead" that Ben claims to have used on the victim's head.[5] Hitchcock likes food, of course, but a sausage is a more surreal weapon than a pencil. The haunted house has the usual frightening wind, banging doors, shadows, vanishing corpse, surprise intruders, and mysterious lights that are played just over the normal tone. Ben is caught in a shadow-web that anticipates Cary Grant's in *Suspicion,* but in *Number Seventeen* every wall quivers with shadows.

The characters are equally strange. The jewel gang arrives after midnight under the arch pretext of seeing a house that's for sale. The detective and the gang don't drop the pretense in the film, though in the novel they do (167). The mute girl and another man do not belong with the gang. The characters share our puzzlement by the whole business, but carry on regardless.

There is much confusion over identity. The latecomer eventually claims to be the famous detective Barton, there to retrieve the jewels, but then our unnamed hero arrests "Detective Barton," revealing him to be the thief Doyle and himself to be Barton. The gang fails to recognize their own leader, Sheldrake, at first falling in behind the good guy, Ayckroyd. In a comic version of this theme, Ben responds to the detective's advice—"It always pays for an innocent man to play straight"—with confused indignation: "Who says I'm an innocent man? I mean, who says I ain't playing straight?"

The characters seem to be aware of themselves as characters in a melodrama. At the clock's chime, Ben's "Twelve o'clock" is corrected by the detective: "Half-past, you fool." In the book it was 4:30 (141; much less promising a time). The gang leader, when he has the detective and Miss Ayckroyd in his thrall, is aware of his "role": "Hadn't we better. . . . I don't know what's done in these cases, but hadn't we better tie them up or something?" "Please," he says, to get their hands for his convenience, and then apologizes for leaving them: "We have to catch a train." "This is just like the pictures," Miss Ayckroyd says later. "Too much for my liking," replies the detective stiffly. "I'm coming back," says the mute lady. "She spoke," says Miss Ayckroyd. "That deaf and dumb business was a fake," observes the shrewd detective, "the trick of a crook." The banal conversations and extravagant situations send up the genre.

Against tradition, the detective pairs off with the reformed criminal "mute" instead of with the original girl, who is left to care for her father. The fallen lady redeems herself by saving the hero and the good girl from falling with the wobbly banister. The romantic switch coheres with the role changing, unreality, and confusion.

Hitchcock shifted the focus from Lion's Ben to the detective. The novel begins with Ben, the irascible Cockney outsider. Hitchcock characteristically opens on an ordered society then introduces chaos, even where the "ordered society" is a foggy, deserted street with the wind blowing thistles and our hero's hat.

Still, Ben has the best lines and the most character in the film. He is the coward's coward, often frightened by his own shadow. What he thinks is blood dripping on him is the wax from his own candle. He points the gun butt at the thieves then aims the gun in his own mouth to check the stiff trigger. He is not an efficient tough. Twice he hits Miss Ayckroyd in a scuffle. Trying to help the detective, he hits him. He knocks out Ayckroyd instead of Sheldrake in another of Hitchcock's antiheroic fights.

Still, Ben has the innocent's blessing. He lands in a shipment of wine on the train. He happens to pick the pocket that contains the missing jewels. Hitchcock drops the original Ben's sentimental gush (e.g., 256).

The film threatens to turn serious when the gang leader shoots the engine fireman and the train rushes out of control. But Hitchcock rarely lingers on the death of an innocent person—the suspect chased into a propeller in *Shadow of a Doubt,* for example, or the man shot by the police in *Strangers on a Train.* His runaway train stays comic.

The film closes on Ben in long johns, soaking his feet, laughing. The spirit of misrule embodied, he unfurls his blanket to show the precious necklace around his grizzled neck. As an image of justice triumphant and beauty and virtue restored to its proper place, this coheres with the film's wacky humor.

Interesting background to *Number Seventeen* comes from scriptwriter Rodney Ackland in his autobiography, *Celluloid Mistress.* Hitchcock and Ackland were enthused about the prospect of filming John van Druten's *London Wall* together. Thomas Bentley was keen to make *Number Seventeen.* "We made the fatal mistake of letting this be known,"[6] Ackland recalls, so Bentley was assigned to make *London Wall* and Hitchcock *Number Seventeen.*

In revenge, Hitchcock planned to

Number Seventeen *(1932). Girl (Ann Casson) and detective (John Stuart) hang around the deserted house.*

make *Number Seventeen* as a burlesque of all the thrillers of which it was a pretty good sample—and do it so subtly that nobody at Elstree would realize the subject was being guyed. Not that Hitch had anything against *Number Seventeen* as a thriller—but he didn't want to make a thriller: he wanted make *London Wall*. . . .

As the heroines of thrillers were invariably dumb, the leading lady of *Number Seventeen,* Hitch decided must be literally dumb—must never utter from beginning to end of the picture. As the climax of a thriller was invariably a chase (generally between a car and a train at this period), *Number Seventeen's* climax must be a chase-to-end-all-chases—its details so preposterous that excitement would give way to gales of laughter. . . .

Neither press nor public seemed to have an inkling that the director had made the picture with his tongue in his chubby cheek.

Leon Lion's attitude to Hitchcock's subversion of his "joyous melodrama" is not known, except that Lion does not mention Hitchcock in his autobiography (*The Surprise of My Life,* 1946) nor differentiate between the silent and talkie versions.

Waltzes from Vienna

1933

Yes, the master of suspense once made a musical: *Waltzes from Vienna*, an unusually free adaptation of the stage libretto by A. M. Willner, Heinz Reichert, and Ernst Marischka.[1] In the United States the film was released as *Strauss' Great Waltz*.

Hitchcock avoids discussing the film. Durgnat retreats to comparing Hitchcock's touch with Lubitsch's.[2] The stars are at best resentful toward it. Esmond Knight recalls Hitchcock's indelicate handling of Jessie Matthews and Fay Compton and his own "hopeless inferiority complex under his direction" and under Hitchcock's practical jokes. "Instead of the romantic rather serious story of the play," Knight remarks, "he turned the whole thing into a light comedy, and his ideas for many of the sequences were extremely funny—on paper."[3]

However disappointed Knight and Matthews felt, the film turned out charming. Several reviews were warm indeed. "A remarkable triumph of intelligence over insufficiency," applauded the *Observer* (March 4, 1934), with "touches of felicitous design" and "a meticulous script." In the October 22, 1933, *Observer*, C. A. Lejeune noted: "It presents a 'musical' unlike any other musical that has ever been filmed, in which the rhythm and melody spring directly from the action, instead of the action being used to amplify the song. . . . The script is full of instances of this kind, intelligent combinations of sound and image, in which the screen is used as an independent medium, and the final effect is assured by a synthesis of deliberate and predetermined shots."[4] And from *Variety* (April 1935): "Picture should never have crossed the ocean."

Hitchcock's musical expresses his somewhat Edwardian aspect: cool, formal, conservative. Like *The Skin Game* it replays the passage of power and social authority from the stiff and old ways to the flexible, cunning, and new. This struggle is within a family, between Johann Strauss the Elder (Edmund Gwenn, this time on the side of the Hillcrists) and young Johann (Schani) Strauss (Esmond Knight).

Schani is in love with the baker's daughter, Rasi (star billing to Jessie Matthews). Jealous of the attentions paid Schani by the countess (Fay Compton), Rasi urges Schani to give up music, marry her, and run the family bakery. Rasi leaves him on the eve of his "Blue Danube Waltz" debut (and spectacular success). It is played by the elder Strauss's orchestra, thanks to some trickery by the countess and her foolish husband, a prince (Frank Vosper). Strauss arrives late for his concert but in time to hear the ovation for his son. "The late Mr. Strauss and his illustrious son," he remarks bitterly. Strauss tells the prince that Schani is having an affair with the countess. Rasi returns to save Schani from the prince's wrath and accepts Schani with his music.

The film celebrates the free spirit, so the villain is regimentation. A marching band impedes the fire truck rushing to the fire at the bakery in the opening sequence ("Where's the fire?" asks the driver, rather sensibly). The models playfully march out in step with the band, to the officious dressmaker's embarrassment. When Schani plays for his father, a somber row of lamps along each wall suggests the enemy regimentation. At his brief bakery job Schani marches in, zombielike under a box of pastries, his face white with flour. The elder Strauss in vain pursues an "Order" (i.e., a decoration). A row of cleaning ladies scrub the floor in unison. They raise their heads as one when Schani kisses Rasi. He leaps over them to exit. Hitchcock contrasts spirited life and art to the mechanical and uniform.

He adds the opening fire-alarm scene to introduce the notion of an intense art, fired by inspiration. So the countess rues the early extinguishing of the fire: "What a pity. So little fire in the world, don't you think? . . . I mean, the sort of fire you put into the song you were playing just now." Schani's fire comically interrupts the dressmaker when he enters instead of a model on her line: "And now I shall show you something attractive for the winter evenings."

Where Schani composes out of personal compulsion, his father exercises the traditional canons. Schani speaks of the soul ("The soul of music is greater than any composer, however great"), while his father sneers at his son's "masterful contempt for form."

The two Strausses differ in another way. Schani draws his inspiration from the world around him, where his father operates in a cerebral vacuum. For his "Blue Danube Waltz," Schani derives the lyrics from the countess (who got the color from her maid), the first musical phrase from Rasi's memory of an earlier composition, and the rhythms from the bakery—the rhythm of the rolls as they are boxed, the bread tossed back and forth, the dough-making machine. Schani is the artist who educes art from real life.[5] For his father, art should be secure from life and from change. The same generation difference obtains in love:

> EBESEDER (ROBERT HALE): Your mother didn't let me kiss her until we were married for six months.
>
> RASI: That explains why I wasn't born till you were 50.

Love, art, and life are for freedom.

When the father rejects his son, Rasi stands between them but is replaced by the fete's sponsor. He stands between the Strausses, back to us, with his hair parted all the way down, heavier on the side where the senior Strauss stands. The head is an image of a divided unity, one half the weightier but both serving a single order. This anticipates Cary Grant's introduction in *Notorious*, where the long close-up of the back of his head suggests chilliness and inscrutability.[6]

The senior Strauss's vanity is parodied by the prince's vain dreams of glory. He duels in his sleep to preserve his honor, which leaves the countess free to compromise hers in daylight. "Needless to say, I killed my man," exults the prince, squashing a fly. The romance between the prince's valet and the countess's maid shows the spark missing from their masters' lives. They also work at translation, changing the countess's "Idiot!" to "An excellent suggestion." Everyone in Hitch-cock's Vienna is artful. Schani's art ideally tempers the prince's ego-tism and Strauss Sr.'s formalism (both vanities) with a warm sense of community.

Hitchcock gives the women will and intelligence. The men are lap-dogs, save for the bullheaded senior Strauss whose vanity renders him putty in women's hands. Publisher Drexler is in awe of the countess. There were wise, strong women in Hitchcock's earlier films, but this is the first one in which the women are so clearly superior to the men, in strength of will, character, and virtue.

This adaptation owes very little to the original libretto. Hitchcock adds the count, the bakery inspiration scene, the gradual composition of the "Blue Danube Waltz," the fire, indeed almost everything of character. From the play Hitchcock kept the quarrel of father and son, the countess's patronage and ploy, and the romantic rival, Leopold. Where the play gives us a slushy reconciliation of father and son but has Rasi marry the unmusical Leopold, Hitchcock spares us the fam-ily scene but reconciles Rasi and Schani.

Hitchcock handles the Strausses' reconciliation without bringing the men together. Strauss Sr. reconciles not directly with his son but with the qualities for which Schani stands. He accepts not just his son but the changing times and values. The reconciliation begins with Schani in deep focus leaving the bandstand to a wild ovation. His fa-ther enters in soft focus on the right foreground. Whether because his fury strengthens or his awareness clears, Strauss Sr. comes into sharp focus. When everyone is off to celebrate Schani's triumph, Strauss Sr. starts miserably home. But a little girl has stayed behind to get the old man's autograph. He signs. As she leaves he calls her back to add "se-nior" after his name. The new waltz swells up as he walks proudly into the shadows.

In changing the signature, Strauss adds to his own name to recog-nize his son. He extends himself by acknowledging his son's success. His pride in his son adds to his own name. Having disowned the son and his music, declaring himself the senior Strauss is like a readop-tion. The resurgent waltz catches the swell of the father's feelings. Finally, the old man is reconciled through the young girl. He accepts the new generation in respect for the little girl honoring him. They mark a new harmony between the generations.

Even in this inapt assignment, Hitchcock achieved an elegance, charm, and formal consistency that few musicals of the period, particularly in England, had. *Waltzes from Vienna* is no misbegotten wreck.

The Man Who Knew Too Much
1934

While Hitchcock was struggling through *Waltzes from Vienna*, he had in his drawer the finished script for the film that would return him to form, *The Man Who Knew Too Much*. In five years, 1934–38, Hitchcock would direct the six films that established "the Hitchcock touch." Contemporary reviews applauded Hitchcock's new film:

> I am very happy about this film. It seems to me, because of its very recklessness, its frank refusal to indulge in subtleties, to be the most promising work that Hitchcock has produced since *Blackmail.* (C. A. Lejeune, *Observer,* December 8, 1934)

> Lately he has been badly served with stories. With *The Man Who Knew Too Much,* based on a celebrated criminal case of the early 1900s, he makes a striking come-back. (*Daily Telegraph,* December 10, 1934)

> After a prolonged spell of "Elstree blues" and a musical confection which was not in his line, Hitchcock leaps once again into the front rank of British directors. (*Daily Express*)[1]

Alistair Cooke heralded Hitchcock's "familiar mastery of a slow ominous tempo, passages of breathless tantalizing cutting, and some psychological detail which advances him in the path previously trodden by Fritz Lang."[2]

At least Cooke attends to the subtleties, something most reviewers in their enjoyment of the thrilling plot failed to do. As late as 1961, Peter John Dyer rued Hitchcock's waste by "being inhibited by respectability," but for his "now legendary injections of 'cinema.'" His audience was play-lovers and "esoteric cine-club types bent on seeking out all manner of functionless technical tricks and often non-existent subtleties." But now, according to Dyer, "Hitchcock lost patience . . . threw compliance overboard and went in for making thrillers for the unsophisticated. *The Man Who Knew Too Much* . . . was outright melodrama, deficient in structure and flawed in its logic. But its very recklessness gave it an excitement hitherto unknown in the British cinema."[3]

Hitchcock admits the film's illogicality. He tells David Castell that he prefers the first version of *The Man Who Knew Too Much* over his 1956 remake with James Stewart and Doris Day: "I think it was more spontaneous—it had less logic. Logic is dull: you always lose the bizarre and the spontaneous."[4] But with the American Bogdanovich, Hitchcock prefers the (American) remake: "The old one is fairly slipshod structurally." Still, "Around that 1935 period, the audience would accept more, the films of the period were full of fantasy, and one didn't have to worry too much about logic or truth. When I came to America, the first thing I had to learn was that the audiences were more questioning. I'll put it another way. Less avant garde."[5] Truffaut's detailed preference for the second version Hitchcock sidesteps discretely with "Let's say that the first version is the work of a talented amateur and the second was made by a professional."[6] Certainly the first version is the wilder, the more fantastic. One need only compare the dentist scene with the taxidermist's, or the fact that the heroine settles the issue with a shootout in the first version and a song in the second.

Hitchcock's "golden period" thrillers are fantasies of varying remoteness from reality. Their primary concern remains the tension between private interest and public duty. Particularly in the first of the series, the ostensible "recklessness" of Hitchcock's narrative style subserves the values of discipline, self-control, and public service.

In the first *The Man Who Knew Too Much* a succession of Swiss travel folders threatens a reprise of *Rich and Strange*. Again an ordinary family is tossed into strange intrigue and threatened with separation. This time Hitchcock is more in control of his material; so is his family. His central characters here are the cause not the butt of the comedy. They are more competent and mature than their earlier counterparts. This married couple works in complete harmony and understanding, even though for most of the film they are apart.

Bob and Jill Lawrence (Leslie Banks and Edna Best) are holidaying in the Alps with their young daughter, Betty (Nova Pilbeam). A new friend, Louis Bernard (Pierre Fresnay), is shot while dancing with Jill. He gives her a message for the British consulate. But the Lawrences are silenced when Betty is kidnapped. An anarchist cell is planning to assassinate a visiting dignitary, Ropa. They hold Betty hostage to keep the Lawrences from warning him. Lawrence and Uncle Clive (Hugh Wakefield) track down the girl's captors: Abbott (Peter Lorre, in his first English film); Nurse Agnes (Cicely Oates); and the assassin Ramon (Frank Vosper). At the last moment, Jill screams, saving Ropa from anything worse than a flesh wound. The police surround the anarchists' refuge, wipe out the cell, and save Bob. To save Betty, Jill shoots Ramon. The film closes on the three Lawrences happily reunited.[7]

The central theme is the Lawrences' conflict between their family interest, saving Betty, and their public duty, preventing the assassination. At first the Lawrences serve Betty, despite the reminder of Sarajevo: "Because one man you never heard of killed another man you never heard of in a place you never heard of, this country was at war." In the original screenplay, the Lawrences see the parallel without that foreign officer's reminder. As Bob says,

> We mustn't get cross at Mr. Gibson, Jill. Betty is ours, not his. He has to think of all the other people, and their Bettys. We went through four and a half years of it and we don't want anybody to do it again. (Shot 153-a)[8]

Hitchcock dropped this for the film, as well as Gibson's brutal parting shot—"If there is trouble I hope you'll remember that you are to blame. It will not be a nice thing to have on your conscience" (shot 163)—and Jill's rejection of the 1914 parallel:

> It couldn't happen again! I don't believe it! And even if it did, don't you realize that I'm a woman, and I've got a child—I'm fighting for her life—Do you realize that? (Shot 153)

With these three omissions Hitchcock tempers the emotional charge of the Lawrence's dilemma, so they make a rational decision.

We are twice given Jill's physical perspective, when her conflict is at its most intense. When she reports Louis Bernard's message to the police, Bob hands her the kidnap note, the room whirls, and Jill faints. She succumbs to the strain of the two secrets, Louis's and the kidnapping.[9] We again share Jill's perspective at the concert in Albert Hall, when she is still uncertain whether or not to warn Ropa. Her eyes cloud over in tears, but she recovers her focus (i.e., her composure, thereby her will) at seeing the gun. Its close-up implies she is at that instant aware of nothing else. That clarity enables her to scream her warning.

The screenplay describes the blurring of her senses more precisely. In shot 336, Jill sees the assassin's empty box, then a policeman, then looks up from Betty's brooch, which Ramon had given her to renew the threat, "and stares out almost defiantly." There follow two images of community, of public connection (shot 337: the arch onstage and the microphone, which will bring the concert and the shot live to Betty's captors). In shot 354, "Her face almost blurs a little as she stares out." In shot 355, "The choir and orchestra are becoming very blurred, while the voices seem to get louder than ever."

With the singing choir in the screenplay, Hitchcock returns to the expressionism of the jury scene in *Murder!* though the effect does not seem as clear in the film itself:

> 357 The voices of the choir, male and female, seem to change the text of what they are singing. The words that come from them sing as though they are crying out for her to settle her problem. The women's voices cry out for her child and the men's to save the victim in the box. These sounds seem to go in waves and as they

do so impressions flit from the screen which help to picture the words she hears.

358   The screen now contains only her eyes.

359   Blurred view of the choir with the various pictorial impressions. The excitement of the sounds is increasing. The screen is filled with impressions. Then slowly from the right side of the screen a long black muzzle appears, moving slowly across until it comes to rest. The image of the choir disappears and the muzzle of the gun is left alone on the screen.

In the film Hitchcock omits the "visual impressions" to focus on Jill's immediate perspective. The intruding gun does not drive the chorus off the screen; between chorus and gun is a black void.

Making the female voices cry for the girl and the male voices for public duty is the sentimental tradition Hitchcock reverses in the film as a whole. He drops Jill's "I'm a mother" speech (see above), has a rather effeminate hero in Leslie Banks, not above play weeping, and makes not the man but the wife the sharpshooter who saves the day. The Lawrence family inflects traditional responsibility in their own, extremely personal, way. Jill is brought to scream her warning by the immediacy of the gun, though her daughter's fate has been her overriding concern.

There are two family clusters in the film. We have the Lawrence family—father, mother, daughter, with a role-reversal between the father and mother signifying the modulation of role by spirit, personality. This family is augmented by a formal uncle (Clive) and an adopted uncle (Louis). As a parody of the Lawrence family we have the anarchist cell—Abbott, Nurse Agnes, and Ramon, as the nucleus, with the dentist as a formal addition (like Uncle Clive) and Mrs. Sprocket the adopted relation (like Louis). In the nucleus, Ramon is the manliest of the three, but he takes the orders so he is like the child in the family. Abbott, the leader, is a cool, cultured, planning man, but he is a grotesque leader on two counts. He has a childish face and manner, particularly vis-à-vis Betty, who is insulted at his impression of her young interests. And he is strangely dependent on the masculine Nurse Agnes. Both families, the Lawrences and the anarchists, are loose in their roles.

Betty is spoiled and undisciplined, Jill manly, and Bob effeminate. But these are but personal inflections of roles. In the anarchist cell the roles are completely distorted, not by personality or spirit, but psychopathology. The theme of duty includes the adults' balance between control and spirit.

The opening scene dramatizes the dangers of lack of self-control. Betty, in her spirit and joy, sets off the disturbances. Rushing to retrieve her dog, she upsets Bernard's ski course, causing him to bump into Abbott and be recognized. Betty's interruption causes Jill to lose the first shooting match to Ramon.

Perhaps Betty is an unwitting catalyst. She no more causes Louis's fall or Jill's defeat than the tangling thread causes Louis's death or the poor cymbalist causes Ropa's being shot. As these innocents become the villains' instruments, perhaps they argue for citizens' engagement for the public good. Like Jill's impulsive scream, they suggest neutrality is impossible when the stakes are high.

Happily, the conclusion provides a rematch, where Jill controls her emotions and with steely resolve, shoots past Betty to kill Ramon. Again Hitchcock brings a new emphasis to the screenplay, where the policeman refuses to shoot at Ramon ("I daren't, sir—I might hit the kiddie"). There is no sign of Jill taking the gun, then:

> 479   Mrs. Lawrence is just lowering a smoking rifle. Her face expresses nothing but horror at what she had to do.
>
> There is no relief in her expression at all. In this terrified state of mind she turns to the nearest to her and almost half consciously murmurs—
> "It's awful—I've killed someone."

Eschewing this sentimentality, the film's Jill very firmly takes the gun, aims, and serves both private and public duties at once. She kills Ramon, throwing a new light on his parting line after their first competition: "I shall live for that moment," the rematch. As the two shooting matches prove, Jill has grown from being distracted to being firm of purpose.

The film contrasts the spiritedness of the young and irresponsible (Betty) and the aware and dutiful (Bernard, Gibson). The anarchist Abbott provides a parody of duty, speaking of his cause but bound by his childish image to seem irresponsible. In his two-shot with Betty, Abbott appears the more childish. And where Betty saves a defenseless dog, Abbott is jokingly dependent. To Louis's "Are you all right?" Abbott replies, "Better ask my nurse. My English isn't good enough to know."

The delicate balance between chaos and control makes for good comedy. Abbott eats nonchalantly while the others pace nervously around the radio. Louis, mortally wounded, points to his heart in disbelief: "Look!" Then he drops and with admirable devotion gives Jill his lengthy message. As in *Murder!* the shaving brush is the pivot to a public duty, here carrying the message the Lawrences must transmit.[10]

Louis's control is discipline, in dying as in his sacrifice while skiing. It should not be confused with that insipidness of character that may seem to be discipline: "The average Englishman is cold, unless he drinks too much." Abbot says the right words with the wrong spirit: "You should learn to control your fatherly feelings." Both Lawrences restrain their emotions for a clear will and decisive action.[11] Hence Jill's improved marksmanship and Bob's coolness when, captured by the anarchists, he sees Betty for the first time. In an addition to the screenplay, Bob greets Betty without any reference to their predicament. He compliments her on her nice dressing gown and her school report card, suppressing his sentiments and his sense of danger. Once wild Betty behaves with poise and maturity throughout her ordeal.

Raymond Durgnat places the church scene at the heart of the film's interplay between the irresponsible and the dutiful:

> In the Tabernacle of the Sun, a thinly cranky disguise for the drab piety of back-street nonconformism, the sleuthing hero and his pal do all the things our childish irreverence dreamed of during those long and dingy services. They sing burlesque words to the hymns, they put their hat on top of the Holy Bible, start a fight and hurl the stacked chairs at the deacons. Of course, they have to pay the wages of sin—the crab-mouthed old lady makes them drop their guns into the collection-plate—but at least the labourer is worthy of his hire.

This childish irreverence contrasts to Betty's maturity and the childish chaos in Abbott (whose name promises ascetic conformity).

Durgnat—in common with most critics—finds this film a succession of bright incidents, "just" an entertainment, as they say: "It seems to be that the theme for which the film gropes, perhaps intuitively, perhaps despite itself, is that of private anguish versus public lies."[12] In *The Man Who Knew Too Much* Hitchcock frees his comic spirit and his adventurous bent to valorize duty and self-control.

Some characters suffer someone else's control, having failed to control themselves. Uncle Clive is hypnotized by the temple priestess. At the dentist's office he suffers a needless extraction. Bob more seriously is threatened by ether, a chemical hypnosis, but turns it on his attacker.

When Bob ties a loose end of Jill's knitting to Bernard's jacket, he sets up a varied metaphor. It shows the husband in a childish prank. Also, it shows such simplicity having destructive effects, both directly—the knitting is destroyed—and coincidentally—pausing to untangle, Bernard is killed. It's also an image of man bound, under restraint if not control, from the outside. The free-spirited skier and playboy is actually bound to an important mission. The thread is an image of unseen consequences winding out of a simple act (like Betty retrieving her dog). It anticipates the quest, leading the heroes through a number of strangers, tripping some, encircling others. It is also an image of community, as separate couples find themselves in a common ring, a common tangle, because of the secret agent's dance/quest. They share a laugh at their discovery. Then there is Hitchcock's reading: "It's the thread of life that gets broken. One could still get pretentious in those days. It was also comic. You combine a little comic action with a break in the thread when the man falls dead."[13] Hitchcock tells Samuels he put in the wool-joke "to show that death comes when you least expect it."[14]

As the heroes represent the unity both of family and social community, the villains cause their fragmentation and are fragmented. They are often represented by parts of the body, either isolated or obtrusive. Ramon is identified by close-ups of his greasy hair. He's introduced with a hairline shot and often shown hair first. Betty satirizes Ramon: "Many too many teeth and wears too much Brilliantine." Lorre's Abbott has a grotesque blond streak in his hair. In Bob's struggles with the foreign policeman, the screenplay is altered slightly to pun on both the hair theme and manliness:

SHOT 100 LAWRENCE: Der—der Britischer.

CONSUL.: He—he is hier?

GENDARME: (Shrugs) Hier? Nein (Gestures round room) Nein.

LAWRENCE: Here, in St. Moritz?

In the film:

LAWRENCE: Der Britischer Consul. Is he here? Is he haire?

GENDARME: Ja, er ist ein herre.

The anarchists meet at the dentist's office, at a sign of a huge mouth of improbable teeth (picking up Betty's other objection to Ramon). In the Tabernacle there is a large close-up of the hypnotist's mouth. Clive sneezes under an oculist's sign of eyes. A single eye dominates the Tabernacle insignia. Abbott describes Clive's arrest with an image of fragmentation: "The arm of the English law needed help in taking our

The Man Who Knew Too Much *(1934). Chaos in the chapel.*

friend to the station." Abbott is given close-ups of his hands in action. When Bob sneaks into Bernard's room for the shaving brush and when he fights the dentist, we see his hands in close-up. Generally the heroes are whole beings and the anarchists are shown in and as pieces, parts of a whole. The heroes represent the principle of wholeness, in self, family, and state. The anarchists represent fragmentation, so they break up the Lawrence family and threaten to break up the world order. They are themselves incomplete or unharmonized.

The cell crumbles. Mrs. Sprocket has to be robbed of her skirt, else she would go home: "My husband wants his supper. Besides I don't want to be mixed up in any nasty business." The anarchists exploit the order of civilization—Abbott's timing of the shot to coincide with the symphony cymbal; Mrs. Sprocket's decorum. Nurse Agnes draws a gun to keep Ramon from walking out on the siege: "You took this on for our cause and you've got to go through with it." The anarchists don't bring freedom but a far more rigid control than the Lawrences enjoy. The church service has ominous political overtones:

> I am therefore going to ask anyone here who is not in tune with us, to submit to a very simple process of control—merely place him or herself under the guidance of the Fourth Circle.
> Before receiving the first degree of the Sevenfold Ray, your mind must be white and blank.

As Abbott is a false image of both the leader and the child, his politics is a fake liberty.

In Hitchcock, of course, innocent objects and situations turn sinister. A gun is felt under a sweet little old lady's gentle line, "You're not going to leave your friend, are you?" The dwarf brooch that Jill gave Betty assumes a definite malevolence when Betty is kidnapped, as do the jingling sleigh bells. When Ramon gives Jill the brooch in the Royal Albert Hall lobby, it suggests the girl's last remains.[15]

The siege depicts the invasion of the private life by the public. The police commandeer a bachelor's flat. One policeman pauses to tinkle the piano but others move it around for a barrier. Two policemen roust a girl out of her bed, joke about its warmth, set the mattress up against the window as a defense, and prepare to take aim. Gunfire kills the joker.

The mattress itself rhymes off the padded doors at the dentist's and at the siege, paralleling the forces of law and disorder the way the hand rubbings did in *Blackmail*. The chief's sweet tooth depletes the candy store stock. Constantly public and private concerns come into conflict:

> POLICEMAN: We've got orders to clear the street.
>
> MAILMAN: I've got orders to clear my box.

No one is a self unto himself, but a meld of self, role, and responsibility. So the dentist is named Barber and the first killed policeman is a Baker. "Looks like an all-night job to me," he worries, sadly wrong. People have private and public selves, roles, and duties. Crises require submergence of the personal into the public. Hitchcock's first *The Man Who Knew Too Much* enjoys the liberty of the fantastic and the comic but promotes man's social responsibility. Not in this film could the heroine sing anything as complacent as "What will be, will be."

The 39 Steps
1935

The 39 Steps is Hitchcock's most popular British film. Ralph Thomas remade it, with Kenneth More in the Robert Donat role, dooming himself to an eternity of unfavorable comparisons.

Hitchcock's film also suffers from its reputation as entertainment. John Russell Taylor makes a typical assumption: "Any idea of the film's being an allegory of good and evil—any more than any conflict between hero and villain, us and them, can be interpreted in this light—seems to me quite unnecessary and at odds with the general impression the film creates on the mind."[1] The story line is so thrilling that it takes a real effort to engage with the film's patterns and themes. The sensational experience quite overwhelms the analytical. But the sensational entertainment is not all there is. A viewer cannot fairly assume that his first take on a work exhausts it, that in the ninety-minute traffic of the stage he has absorbed all that the director and his crew could have implanted there. "The general impression the film creates on the mind" can't cover it.

Richard Hannay (Robert Donat) is a Canadian holidaying in London. At a music hall performance by Mr. Memory (Wylie Watson), a skirmish erupts between a guard and an audience member. After two shots are fired, the audience rushes out. Hannay is accompanied home by a strange German lady who claims to have fired the shots in order to escape two men who are trying to prevent her from telling the authorities a secret message vital to England's air defense. The next morning Hannay finds her dead in his flat. He flees, pursued by the foreign agents and the police, who suspect him of the lady's murder.

Each refuge Hannay finds becomes a greater danger. He feigns friendship with a beautiful blonde in the railway car, Pamela (Madeleine Carroll), but she turns him over to the police. A dour crofter (John Laurie) is cruelly jealous of his wife (Peggy Ashcroft). The urbane country squire, Professor Jordan (Godfrey Tearle), turns out to be the gang leader. The sheriff (Frank Cellier) pretends to believe Hannay's story, then gives him to the spies. After an awkward period of being handcuffed together, Hannay wins Pamela's trust. Back at the Palladium, Mr. Memory clears up the mystery before being shot by Professor Jordan.

For all its thrills, the film has at least three themes. In one, a chaotic world returns to harmony and order. Another is the growth of the Donat and Carroll characters as they handle the upsets of their lives. A third theme reflects on the function of storytelling.

In the opening sequence, visitor Hannay is drawn to a theater's brightness and community. A quick montage conveys Hannay's perspective as he buys a ticket, then we watch him enter the music hall. The show will end in chaos, but the theater offers refuge from the city's loneliness and confusion. Nor is this the exclusive trait of city life. The episode at the crofter's, where "the Lord made the country," offers as much danger and alienation as the city does.

The first Mr. Memory scene is a familiar Hitchcock exposure of people displaying their narrow self-concern. Inviting questions from the floor, Mr. Memory uncovers a mine of personal obsessions. "How old is Mae West?" To one lad "cup" can only refer to football. "Where's my old man been since last Saturday?" "What causes pip in poultry?" a timid thin man asks, despite his wife's "Don't make yourself common!" Pip is a common poultry problem but is also suggestive of venereal disease.[2] Even Hannay draws his question from his own experience ("How far is Winnipeg from Montreal?"). The only serious question is the poultryman's, and that is called common. For everyone else the invitation to test Mr. Memory is the questioner's chance to show off.

The 39 Steps *(1935). Richard Hannay (Robert Donat) finds the villainous Professor Jordan (Godfrey Tearle).*

In a parallel conversation on the train, two traveling salesmen reduce world concerns to the girdles and bras they sell. "Is there no honesty in the world?" The reference is not to the front-page news of the murder or the spy threat to the country but to a commercial rival.

Hannay reacts to the female agent with bored disinterest, as if he has been numbed by the city's sensations and chaos:

SHE: Can I come home with you?

HE: What's the idea?

SHE: I'd like to.

HE: Well, it's your funeral.

SHE: I owe you an explanation.

HE: Don't bother about me. I'm nobody.

On their bus ride a sign advertises "Cooperative Permanent." At that point their cooperation seems hardly permanent, but she will haunt him.[3] Hannay's disinterest and skepticism will be returned tenfold when he needs Pamela's help. Cooperation will remain his permanent need.

Hannay is slow to get involved because the female agent, to protect him, is reluctant to involve him. He only joins her cause to clear himself of her murder. As Hannay passes through the blonde lady's life, the terribly dull life of the crofter's wife, and the political rally, he develops sensitivity to others.

The film contrasts the rigid, habitual response to life with the livelier life of the instincts. Those questions Mr. Memory fielded sprang from habit. By instinct Hannay realizes that Mr. Memory is the clue to the mystery, so he leaps up and asks him about the thirty-nine steps. Mr. Memory by habit provides his fatal total recall. With a perfectly mechanical mind, Mr. Memory can't not answer, so he is killed for divulging the spies' secret. Noble in his powers, relieved to unload the secret, Mr. Memory is an impressive victim of rigidity.

So is Pamela in her skepticism of strange men popping into her cabin for a kiss and a cover. "All bones and no bend," as the traveling salesman dismisses his rival's girdle. Hannay begins this stiff but grows flexible through his trials.

The crofter embodies a worse rigidity. His rote religion contrasts to his wife's intuitive sentiment. Despite his moral pretense, the crofter will sell out either Hannay or his pursuers for the greater sum. "But he took the money," Hannay tells the crofter's wife: "He couldna resist it." The crofter's rigidity is (1) corrupt, (2) shifting to suit himself best, and (3) an abuse of the positive values of life, as embodied by his warm and wasted wife. Because she knows fear, she can understand Hannay's plight. Her sense of his innocence and her risk to help him suggest a true moral constant. For the religious crofter the hymnary only lends sanctimonious cover. But as part of his wife's charity, it saves Hannay's life. The crofter wears religion like a fancy coat, for appearance. Hannay wears a coat for a coat and finds the religion an incidental aid. So, too, the Salvation Army parade covers Hannay's escape from the sheriff, but only gets him to the political meeting.[4]

The crofter's religion has two other analogues. The elderly priest on the train, driven off by the underwear salesmen's repartee, demonstrates a religion of disengagement. The crofter's grace—"Sanctify

149

The 39 Steps *(1935). Caught between them, the oppressed crofter's wife (Peggy Ashcroft) seems drawn to the fugitive Hannay (Robert Donat) instead of her cold husband (John Laurie).*

these mercies for us miserable sinners"—might have served that priest better than his flight. The other is the Jordans, who live half an hour from church. Their religious citizenship is hypocrisy. Jordan anticipates the suave villains of *Saboteur* and *North by Northwest*. In his normal home life, he would kill Hannay to preserve his wife and daughter's respectability. While Jordan holds a gun on Hannay, Mrs. Jordan sweetly announces lunch then returns with an impatient reminder. Their harmony is a happy contrast to the crofter's marriage, yet it too lacks a moral base. Hitchcock cuts from Jordan shooting Hannay to the crofter slapping his wife for giving away his hymnary! As the sheriff concludes, "It's a lesson to be learned by us all, not to mix with doubtful company on the Sabbath."

Perhaps the "McCrocodile" that Hannay misreads off the McCorquadale election poster suggests the Jordans' false sentiment. To explain his mistake, Hannay pretends that the candidate is already so "in" with the Parliament gang that he has an affectionate nickname. Hannay identifies with the candidate because he is himself an outsider there, pretending to belong.

As in that fiction, Hannay becomes an artist when he tells stories. He finds people will believe familiar lurid tales more than any unusual truth. The true story doesn't win the milkman's help, but inventing a cuckolded husband does. Still the milkman sticks to his habits: "Oi, the empties," he calls after the fleeing Hannay. Pamela remains antagonistic until Hannay cows her with a fiction: "All right, then, I'm just a plain, common murderer who stabbed an innocent, defenseless woman in the back not four days ago."[5]

Hannay's triumph as an artist is his extemporaneous speech at the election meeting. Even his platitudes are true:

> May I say from the bottom of my heart and with the utmost sincerity how delighted and relieved I am to find myself in your presence at this moment.

Soliciting topics from his audience, he finds their range of concerns as personal as Mr. Memory's: herring fisheries, unemployment, the idle rich. Hannay finds himself holding forth on the human condition, as he has been experiencing it and as it holds true for the city tourist and the crofter alike:

> And I've known what it is to feel lonely and helpless and to have the whole world against me. And those are things that no man or woman ought to feel.

Throughout this speech, an inverted top hat in the foreground suggests Hannay is magically pulling out a verbal rabbit. But Hannay delivers sincere emotion that invites our sympathy even for the crofter. When he leaves his house to test his wife's fidelity, he too is a frightened outsider.

Hannay envisions

> a world where no nation plots against nation, a world where no neighbor plots against neighbor, where there's no persecution or hunting down, where everybody gets a square deal and a sporting

chance . . . a world from which suspicion, cruelty and fear have been forever banished. That's the sort of world I want. Is that the sort of world you want?

Of course, he has caught the spirit—the anxiety and the hope both—of the common people. He has articulately generalized from his own experience an understanding of his audience.[6] However idyllic, in that vision an artist fashions his own experience into a connection with his audience. This scene is one of the most important in the film. Immediately after, Hannay is handcuffed to Pamela and taken away by the spies, who pose as police. Pamela provides an unexpected antidote to his vision of the lonely prey.[7]

Hannay, of course, is not a professional artist. But as he discovers his intuition, voice, and spontaneity, he achieves a moment of intense art at that rally. Other characters are laughable by their lack of instinct or sense. The policeman in the train station has more confidence than discretion when he remarks about Hannay's newspaper report: "There's enough evidence there to hang any man." Vain, he doesn't recognize Hannay and sends him away: "Do you think I'm a railway porter? Go and find out for yourself."[8] As Hannay gets no help from the police, he calls the delaying sheep "a whole flock of detectives." The "detectives" (sheep) actually impede the villains, while the detectives ("sheep") help them. In assuming Hannay's guilt they fall short of the crofter's wife's intuition.

So, too, the delightful couple who runs the inn where Hannay and Pamela spend the night. As in *Saboteur* later, the old couple twigs to the love between the two antagonistic young people. Asked if the couple is married, the Scottish lady replies, "I dinna know and I dinna care. They're so terribly in love." This is a mix of insight and prophecy. Hannay has revealed his growing affection for Pamela. As he tells her his plight, he gently picks a loose pin from her hair. Pamela suppresses her affection for Hannay until she overhears the villains confirm his story. Her sudden trust is expressed in the landlady's loving scold of her husband: "Ye fool ye, ye wouldna give away a young couple, would ye?" Even when she returns to Hannay, Pamela is not so much in love that she won't take back the blanket to cover herself. Intuition teaches practicality as well as sentiment.[9]

The 39 Steps *(1935). The dangerous Hannay (Robert Donat) holds the beautiful blonde Pamela (Madeleine Carroll) with handcuffs.*

In Hitchcock's last shot the lovers harmonize all the discordant elements. The policeman arresting Hannay in the Palladium separates Hannay's political concern from the diversion: "You don't want to cause any trouble and spoil people's entertainment." But Hannay has survived through his storytelling. The film begins and concludes at an entertainment. In between, people crave an exciting address to mobilize their emotions and their political or community spirits. Hannay gives just that to the milkman, to the crofter's wife, to the political rally, to Pamela, and to the sheriff.

The last shot reconciles the entertainment with the romantic and political interests. The political theater has overrun the music hall. As Mr. Memory unburdens himself of his secret, the music and the dancing girls continue in the background behind him. Mr. Memory failed to distinguish between politics and entertainment, so he turned his skill to treachery. Jordan's arrest is viewed from the balcony. With the proper proportion restored, the dancing girls are small in the background.

As the camera draws back from the dying Mr. Memory ("I'm glad it's off me mind. At last."), the foreground shows the backs of Hannay and Pamela. Having spent so much of the film trying to escape him, Pamela now takes Hannay's cuffed hand. Her arm is in a long, elegant black glove, in erotic juxtaposition to the dangling handcuff. As Mr. Memory's "confession" superseded the dancing girls, the lovers now take the center foreground, consigning the politics to the back.[10]

This final image is a temporary balance, for can we believe in that "Cooperative Permanent"? The political story in the middle draws to an end. The musical in the background goes on. The romantic match in the foreground is a momentary consolation, still carrying signs of mismatch—a lonely handcuff still Hannay's mark of the outsider, the glove promising a world of civility, elegance, and comfort that the entire film has undercut. The last shot is a romantic conclusion to the film's disparate tensions. Like the staged romance that closes *Murder!*, it stops short of total assurance.

Secret Agent
1936

The tentative resolution of *The 39 Steps* and the embroilment of innocents in a political tangle (Hannay, Pamela, Mr. Memory) return in *Secret Agent,* a surprisingly faithful adaptation of Somerset Maugham's *Ashenden. Secret Agent* is the grimmest of Hitchcock's 1930s thriller series. It was not a commercial success, he explains, "because it was the story of a man who did not want to do something. . . . You can't root for a hero who doesn't want to be a hero."[1]

Famous writer Edgar Brodie (John Gielgud) is a British secret agent during the First World War. He's given a fake death and funeral so that he can be spirited out to Switzerland to track down and kill a German spy. He is assigned a new name (Ashenden); a Mexican assassin, the factitious "General" (Peter Lorre); and—he finds to his surprise on arrival—a cover "wife," Elsa (Madeleine Carroll). Elsa is playfully courted by an infectious American, Marvin (Robert Young), who turns out to be the German spy, but only after the General has killed an innocent man, Caypor (Percy Marmont), in his stead. Ashenden and Elsa fall in love and abandon the spy business.

The personal story is framed by war footage. The credits appear over silhouettes of soldiers. The film concludes with newsreel footage of the British routing the Turks. The film has two famous scenes, a chase through the spy-infested chocolate factory and the contact man lying dead on his church organ, emitting a single, continuous note.[2]

The characters function as a triangle on two levels. As spies the basic tension is between the cold-blooded Lorre, the conscience-saddled Gielgud, and the playful but sinister Young. The Madeleine Carroll figure stands apart, judging all three points. Lorre's character is the most savage, the heartiest in appetite both alimentary and sexual. Beside his robust life spirit the other two men pale. Lorre's pragmatic morality here lacks the pathology of his roles in *The Man Who Knew Too Much* and Fritz Lang's *M*.

Young's Marvin is immediately at odds with both Lorre's General and Gielgud's Ashenden. "This college boy, no simpatico," the General remarks. On their first meeting, Ashenden calls Marvin Larkin and Marvin calls Ashenden variations on Ashincan. Typically, Ashenden's cerebral response contrasts to General's instinctive one. Not until the end do they learn the political basis for their resentment. The audience prefers the genteel Ashenden and the sensual General.

As the General puts it, "Heaven is always with the good cause." But rooting for the General is not easy for a moral audience after seeing his indifference to killing an innocent man and leaving a bereft widow—and dog. That drives Ashenden deep into his conscience and Elsa out of the service. The General proves the original Ashenden's point: "Well, that was war, and only fools thought it could be waged with kid gloves on."[3]

Our affection for the murderous General muddies the ending. Truffaut and Hitchcock both refer to him as the hero. Hitchcock says, "The hero finally agrees to do the killing" but "botches the job by killing the wrong man." Truffaut says the villain shoots the hero before dying.[4] Durgnat corrects them but claims the villain is shot by the General, the ur-ending that the censor forced Hitchcock to change.[5]

The film ends with English planes (the wartime deus ex machina) bombing the tracks behind enemy lines, crashing the train. Our principals are stuck in the rubble. Ashenden reaches out to strangle the German spy Marvin but cannot bring himself to do it, weakened by his conscience and Elsa's sentimental morality. (Hitchcock had promised Gielgud the role was a modern Hamlet.) That enables Marvin to shoot the General before dying from the crash (natural causes, that is, or the heaven presumed to side with the good). The General is thus either punished for having killed Caypor or granted the hero-martyr's death as likable rogue. The uncertainty is owing to the censor's coauthorship.[6]

Ashenden is clearly the hero in the romantic triangle. He is ostensibly married to Elsa, whom Marvin courts in another false guise, as an American playboy. In this clash of masks, the supposedly neutral "American" besieges the supposed "Mrs. Ashenden." Outside this triangle stands the General, a self-respecting lecher. His directness outdoes the others' civilized formalities. Through the General's sexual exploits our heroes find the factory worker who identifies Marvin as the spy. For all the General's callousness, he feels distaste and confusion at the woman Elsa being "issued like a passport."

Love and politics mingle; the triangles intersect. When Ashenden first learns of the General he asks, "Ladykiller, eh?" "Not just ladies," Commander R replies. Marvin's betrayer needs the money to marry his girlfriend (the General's conquest). Elsa turns on the sexual charm to keep Marvin from searching the German train for Ashenden. Caypor's death is made all the more tragic by the loss of his loving marriage.

In a harsh convergence of the two triangles, Marvin tells Elsa, before kissing her, "Too bad I didn't love you. Never did. You know that, don't you?" As this humiliation violates romantic convention, it diminishes Marvin. He can't sustain even a pretense of love when at risk to his ego. The murderous General's lechery is superior to the attractive Marvin's emotional vacuum. Hitchcock also distinguishes between "enemy" and "German" by having his German spy hide behind the cover of an American neutral, and in presenting the loving Caypors as the most touching casualty of the war.

The triangles can be defined in other ways, for the film is much livelier than any geometric scheme. One can take Gielgud and Carroll as the base with Young or Lorre as hypotenuse, separate threats to the stars' unity. Hitchcock usually shoots Young and Lorre in triangular relationships to the couple, either behind or between them. But the triangle is a central theme, as in Marvin's "Now is the time for the triangle to retire from the family circle." His American guise makes him a triangular threat only as a lover. As the German spy he is the political threat.

Secret Agent *(1936). The climactic crash. Left to right: Elsa (Madeleine Carroll), Ashenden (John Gielgud), Marvin (Robert Young), and the General (Peter Lorre).*

Commander R makes Ashenden "a married man just to round off your character." That rounding sets up the triangles.

The combination of the triangles sets the main theme, the dangers of neutrality, the necessity for commitment.[7] American neutrality provides Marvin's cover in Switzerland and Ashenden's on the German train ("Fine, baby," replies a German soldier, anticipating the colloquial Gromeck in *Torn Curtain*). No honest neutrality survives here. The Swiss chocolate factory has not only an enclave of German spies but an anti-English spirit, so the police are called to catch the English spies. The Caypors, an English man and a German woman, find in marriage a refuge from nationalist strife, but the war destroys them.

With neutrality impossible, the virtue is involvement. Marvin is uninvolved in the romantic triangle but involved in the political one. As his fault is to kiss without feeling, the General's is to kill without feeling. Ashenden's emotions make him try to stop the General from killing Caypor, but he's not firm enough to insist. That moderation also prevents his saving the General.

The General is almost animal in consciousness. He makes love with a dog's sincerity and fidelity. Indeed, he pretends to be a dog, sniffing and scratching at the Ashendens' door, on the chairlift to amuse the little girl, and in his social indecorum. He sniffs along the chocolate assembly line, brags, "Me certainly well-trained bloodhound. Me first-class bloodhound," and compliments Elsa with, "She is the first classest bloodhound of all of us." He says he hates dogs, perhaps because he is disturbed by the identification.

Elsa and Ashenden's ineffectual civilization make the canine General a necessary evil, but he is shown up by the loyalty and love of the Caypors' pet dog. In a long poignant scene Hitchcock intercuts Caypor's killing with his dog's increasing restlessness at home, his howling, then his horrible whimper. This dog is not subcivilized but in loyalty, emotion, and intuition superior to the civilized Marvin, "a caveman with a college education." The dog's howl is heard over the mountain footage but ends when the General cites his motive for killing Caypor as "honor." The mendacious term seems to silence the indignant dog, so outrageous the claim, so futile the response. Or the dog is stilled at that word because it's the truth; the General's honor as a political assassin is at stake.

Ashenden absents himself from Caypor's killing but watches it, horrified, impotent, through the telescope. While the dog howls his understanding, his warning, and his grief, the American spy Marvin and the English spy Elsa sit in a civilized language lesson with the woman Elsa knows she is helping to widow. The most carefree is Marvin, in whose stead Caypor is killed. From the salon to the mountain the dog sends out an ambiguous message, a warning to his master or a plea to his kindred General. The scene is a high point in Hitchcock's suspense and psychology.

As folk art runs truer than language, the dog's howl segues into the festival yodeling. The howl also rhymes off the dead organist's long, single note, an eloquence that transcends melody. Ashenden and Elsa's guilt at Caypor's death echoes in the coin's whirling music, growing into a shrill, metallic scream. Against this noise, man's civilized vocabulary seems feeble. The General struggles with language:

"I'm still blind on this ear." Precivilized, he expresses himself in gestures, a slit of his throat, say, or taking his jacket half off in the lobby to say he's going to go change. For women he has another vocabulary of action altogether.

In contrast, civilized Marvin pretends to be "just the well-equipped young man at home in every language," but ostensibly unable to communicate with the German cabbie. As a writer, of course, Brodie/ Ashenden is a merchant of words, of observing detachment, and thus a pole apart from the General's naked nature. Marvin's use of language can be playfully deceptive or outright dishonest, as when Mrs. Caypor asks if he understands German: "Not a word, but I speak it fluently." His duplicity is like Elsa's visit, knowing but not revealing Caypor's fate.

R's speech is sanitized. When Ashenden asks what he should do when he identifies the spy, R replies, "That sounded like a gunshot, didn't it? Report to me." His "report" is a bureaucrat's ambiguity that contains "gunshot."[8]

In the opening scene a social civility is as false as this language. After a military funeral, the one-armed veteran lights a cigarette, picks up the casket under one arm, drops it (showing it's empty), and walks off. The scene must have thematic purposes because the plot doesn't need it. Even before the organist is found dead, the Swiss know that Ashenden is Brodie. The funeral scene exemplifies the pointless exercises that constitute civilization. The General would have no truck with anything like that, though Marvin would. Indeed, he does when he tags along to Elsa's "language lesson," Caypor's funeral scene in disguise. The attendant's irreverence expresses the emptiness of decorum.

Like this scene, the film disturbs us because it denies the possibility of heroism in war. Our funeral sentiments are aroused then found irrelevant and falsely generated. We are again upset when the old Swiss man buys a large chocolate, throws away the bar, and keeps the wrapper that identifies Ashenden. We are disturbed when the supposedly neutral Swiss are infiltrated by danger—a corpse in the church, spies in the chocolate factory.[9]

In a domestic upset, the General invades the ersatz couple's chat in their bathroom. Films did not often show toilets before *Psycho*. So here Hitchcock and the General violate privacy. In dubious decorum, Hitchcock puts a phonograph on the toilet seat. When the General shreds the toilet paper in indignation at not having a wife assigned to him, language and civility suffer again. Even music has a savage power, of course, particularly in a story where the hero rises like Orpheus from his funeral—and stays at the Excelsior Hotel.

According to Ivor Montagu, the film as originally planned was to be even more upsetting than it is. After the train crash at the end, "We decided to heighten the climax by a change to colour, and we got Len Lye to hand-paint scarlet and yellow flames across the picture frames at the same time as we stuck sprocket holes from the side of a torn strip of film across them. The effect we wanted, and got, was to bring the fire resulting from the train-crash right into the audience. When we first ran the scene in the projection theatre, the projectionist stopped the film immediately and emerged from his box threatening to punch us on the nose."[10] This brilliant anticipation of *Persona* would have extended the audience's dislocation from the funeral scene at the start of the film, coherent with the themes of deceptive appearances, false values, and the lack of truth. The film's identity itself would have been wiped away like Marvin's American innocence or the General's animal otherness. Perhaps then the film's disturbing effect would have been recognized as its basic intention and celebrated.[11]

Instead *Secret Agent* is underestimated because it didn't meet the critics' expectations. Once one sees the General as Hitchcock's bare forked politico stripped of pretensions, one can understand why the passionless characters played by Gielgud, Young, and Carroll *should have been* "merely projected, pretty bloodlessly," as Peter John Dyer complains, and why the film is "filled with cold-blooded assassinations."[12] The film declares the impossibility of preserving passion from politics (the Caypors tried), and the price—in man, honor, innocence, truth—that civilization pays to protect itself. That's the main secret our agents keep.

Finally, a defense of *Secret Agent* as an adaptation of W. Somerset Maugham's original stories. Until *The 39 Steps* we found Hitchcock close to the texts he adapted, allowing for his right to shift emphasis and to trim or to expand his material to suit his camera. With the Buchan and Maugham works, however, he takes serious liberties. Hitchcock lists his changes on Maugham's *Ashenden* stories "The Traitor" and "The Hairless Mexican": "We switched the two stories round completely; made Caypor the innocent victim; turned the Greek into an American; introduced a train smash for dramatic purposes; and obtained the love interest from the play" by Campbell Dixon. The romantic triangle interwove the two stories and brought the American in earlier.[13]

His changes go further. Making Marvin an American expands the theme of neutrality throughout Maugham's *Ashenden* stories. For most of the book, the Swiss protect their neutrality:

> Now, taught presumably by past experience, the authorities are watchful and it would go ill with any alien who displayed unseasonable curiosity. (8)

> Jealous of their neutrality, they were determined to prevent conduct that might embroil them with any of the belligerent powers. (17)

Hitchcock rather shows the Swiss to be pro-German. In the German infiltration of Switzerland, neutrality (like uninvolvement in the romantic parallel) is bad. As Maugham's Caypor observes:

> I'm sure you wouldn't tell me anything that anyone shouldn't know, but after all these Swiss are absolutely pro-German and we don't want to give anyone the chance of over-hearing. (138)

Similarly Hitchcock's opening red herring, the fake funeral, dramatizes Ashenden's occasional whimsy:

> He was often slightly tired of himself and it diverted him for a while to be merely a creature of R's facile invention.

Hitchcock's R invents a death for Brodie before his new character is created. His love plot has a root in Maugham's episode of "Giulia Lazzari," where a woman and her lover are entangled in international skullduggery. Marvin and Ashenden's game of diplomatic one-upmanship, particularly in the casino over Caypor's dog, dramatizes the pecking order in "Behind the Scenes." The button clue and gamble come from "Flip of a Coin."

More importantly, Hitchcock preserves the witty skepticism of the *Ashenden* stories. Indeed, the central thrust stems from R's words, "Once more the cool and astute judge of his fellows":

> I've not yet made up my mind whether the best men for this kind of job are those who do it with passion or those who keep their heads. Some of them are filled with hatred for the people we're up against and when we down them it gives them a sort of satisfaction like satisfying a personal grudge. (94)

There is the clue to the General's "honor," perhaps. And Hitchcock's Ashenden is true to Maugham's, not emotionless, but stepping beyond his emotions to arrange what must be done, though not quite doing it himself.

Hitchcock's General grows out of Maugham's:

> If he had half a chance he'd seduce your wife, but if you were up against it he'd share his last crust with you. (47)

But he is much more physically appealing than Maugham's to facilitate the audience's identification. He is the underbelly to Ashenden's image of Western civilization. The crust he is willing to share becomes brandy and water in the script and film endings respectively, but why quibble?

Hitchcock exceeds Maugham in the harshness of Ashenden's detachment. Hitchcock amplifies the humanity of his victim, Caypor, and of his wife (and dog). The telescope, like a gun-sight, undercuts Elsa's naive belief that "long-range assassins" are not as guilty as the killers themselves. As if to refute this, Commander R in London runs a fake funeral that leads to all the deaths we see. When Elsa draws the gun on the train to protect Marvin, she sets up the General's death. Wanting to not see a murder, she enables his killing. Around Caypor's murder, Hitchcock extends Maugham into scenes of such emotion and irony any writer would be proud to inspire.

Sabotage

1936

Having based *Secret Agent* on Maugham's *Ashenden*, Hitchcock turned to adapt Joseph Conrad's *The Secret Agent*. As secret agents communicate in code, he changed the title to *Sabotage*. In America the film was known as *The Woman Alone* and *Hidden Power*. Hitchcock fed the confusion in 1942 when he made *Saboteur*. To summarize: *Secret Agent* is *Ashenden*, *Sabotage* is *The Secret Agent*, and *Saboteur* is a different film altogether.

In *Sabotage* Verloc (Oscar Homolka) manages a small London cinema, but secretly serves a gang of anarchists trying to throw London into panic. He is married to the much younger Sylvia (Sylvia Sidney), who devotedly raises her young brother, Stevie (Desmond Tester). They are befriended by a handsome detective, Ted (John Loder), who poses as a grocer's assistant in order to spy on Verloc. Conscious of the scrutiny, Verloc dispatches Stevie to plant a bomb at Picadilly Circus. Stevie is delayed by the crowds and blown to bits. Sylvia murders Verloc. She wants to give herself up to the police but Ted, in love with her, won't let her. Verloc's bomb supplier, the professor (William Dewhurst), goes to the cinema to retrieve the cage in which he sent the bomb. Finding the dead Verloc and hearing the police approach, the professor sets off another bomb, blowing up himself, Verloc, and any evidence that would have incriminated Sylvia. She and Ted can remain together.

Sabotage was immediately hailed as a brilliant work and has lost very little ground since. Mark Van Doren lauded its "old-fashioned" quality: "Its dialogue is unnecessary without being precisely superfluous."[1] Graham Greene found that "in *Sabotage* for the first time (Hitchcock) has really 'come off,'" overcoming the objections of credibility that Greene had raised against *Secret Agent.*[2] To Hitchcock the film is "sabotaged" by Loder's weakness and Sydney's inexpressiveness.[3] But to Durgnat *Sabotage* is "the profoundest film of Hitchcock's thriller period, and perhaps of his career."[4]

The film is famous for three technical tours de force. One is Verloc's interview with his superior in an aquarium, first in front of a huge glass cage enclosing giant turtles, then against an empty case. Having vowed not to take a human life, Verloc imagines a teeming Picadilly Circus blown up, then swirling down the drain like the silt from his hands in the sink. As he leaves, Verloc is stuck in the revolving door and needs to be redirected by his boss. The scene dramatizes Verloc's confusion and compulsion and how a brief memory can swell into fancy. The anarchists' threat turns familiar settings and props sinister. The bomb maker keeps his explosives in a ketchup bottle.

Stevie's delay by a policeman, crowds, and sights in the London streets builds the suspense before he and the bus are blown up. Our attention to the boy and his last moments' play with a puppy make his death more disturbing than Caypor's in *Secret Agent,* or the reformed Marion Crane's in *Psycho,* or the motiveless malignity of the birds in *The Birds. Sabotage* presents a terrible coincidence of human deed and mishap. Hitchcock customarily apologizes for his error in killing the boy, but it's hardly a mistake.[5] It is Hitchcock's purest statement of societal insecurity in the mid-1930s, as calculated as Smith/Schmidt's amputation and suicide in *Lifeboat.*

The third classic sequence is the murder scene. Numbed by her discovery that her husband caused her brother's death, Sylvia drifts into the family cinema and dissolves into the children's laughter at the Disney cartoon. But the comedy turns macabre when the Mae West chicken and Bing Crosby bird give way to a deep bass: "Who killed Cock Robin?" Even her diversion allows no escape. At the dinner table her hand returns to the carving knife, to serve the cabbage, to serve the potatoes, as if the hand—or the knife—controlled her will. A montage alternates Sylvia's and Verloc's reactions in tight close-up, between her eyes and his, her hands and his terror, conveying the characters' emotions and intuitions.[6]

Behind all three technical high points we find the grimmest Hitchcock mood before *Psycho*. The aquarium scene makes a small political point: three such giant turtles will be sacrificed for the soup for the lord mayor's banquet. So will Stevie. Even the safe entertainments of a museum are fraught with politics. Even that refuge breeds danger.

Here human life is a miserable and worsening lot. The professor's daughter (Martita Hunt) is haggard, defeated, endlessly polishing her tabletop while her father shelters and recites her shame of an illegitimate daughter. Her life story is replayed when she recovers her courage, flares up, and sends him to retrieve the incriminating birdcage. Her one self-assertion sends her father to his death. "Tell him he has got to keep your name out of this business," she says, "because your name is my name." The professor earlier told Verloc (in her presence), "It's her cross and she has to bear it. We all have our crosses to bear, hmm?" Where the father shared the daughter's shame, she now bridles at sharing his. This family is bound in shame. For that beaten girl there is no escape, no self-respect, only one loss after another.

Then there is Stevie, struggling manfully against a conspiracy of hot roast, slippery plate, blinding towel, and tripping apron for a simple task. And if a trip from stove to table can be so challenging, we know what to expect of his errand to Picadilly.

Two comic scenes reflect Hitchcock's grimness. To mollify the disgruntled cinemagoers, Ted distinguishes between acts of providence and acts of man. But their effect is the same, to sabotage man's comfort and desires. Stevie's death is a combination of the anarchists' designs, Ted's innocent spying on Verloc, Verloc's dispatch of Stevie, and the combination of mob, salesman, police, lord mayor's show, and traffic jam that impede his safe delivery of the package. In that horror, where the human element leaves off and the divine begins doesn't matter. Rohmer and Chabrol refer to the *explosion providentielle* by which the professor assumes Sylvia's guilt.[7] To consider that explosion

Sabotage (1936). Turning away from the fresh air and freedom of the open window, Sylvia Verloc (Sylvia Sidney) contemplates the shadowy burden of her murderous husband (Oscar Homolka).

but not Stevie's to be a help from the gods is to impose on the world an order, divinity, and justice that the film denies.

There is no God in *Sabotage,* though Ted claims that only he and God will know Sylvia killed Verloc. That God is a figure of speech, as when the toothpaste vendor sends Stevie off "groomed for stardom, as the saying is" and the police inspector tells Ted that Verloc has been "blown to glory." The heaven that awaits the mortals, whatever their innocence or guilt, is a figure of speech, like Ted's God, a colloquial fossilization of faith, with no spiritual or moral dimension. As Arnie asks in *The Trouble with Harry:* "Who's Providence, Mummy?"

The toothpaste seller encounters the same distinction between the act of man and the act of God:

SELLER: What causes teeth to fall out?

VOICE: A punch in the jaw.

SELLER: The process of decay, inevitable in all human organisms, decay can be arrested . . . arrested instantaneously . . . by what?

VOICE: By a copper.

SELLER: Exactly, but if I may say so, just a little more than one . . . a few coppers.

The punch on the jaw is an act of man, of the king's enemies, as Ted puts it. But more frightening is decay as the natural condition of providence. Against our natural decay, our defense by coppers (coins; police) is futile.

The other danger is that humanity might be lost in man's flight from this decay. The vendor's hair oil is "guaranteed to produce the appearance of patent leather upon the human thatch." As in *Blackmail,* the policeman is torn between his lover's duty to Sylvia and his police duty to enforce justice. The flesh can sabotage the system and the system can sabotage the flesh.

The title's "sabotage" goes beyond the dictionary definition that opens the film: "Wilful destruction of buildings or machinery with the object of alarming a group of persons or inspiring public uneasiness." The dictionary page leads into documentary shots of machinery breaking down, a power failure, and a large lightbulb dying out. The definition's light similarly fades, for *Sabotage* details disasters not just by the malevolent but those without human motive.

The two parallel families demonstrate the sabotage of an emotional unit. In the central family—Sylvia, Stevie, and Verloc—the marriage is chaste, the husband paternal toward both Stevie and Sylvia. She freezes when he suggests that having a child might help her get over Stevie. Sylvia clearly married Verloc just for Stevie's security. From Conrad's story, Hitchcock drops the predatory mother-in-law and Stevie's advanced age and mental deficiency. The film Verloc is an attentive family head who raises his voice against Stevie only—paradoxically—in Stevie's interest, to hie him out to deliver the bomb on time.

In the professor's family another elderly man heads a family comprising an unfulfilled woman and a fatherless child, but with none of the Verlocs' warmth. The contrast increases our sympathy for Verloc. The two fatherless families might suggest a society deprived of traditional leadership, therefore struggling along the parallel roads of introjected despair (the professor's family) and a broadening community spirit (Verloc's family, calling the cinema patrons family and receptive to the addition of Ted; that is, Verloc's family without Verloc).

Ted shatters both families. He lets the professor die bearing Sylvia's guilt. He hounds Verloc as a detective and undercuts his marriage. Like Verloc, Ted gets to Sylvia through his friendliness with Stevie, brings in the cabbage, and finally sabotages justice for personal benefit. These two anarchists recall the two avengers in *The Lodger*. Verloc is prompted to his espionage less by political conviction than to improve his family's financial lot. So between Verloc and Ted there is as thin a distinction as we found between the acts of God and man. So Conrad:

> The terrorist and the policeman both come from the same basket. Revolution, legality—counter moves in the same game; forms of idleness at bottom identical.
>
> Chief Inspector Heat . . . could understand the mind of a burglar, because, as a matter of fact, the mind and the instincts of a burglar are of the same kind as the mind and the instincts of a police officer.[8]

Hitchcock often paralleled the law and the outlaw. Like the more negative professor, Verloc and Ted are self-serving paternalists.

Ted remains our preferred. His younger and more attractive image and his romantic suitability to Sylvia offer a healthier relationship. When Ted coaxes Sylvia out of surrendering herself to the (other) police, she stands against a milk ad promising "Health!" When she rushes away from him, it's toward a gloomy religious procession urging sinners be punished and repent. Ted's apples, cabbages, and milk are the preferable life.

What finally justifies Ted is his capacity to sympathize with others that Verloc lacks. So Conrad: "Chief Inspector Heat rose by the force of sympathy, which is a form of fear, above the vulgar conception of time."[9] Empathy and sympathy are the precise antithesis of "sabotage." Sylvia expresses her extension into Stevie: "If you're good to him you're good to me. You know that." The professor wishes he were a frontline fighter like Verloc, not just a supplier: "I would rather be in your shoes." Empathy is played comically when a child in the aquarium asks, "What's them bubbles, Dad? Has that fish got the 'iccups?" The father replies: "You'd get 'iccups if you 'ad to live off ants' eggs." And later:

> BOY: After laying a million eggs the female oyster changes her sex.
>
> GIRL: I don't blame her.

Stevie jokes about his male birds laying eggs, just before he goes off to Picadilly. The shooting script has a similar scene, where Sylvia and Stevie feed the pigeons:

> STEVIE: Ow—their feet are cold. Aren't they fat?
>
> SYLVIA: You'd be fat if people fed you all day with corn and bits of bread.[10]

A customer complaining about her canary asks, "Perhaps you want me to sit in the cage and him do the housework?" In these jokes, the point is one's sympathetic identification with another creature, as Sir John did in *Murder!* As substitute fathers/husbands, Verloc and the professor are in another's position, but they lack emotional understanding. Ted's sympathy makes his sabotage of justice superior to their self-sacrifice.

Like *Murder!*, *Sabotage* demonstrates the service of dramatic art to truth and justice in the real world. Hitchcock changed Verloc from a dealer in pornographic literature to a cinema owner. That helps some of us identify with him.

Here life is permeated by theatricality, pretense, roles, "shows." Stevie's journey is impeded by "shows": the sidewalk vendor's, the lord mayor's. The obviously flat back-projections of the parade and the bus make even the character's "reality" a show, like the image on our screen. Both saboteurs' fronts involve diversion: a pet shop, a cinema. In Verloc's first sabotage attempt the people laughing in the dark underground could be a cinema audience. The aquarium is another cinema-like entertainment, its glass cases like screens, particularly for Verloc's vision of an exploded and drained Picadilly.

The film often refers to films. The anarchist cell lives the genre style; one member has a James Mason accent. During the cell meeting the cinema runs a Robertson Hare potboiler reminiscent of Hitchcock's *Number Seventeen*. It repeats the motif of extended family: "I'm your nephew." "Oh, are you?" Then a man burns some papers and assures the lady, "All our troubles are over now," anticipating the conclusion of *Sabotage*. In the surrealist expression of Sylvia's mind in "Who Killed Cock Robin?" the child and woman, laughter and agony, community and isolation, refuge and attack, are all expressed at once. The fatal *Bartholomew the Strangler* anticipates the professor's strangling hands, though he will save Sylvia as the film tin kills Stevie.[11]

Verloc, of course, hates murder films, but he books them so as not to antagonize his audience—an odd concern for a saboteur. Ted and the grocer tease him about his programs. Hitchcock may be having some personal fun at the audience's bloodlust and squeamishness. The bus conductor's reluctance to allow the film can on board reminds us that films are literally inflammatory, as well as metaphorically. He fears the film independent of its bomb.

Related to the film motif is the use of eyes, as spying rather than voyeurism.[12] To an uncommon degree the characters express themselves by their eyes—Verloc pretending to be waking from a sleep, Verloc answering Ted's interrogation, Verloc's and Sylvia's eyes clashing across the kitchen table, Ted's suspicion growing as he watches. Our vision is often impeded: our rear views of the conspirators in the aquarium, the professor retreating, Verloc cleaning his hands in the background while large in the fore a cat preens herself, a deceptively innocent analogue. The murder of Verloc escapes us, as the stabbing happens just below the frame and we don't know if Sylvia plunged the knife or he strode into it. The distinction is as irrelevant as that between a disaster by man or God, or whether the professor or his daughter was the heavier cross to bear.[13]

Because the eyes here don't just watch but act, they are in harmony with the hands. There are many close-ups of Verloc's hands, dirty, being cleaned, twisting in anxiety. The professor is characterized by his strangling hands. In the climactic murder scene Hitchcock alternates shots of the eyes and shots of the hands, which enact the mood and the mind.

Sabotage looks ahead to *Rear Window,* where Hitchcock more fully explored being one's brother's watcher. Here Ted is held accountable for his spying. Sylvia's first words to him are "Will you kindly not interfere." Verloc blames Ted's spying for having to send Stevie with the bomb. The grocer apologizes to Verloc for having let Ted spy on him. But the hero's spying is justified by two things. One is the villain's covertness. Verloc lies, hides behind newspapers and cats, and frustrates our desire to see. More importantly, Ted's spying is justified by his sympathy for the society threatened by the anarchists, as well as his feelings for Sylvia and Stevie.

One gesture absolves Ted of abusing his position. Deciding that Sylvia is not aware of Verloc's activities, Ted makes their lunch a personal expense, however dear—one pound for the three of them. He tears up the police reimbursement slip. Ted has scruples. So had Verloc. But Ted's capacity for sympathy justifies his exploitation of Stevie and Sylvia, his spying, his maneuvering.

And in a world characterized by decay, by frustrations, by acts of God and acts of man indistinguishable in disastrous effect, the understanding of such lovers is the best we can expect.

Young and Innocent

1937

Of Hitchcock's classic British thriller period, the most under-rated film is *Young and Innocent*. It has been praised for catching the British flavor:

> Hitchcock's direction is painstaking, revealing brilliance of characterisation and attention to detail. This is an outstanding example of realism in entertainment. (*Cinema*, November 25, 1937)

> This is Hitchcock at his best. As you watch the story unfold it comes to you that here, in the best sense of the phrase, is a typically English picture. It has something native in its people, background, humours and ways of thought; and all of those things unforced. (*Film Weekly*, February 5, 1938)

Durgnat suggests that it was the most popular Hitchcock film of the period in America because of its simplicity and its lack of "dramatic uneasiness and moral dissent."[1] Its strength lies in its psychological interest more than in its effectiveness as a thriller, effective though it certainly is.[2] It eschews the frissons of *The Man Who Knew Too Much* and *The 39 Steps* and the plot complexity of *Secret Agent*, preferring domestic character. It extends from *The Man Who Knew Too Much* and *Sabotage* Hitchcock's interest in the family unit. As a result it is a homier, more personal film than any other in the sequence.

Movie star Christine Clay (Pamela Carme) is found murdered on a beach. Police suspicion falls on the struggling young writer Robert Tisdall (Derrick de Marney) to whom the actress bequeathed 2,500 pounds and whose raincoat belt was found near the body. Circumstantial evidence and a ludicrous lawyer prompt Tisdall to escape during his first appearance in court. He wins the confidence of Erica Burgoyne (Nova Pilbeam), the daughter of the local police superintendent, Colonel Burgoyne (Percy Marmont). Erica hides Tisdall, brings him food, helps him locate his lost raincoat, and sees him through a riot in a truckers' cafe, a cousin's birthday party, and a cave-in of a deserted mine. Tisdall decides to surrender rather than implicate Erica further. At the moment of his arrest, however, the hobo Old Will (Edward Rigby) spots the murderer, who gave him the coat. The villain is a jazz drummer. At the sight of the tramp and the police he panics and confesses. Erica and Tisdall look ahead to a romantic life together.

Again Hitchcock prefers intuition over seeing the obvious. Both Erica and her aunt (Mary Clare) are strong willed and intuitive. When Erica brings Tisdall to the cousin's birthday party, the aunt senses trouble so she probes until her husband blindfolds her for a party game. Erica senses Tisdall's innocence and helplessness when she first meets him. Later, when her car has stalled and she sends her police friends away, she senses that she is not alone, that the fugitive is helping to push her car. Tisdall maneuvers her by imputing nobler motives than she realizes she has (that she is planning to hide him in the mill, bring him food, etc.). For all his playfulness and without presumption, he senses her Girl Guide virtues. Her instinct is to help. So she rushes over to help Tisdall when he faints in the police station. That involves her in his case, which she solves when she rushes to help the fallen drummer. Erica's knowledge and her charity are both rooted in instinct.

Primarily the film is about a girl's growing up, the point at which the child becomes a responsible adult. This is implicit in the title of *Young and Innocent.* In America it was *The Girl Was Young,* perhaps because there a girl's innocence is box office anathema. Hitchcock refers to the American title.[3]

The film centers on Nova Pilbeam, who played the kidnapped child in *The Man Who Knew Too Much* with aplomb and maturity. Where his source, Josephine Tey's novel *A Shilling for Candles,* centered on the police detective Grant, Hitchcock focuses on Erica and displaces Grant (Kent in the film, played by John Longden) with the fugitive Tisdall in the romance.

Erica is divided by her conflicting loyalties to her police chief father and to the fugitive to whom she is drawn. In *The 39 Steps, Sabotage,* and *Saboteur,* the antagonistic couple gradually slips into love for a romantic close. In *Young and Innocent* the love is central to the film. It leads the girl from her father's authority to assert her own.[4]

The film first introduces the tension in terms of sides. "I'm on their side," Erica tells Tisdall as they flee the police. He intuits she's on his but she doesn't know it yet. When they are separated in the mine shaft, the police "naturally surmise" she is trying to trap him for them. In "Can't you see what a mistake you're making?" she implies their error in assuming his guilt but also in assuming her support. There is a comic variation on this theme when Tisdall loses patience with his incompetent solicitor, Biggs (J. H. Roberts), who seems to prefer the prosecution case:

TISDALL: Are you representing the police by any chance?

BIGGS: Oh no, dear fellow. I'm on your side.

He inadvertently is when Tisdall dons Biggs's misplaced spectacles to escape.

The emotional index to Erica's divided interest and responsibility is provided by her father. A close-up of Colonel Burgoyne catches his rue at having been displaced when he overhears her telling the police the fugitive

> couldn't kill anything. He's much too kind and gentle. He's the finest person . . .

At that her father gently interrupts her to prevent a superlative that would hurt him: "I'm sorry I kept you waiting." The next scene shows Erica at the head of the family table saying grace, her father's chair gaping empty in the opposite foreground. He is in his study writing his resignation from the force. His daughter has replaced him at the table, as he feels the stranger has replaced him in her sentiments and in her moral sense.

When Erica refuses to help her father find Tisdall, he sends her to her room, as if a child's punishment could prolong her childhood. She retires to the obligatory fetal pose on her bed. Then an ominous shadow falls across her, and Tisdall enters her bedroom for the first time. She runs to hug him. The situation suggests sexual culmination, but Robert has only come to tell her he will turn himself in. Earlier, a policeman tried to reassure Colonel Burgoyne of Erica's safety, but his consoling tone is belied by sexual danger:

> He's probably forced her to go to Ashcroft Forest. There'll be less chance of their being found there. We're combing the forest now, sir.

His assurance is undercut by the single thin light brushing across the deep forest. The policeman's consolation is funnier to us than to her father, who fears his daughter is helpless in the forest with the gigolo who murdered the actress. In another policeman's deliberate innuendo, the fact that Tisdall sold the actress a story becomes "I received money from her on former occasions."

Hitchcock's focus on the father improves on the novel, where Erica's maturing is calibrated by the attracted detective. There she enters, "a small, skinny child of sixteen in shabby tweeds,"[5] looking for her father, as in the movie. She herself feels a brief pang of disloyalty to her father (98) but sees her interest in the case as serving Detective Grant (112). At the end she invites the detective to take her to the circus (188). Hitchcock's triangle of fugitive-daughter-father is more stirring.

At the end another close-up catches Colonel Burgoyne's rue at Robert kissing Erica's hand. She runs to Burgoyne, takes his lapels, kisses him, and says, "Father, don't you think we ought to ask Mr. Tisdall to dinner?" The line is important, particularly after the earlier dinner scenes. Erica restores her father's authority by letting him invite Tisdall into the family circle. In the last shot Erica beams up first at her father and then at her young man, both off camera.

Young and Innocent (1937). The daughter rebels against her father's orders. Erica (Nova Pilbeam) confronts Colonel Burgoyne (Percy Marmont).

Erica grows out of Girl Guide by helping the stranger in distress, having briskly deflected Detective Kent's flirtation. She seems mature in her authority over her four brothers, not having a mother. She seems girlish as she defends her car against insults, in Tey's words:

> Never in her indignation, never in the moments of her friends' laughter, had she ever been tempted to disown Tinny. Still less to give her up.
>
> But now she thought quite calmly, I shall really have to get a new car.
>
> Erica was growing up. (92)

When the car sinks down the mine shaft, Erica openly sides with Tisdall. Her youth and innocence sank with the car.[6] Erica expresses girlishness in her care for her dog and cheekiness toward the truckers. Her increasing maturity is not sexually conscious, despite the erotic potential of that shadow-bedroom scene. In a comic parallel, Old Will, whom Erica dresses for the visit to the hotel, says, "I feel like a shy bride," as he peels off layers of overcoat to get down to Tisdall's. A bobby who sees him dressed up calls him Cinderella. Will's business of repairing broken china has a sexual association, glass and bottles often emblematic of virginity.[7]

Erica's adventure socializes her. When she rejects the detective she prefers being a Girl Guide rather than a woman. When her car breaks down she accepts the new man's help. At the subsequent family dinner, her new relationship puts her at odds with the old one, as the family's discussion of the fugitive makes her feel nervous.

Erica's union with Tisdall begins in the mill, a lovers' setting familiar from *The Manxman*. In their first social exposure, the community of truckers, the couple is a catalyst to a donnybrook. They proceed to the more civilized party, the cousin's birthday celebrations. As her Uncle Basil (Basil Radford) puts it, "Something would have to be radically wrong for her to forget Felicity's birthday." Of course, something is radically different, and from her family's perspective, wrong. The child's mind is lost in the woman's. Erica arrives having forgotten both present and birthday. Tisdall gives the family their own stone garden dwarf as a birthday present, which he picked up in front of the house. He restores to the family its own, as he will later do with Erica.

The couple's movement from the mill culminates in the most civilized setting, the Grand Hotel with its afternoon tea dance. Will's spiffing parodies Erica's socialization. She has been assuming womanhood as now he carefully becomes a proper man: "I'd better order because I'm the man, eh?"[8]

But Will cannot escape his past associations with china, even in ordering tea:

WILL: Two cups of tea, please.

WAITER: India or China?

WILL: Tea!

He confuses his sign and his self. Will assumes the innocent "china" refers to his work, his hidden past. Later the drummer, identified as the murderer by the twitch in his eyes, says, "This twitch has got to be stopped. It's getting on my nerves." The twitch *is* his nerves. He confuses what he does with what he is. Earlier the hysterical girl who discovered the corpse says, "No, I'm not. I'm never hysterical." And when Tisdall recovers from passing out he says, "Don't be ridiculous. I never pass out." People do uncharacteristic things as they develop and as they respond to different situations. Indeed growing up may mean changes in one's patterns of behavior, as one discovers one's new self. Certainly that is true with Erica, who seems to her father and aunt to be acting wrongly because she is acting differently as she blossoms.

In the case of adults, the self can be fossilized and grow unsympathetic to natural processes. The couple's brief service station stop shows a comfortable crossing of the generation gap. The father (whether out of laziness or considerateness) dispatches his extremely small son to pump gas. Like Erica, the child has assumed adult responsibility. But unlike the gas man, Erica's father would extend her childhood.

Colonel Burgoyne's anxiety about his daughter is prefigured in Christine Clay's husband, who sneers at the "boys" in his wife's life. Both men fear ouster by youth, where the gas seller relishes the prospect. Where the drummer breaks up the Clay family, then his rhythms, then himself, Burgoyne can preserve his family by embracing Tisdall. To both police chief and drummer, Tisdall is the threat. Like a (bad) father, the drummer nags Christine for all he did for her (he "made" her). Of course, Mrs. Clay shares Chloe's name and vulnerability from *The Skin Game.*

The tendency of each new generation to break away from its parents to find romance will go on, won't it? By this inexorable movement a community survives and the family is tested. Our natural drift from chaotic impulses toward a traditional pattern is given two important pieces of technique in *Young and Innocent.*

First, a pattern may seem to be waiting for our sense to find it. The opening music is the song that will be playing when we see the killer caught.[9] The song is "The Drummer Man" but the music will not mean much to us until we hear the words at the end:

> I'm right here to tell you, mister
> No one can like the drummer man

Young and Innocent *(1937). The coffeehouse brawl, with Erica Burgoyne (Nova Pilbeam) the still center of the storm.*

Then we discover the pattern and the irony of the drummer fingered as the man who can and did "do it." The nervous drummer may be unable to make rhythm anymore, but he is locked into the rhythm of justice and is caught.

He is caught in the second of Hitchcock's brilliant devices, that magnificent camera swoop in on his twitching eye. The shot took two days to film. It was set up in the largest sound stage at the newly opened Pinewood Studios. A special lens and mount were invented for it, the crane enabling Hitchcock to begin with a general shot down, then gradually swoop in from 145 feet away and come to rest 4 inches from the drummer's right eye.[10]

As usual, Hitchcock's most brilliant technical device makes a key point. The shot reduces the drummer to his twitch, the man to his sign, the maker of music to the cause of disorder. As in a similar shot at the party in *Notorious*, Hitchcock begins with a large room full of people at civilized leisure, then strips away the glamour by zeroing in

Young and Innocent (1937). The filming of the famous dolly in on the drummer's eye.

on a private concern and tension. This is a basic Hitchcock idea: civilized order conceals a livelier chaos. Further, the inexorable swoop down to the guilty eye suggests the relentless fate we wish we could call reliable justice.

That swoop also expresses the drummer's paranoia, his feeling singled out. He fears losing Christina and that the tramp has spotted him and the police are there for him, not for Tisdall. The camera swoop helps explain why the drummer cracks under Erica's "pressure":

> ERICA: What did you do with the belt that belonged to it?
>
> DRUMMER: What did I do with the belt? (laughing manically) I twisted it around her neck and I squeezed the life out of her.

The camera movement suggests the guilt that drives the drummer to confess in despair. After the famous zoom in, Hitchcock reverses and pulls back so we get the long view of the drummer going to pieces.

The camera takes an unpitying perspective on the man's collapse yet allows him some dignity.

The sequence relates back to the birthday party, as the camera's supreme power to see contrasts to the aunt stumbling about blindfolded. The drummer's helplessness also contrasts to the courtroom scene, where the hero because he is innocent can scamper out of the chaotic court into freedom.

The shot is also an important incident in Hitchcock's continuing obsession with the eye, with sight, with the ambivalence of watching, as Peter Wollen has outlined in "Hitchcock's Vision," too rich a mine of insights to paraphrase here.[11] The swoop in *Young and Innocent* anticipates the swoop into that random hotel room that opens *Psycho* and the swoopers in *The Birds*. It harkens back to the unseeing, all-seeing eye of the gods in the British Museum in *Blackmail*, back to the spying in *The Ring* and *The Lodger*, indeed back to the monocle in *The Pleasure Garden*.

Young and Innocent also confirms Hitchcock's interest in the essential social unit, the family. In *The Pleasure Garden*, *The Lodger*, *The Manxman*, and *Blackmail*, families are threatened by intruders. In *The Birds*, the schoolteacher Annie's foray into Lydia's family is repelled, but Melanie's is more successful, before the birds' invasion.

Colonel Burgoyne foreshadows Lydia's threatened position. Melanie joins the family by becoming childlike, helpless, joining Lydia as a daughter, not a rival for Mitch. Between these films comes the detective's replacement of Uncle Charlie in Charlie's life in *Shadow of a Doubt*. In *Psycho*, child Norman not only kills his mother but hides behind her shadow. The violated families of *Frenzy*, the deceived families of *Topaz*, the separated families of *The Man Who Knew Too Much*, *The Trouble with Harry*, *Stage Fright*—their test is explored in *Young and Innocent*. The film is crucial to the Hitchcock canon.

Here Hitchcock is still confident enough to see a happy continuity surviving the tensions. In his American period family continuity proves costlier. In *Young and Innocent*, however, Hitchcock could still talk of balances, between past and future, old and new, between the ocular proof and the intuitive, even between love and honor. Over the police's interrogation table hangs a lamp with a string that pulls both ways, a light parody of the scales of justice. The string tips come to life and sparkle when the shades are opened and natural light pours in, that is, when the lights/scales are not needed. Then Hitchcock had faith in such balance.

The Lady Vanishes
1938

The Lady Vanishes is the high point in Hitchcock's British period and was the most enthusiastically received. Reviewers applauded how Hitchcock's verve and style make one overlook the logical gaps and improbabilities.[1] It remains the most frequently shown British Hitchcock film even today.[2]

Thematically, the film continues from *Young and Innocent* the focus on an affluent young girl's awakening to maturity. Its political vein connects the concerns of *Secret Agent* and *Sabotage* to *Jamaica Inn*.

The Lady Vanishes opens in a snowbound inn in the fictitious Tyrolean country of Bandrieka. Iris Henderson (Margaret Lockwood) celebrates with girlfriends her last freedom before marrying into the stiff upper crust. Jaded by her freedom and experience, she is resigned to wedding her "blue-blooded cheque chaser." She meets a collector of folk music, Gilbert (Michael Redgrave in his screen debut),[3] and has him evicted from his room for his noisy research into country dances. When he threatens to move in with her she has him reinstated.

On the train the next day, Iris befriends an elderly English nanny, Miss Froy (Dame May Whitty), but after a nap finds that Miss Froy has disappeared. The other passengers deny Miss Froy's existence.

Brain surgeon Dr. Hartz (Paul Lukas) attributes Iris's hallucination to a bump on the head. Finally Gilbert and Iris find Miss Froy, whom Hartz and his accomplices planned to kill to prevent her giving the British government the secret clause of a treaty. The railway car is sidelined in enemy territory and the English besieged, but Miss Froy and then the others escape. When Gilbert and Iris reach London, their bickering has already turned to love. Iris abandons her fiancé and goes with Gilbert to the Foreign Office where they are welcomed by the safe Miss Froy.

Family is central to *The Lady Vanishes* but not the fractured and fragile personal community of *Sabotage* or the expanding personal unit of *Young and Innocent*. Here family is the metaphor for the international community of man, which the villains seek to disrupt.

The minor characters provide a range of false-family or failed-family types. The solicitor and his mistress, the Todhunters, off on a dirty fortnight, are not just a pretend-family but the violation of the two families they left behind. The Doppo family sharing Iris and Miss Froy's compartment is a political cell, with the countess and the doctor domineering parental figures.

The two cricket fans, Caldicott (Naunton Wayne) and Charters (Basil Radford), are a parody of a couple. Inseparable, of one mind on all issues, the two sports are a sterile, narcissistic coupling. They parody the Gilbert and Iris romance in the inn scene, when the maid returns to her room to change. As they search the paper for cricket scores they share a single bed and a pair of pajamas. They disdain the maid's bawdry as "primitive humor." One man hides the other's bare chest from her view, later to be caught pantless himself.

In contrast to the cricket couple's insularity, the Gilbert-Iris affair develops in natural romantic order. Before meeting Gilbert, Iris jokes of her romantic isolation:

I, Iris Matilda Henderson, a spinster of no particular parish, do hereby solemnly renounce my maidenly past.

I've no regrets. I've been everywhere and done everything. . . . What is there left for me but marriage?

The Lady Vanishes *(1938). An ad with a variety of shots from the film. Note the censor's "A" certificate.*

She is marrying Sir Charles Fotheringale—a young Caldicott and Charters—out of boredom and out of her father's hunger for status:

> Father is simply aching to have a coat of arms on the jam label.

Gilbert will save her from remaining a feather-in-a-gale. "It's a bad wind that blow nowhere no good," quoth hotel manager Boris (Emile Boreo). Her planned marriage denies the normal cycle of passion, fertility, and love. Retiring to bed she kisses each of her two girlfriends maternally on the forehead and says, "Goodnight, my children." Of course her motherhood is premature but not *that* premature, as the next scene will put her on her bed with Gilbert.

Gilbert on Iris's bed bodes a more fertile romance than Charters and Caldicott in the maid's. Innocently lying in bed with the paper, they seem presexual boys. Projecting, they call Boris and the maid "grown up children, you know," as later they will accuse the American papers of no sense of proportion for omitting the cricket scores.

Iris is extrasexual in her scene with her girlfriends, aware of the process but outside it. She stands semidressed on a table and teases the waiter Rudolph, detached from his embarrassment. Gilbert moves in on her bed with images of discipline and romance, force and courtship, putting his walking stick on one side of the bed (kissing the rod first) and his flute on the other. Iris, initially a passive victim—

> This time next week I shall be a slightly sunburned offering on an altar in Hanover Square.

—ultimately takes the initiative to dump her fiancé for Gilbert.

In a parody of the main romance, Miss Froy is serenaded in her bedroom by an elderly troubadour. He is conveying the coded secret and is strangled for his efforts. But the old blood serenading a grandmotherly spinster reads romantic. With Miss Froy the family metaphor transcends the fertility archetype.

For Miss Froy family is macrocosmic. However elderly, she still has parents to visit. Her family's unusual range is metaphoric. She considers the Bandriekans "just like happy children, with laughter on their lips and music in their hearts," by implication *her* children. Her political engagement is based in her feeling of parental responsibility for their security. She embraces the country as if it were her family.

So too her parents' tea is drunk by fifty million Mexicans, family and international brotherhood together in a single cuppa. The tea label will later reassure Iris of Miss Froy's existence. Her familial affection extends to nature, as she describes a mountain range as a family, large hills parents, small ones children. She prescribes family to Iris:

> You'll have children, won't you? They make such a difference. I always think it's being with kiddies so much that's made me, if I may say so, so young for my age.

Miss Froy exorcises the family of sexual demons when she spells out her name. "It's Froy," she says.

IRIS: Did you say Freud?
FROY: No, O.Y., not E.U.D. Froy. It rhymes with joy.

In the last shot a beaming Miss Froy holds out her arms to welcome Gilbert and Iris, like the last shot of Erica uniting father and lover in *Young and Innocent*. In Gilbert's mind, Miss Froy's musical message has been driven out by the Wedding March, but that's her other message, not failure. This secret agent's primary function is to promote new families.

In some ways Gilbert is a lighter version of Miss Froy. He has her devotion to family traditions and old songs. So he turns on Boris:

> You dare to call it a noise? The ancient music with which your present ancestors celebrated every wedding for countless generations!

In contrast to Gilbert's devotion to other cultures' music, the stiff Caldicott and Charters stand through the entire Hungarian Rhapsody (alone), believing it to be the national anthem. Like Miss Froy, Gilbert extends family feeling beyond the term's formal limits, but bawdily. So to Boris:

> The dance they danced when your father married your mother, always supposing you were born in wedlock, which I doubt.

And to Iris:

> My father always taught me never desert a lady in trouble. He even carried that as far as marrying Mother.

When he tells Iris his life story he emphasizes his father:

> I'll begin with my father. You know it's remarkable how many great men began with their fathers.

His father is a responsibility—

> Well, after I'd, er . . . paid my father's debts, I started to travel, before they tried to cash the cheques.

—as Iris attributed her inapt engagement to her father's desire for status. Gilbert's father lost his status; Iris's wants to raise her father's.

The Todhunters are a neat parallel, the solicitor nervous about his reputation and his mistress craving promotion to wife.

> MR. TODHUNTER: You must think of it from my point of view. The law like Caesar's wife must be above suspicion.
>
> MRS. TODHUNTER: Even when the law spends six weeks with Caesar's wife?

In contrast to the Todhunters' isolated affair, Iris and Gilbert are emotionally united by their engagement with Miss Froy. As Gilbert recasts a proverb, "Faint heart never found old lady." By finding the old lady he wins the proverb's fair lady.

The treacherous nun inflects the family/fertility pattern. As a nun she seems beyond (but still outside) the family and fertility pattern. But her image belies her nature. Her habit is betrayed by her high-heeled shoes. Like Chaucer's prioress, the woman is incompletely submerged in the nun role. She works for the villains for reasons of marriage—her husband was Bandriekan. She leaves the villains to serve her larger family:

> This was murder, and she was an Englishwoman. . . . I'm English and you were going to butcher her in cold blood.

Of course, the "nun" redeems herself—like the "mute" criminal in *Number Seventeen*. She enables the English's escape by switching the train tracks, suffering—aptly, given her earlier vanity—a leg wound.

The family and fertility theme includes several references to rabbits. Blanche tells Iris, "Well, I'm fond of rabbits, but they have to be kept down." Todhunter's mistress tells him, "Now I know why you lied like a scared rabbit." The maiden Blanche controls the rabbit (proverbial emblem of rampant fertility), while the Todhunters associate it with fear. When Iris and Gilbert stumble through the baggage car, Iris steps into the magician's disappearing cabinet and seems to have turned into a rabbit.

Through the adventure the spoiled, complacent Iris develops courage, self-sacrifice, and both responsiveness to and responsibility for other people. The family motif marks her growth from selfishness to feeling for others. In the source novel, Ethel Lina White's *The Wheel Spins*,[4] Iris Carr

> was used to the protection of a crowd, whom—with unconscious flattery—she called "her friends." An attractive orphan of independent means, she had been surrounded always with clumps of people. They thought for her—or rather she accepted their opinions, and they shouted for her—since her voice was rather too low in register, for mass social intercourse. (7)

> Iris appeared just one of her crowd, and a typical semi-Society girl—vain, selfish, and useless. (8)

> She was only vaguely conscious of fugitive moments of discontent and self-contempt. (9)

Hitchcock gives Iris a forceful but absent father. In the novel her sympathy for Miss Froy is based on having been lost in the mountains and then among the townsfolk when she falls ill with sunstroke. In Hitchcock a pot falls on her instead of on Miss Froy. Iris's problem is not being lost in the mountains but being besieged by the man in her room. After her spinsterish recoil from him (unlike the true spinster's response to her serenader), her sympathy for Miss Froy grows into love for both Froy and Gilbert.

A second major theme is language, from meaningless noise at one extreme, to verbal and nonverbal communication, to the highest form, music. Miss Froy has the liveliest values so she commands several languages. She has to translate for Caldicott and Charters, despite their superior education, class, and attitude. She can even criticize in gentle language:

> I never think you should judge any country by its politics. After all, we English are quite honest by nature, aren't we? You'll excuse me if I run away?

She teaches English and music. In the opening scene the inn is quiet until the instant Miss Froy leaves, whereupon a chaotic babble and tumult break out. Miss Froy embodies harmony.

Gilbert shares her lively sentiments, human interest, cultural range, and engagement with music. The soul he hears in the folk music Iris considers just noise. Music plays no part in her life until her Wedding March supplants the politics in Gilbert. Music is the emblem of harmony, traditionally; here it works romantically in Miss Froy's connection of Gilbert and Iris and as international harmony in her coded message. At first Gilbert's music interrupts Miss Froy's. He, like Iris, must learn considerateness.

Hitchcock added music to the novel's language theme:

> Her [Iris's] ignorance of foreign languages was the result of being finished at Paris and Dresden. During the time she was at school, she mixed exclusively with other English girls, while the natives who taught her acquired excellent English accents.
>   This was her rendering of the line in the National Anthem— "Send us victorious." (18–19)

> She was acutely aware of her own impotence, as though she were some maimed creature, whose tongue had been torn out. . . . Feeling that she had lapsed from the dignity of a rational being, she was forced to make pantomimic gestures. (10)

Hitchcock dropped White's vicar, who goes daily into the village to chat with the natives even though he does not know their language:

> "Oh, he *makes* them understand," explained his wife proudly. "Sympathy, you know, and common humanity. He'd rub noses with a savage." (26)

Perhaps Hitchcock dropped the vicar and his family so as not to deflect sentiment from the Froy-Iris-Gilbert unit.

Hitchcock elaborates on the novel's use of language as an index to human relationships. Characters' selfishness is presented in terms of language. Boris, a parody of Gilbert and Miss Froy's internationalism, panics in five or six languages. Inconsistent in morals as in tongue, he is open to bribes, impersonal toward his customers, and an unscrupulous translator. He embellishes Gilbert's remarks about Iris:

> And do you know what he said? "Who does she think she is, the Queen of Sheba? She thinks she owns this hotel?"

Boris is a comic version of Dr. Hartz, flustered to the doctor's cool, resentful of outsiders' intrusions, and corrupt. They're connected in Boris's malapropism for "eject":

> We will inject him with a little . . . he'll never forget as long as he live.

This anticipates Dr. Hartz's plan to drug Gilbert and Iris. Otherwise Boris's knowledge of English might be called alimentary: "the have-lunch" he calls the avalanche; the train has no "eating" (heating).

Language separates the English from the conspirators. Doppo (Philip Leaver), who looks like a working man but is a magician, cannot speak English. The baroness (Mary Clare) could if she deigned, as in the novel:

> "Do you speak English?" Apparently the question was an insult, for the lady closed her heavy lids with studied insolence, as though she could not endure a plebeian spectacle. (66)

But language does not guarantee community. The soldier who boards the train speaks English—he was educated at Oxford—but is rejected on the "nun's" warning. Gilbert knocks him out and explains, "I went to Cambridge." Politics threatens even communities of language.

Though masters of English, the Todhunters are cowards and liars in its use. "I would rather be called a rat than die like one." Where Doppo, the baroness, and Hartz are committed to a cause, however bad, the Todhunters drift with their own best interest. The woman admits to having seen Miss Froy when she thinks the scandal might win her man, but lies when she learns a delay or scandal would lose him. Deviants from the social system, the Todhunters are denied redemption.

Not so the grown boys Caldicott and Charters, who are only slightly less narrow and selfish than the Todhunters. The cricket-lovers redeem themselves at the end by proving generous, brave, and crack shots. For all their ludicrous triviality, Caldicott and Charters are a familiar and respectable English type. They deny the validity of any language but their own. So Charters, of Boris's third explanation of the train's delay: "Why the deuce didn't he say so in the first place?"

—Awful being in the dark like this, you know, Caldicott.

—Our communications cut off in a time of crisis.

Their "communications" with each other and with the outside world is solely concerned with the cricket test match. Charters breaks a businessman's important phone call from London in a pique at not being able to get the score. Their cricket talk parallels language of political concern and saps its weight and seriousness:

—That last report was pretty ghastly, do you remember? England on the brink.

—Yes, but that's newspaper sensationalism. The old country's been in some tight corners before.

—It's this hanging about that gets me. If only we knew what was happening in England.

—Mustn't lose grip, Charters.

They shrink the world to their own concerns. They leave Iris to doubt her own sanity and Miss Froy to death rather than risk arriving too late for the test match (which, in the tradition of Hitchcock Macguffins, is rained out anyway). The men are not immoral. They just have a naive confidence that all is well and orderly in the world. "Things like that just don't happen," Caldicott reiterates as their peril grows. They are certain there is a unifying order in the world and that power is English, cricket its primary service. If one behaves English, wearing proper dinner dress to a foodless dinner in a snowbound inn, all will be right in the world.[5]

The nun is a variation on the Todhunters' and cricket-boys' uninvolvement. Playing mute denies her expression and her community, both being English. She shocks us twice with her first words: "How the devil should I know?"

Dr. Hartz has Miss Froy's range of languages but chills them with his crust of science—cold, formulaic, glib in declaring Iris's fantasy a danger. As to the brain surgeon's name, Hartz is "heart" in German, Austrian, and points Tyrolean, but his politics renders him heartless. The Heart operating on the Head applies to Iris, Gilbert, and Froy, not to Hartz. Even his professional concern for Iris serves only his interest.

With scientific confidence, Hartz asserts, "There never was a Miss Froy. Merely a vivid subjective image." Proved wrong, he holds his ground: "My theory was a perfectly good one; the facts were misleading." He accused Iris of just such subjective projection. Hartz's ambiguities grow sinister, as in his toast over the heroes' drugged drinks:

To our health. And may our enemies, if they exist, be unconscious of our purpose.

They are his enemies whom he would now render unconscious. For a brain surgeon to wish anyone unconsciousness is perverse.

By dismissing Iris's concern for Miss Froy as a hallucination, Hartz would force her regression back into her own mind instead of out to concern for another. Fortunately, nature—or fate—or accident—or God—or the physical world in all its healthy intransigence—conspires to check his cold psychology. A signature in dust on a window and a flapping tea wrapper renew Iris's confidence in her sanity. Even in defeat, Hartz is the detached scientist. As the English speed off to safety he is surprisingly bright: "Car marniblon. Or as they say in English: jolly good luck to them."[6]

The Hartz scenes establish the spectrum between madness and sanity. "We'll be off in a jiffy," says Gilbert, just as their car is being detached from the remainder of the train. Paradoxically, in this film's politics detachment is madness, involvement sane. All the outside shots of the train show it going around the bend. Gilbert goes outside the train to begin his attack, as if off the rails. The train itself can be taken as a fantasy speeding uncontrollably through the mind. Durgnat brilliantly explains a surreal shot:

> Shortly after Iris is hit on the head, Hitchcock interposes a strange, dreamlike shot of three men, shovelling sand or ballast, tiny against a back-projection of huge locomotive wheels. The perspective is wrong, the tonal register is wrong, the size is wrong, and today's sophisticated audience may see only the least convincing of the film's many unconvincing backgrounds, but, one suspects, this back-projection read as a kind of entry into dream to the less analytical, more rapidly and intensely emotive audiences of forty years ago.[7]

The train is introduced in an image of perceptual dislocation, tempting us to adopt Hartz's explanation not just for Miss Froy but for the entire adventure on the train. Gilbert has an easy line deprecating the English cabinet minister on whose brain Hartz just operated: "Find anything?" But through these fantastic adventures, a variety of characters "come to their senses": Mrs. Todhunter, the cricketers, the nun, Iris, perhaps even Hartz in his shift from cold killer to sporting loser. Even if she were a phantom, the lady didn't just vanish but snapped people back into a commitment to the real world.

Love and games are fine but private things. Sometimes the world demands more strenuous engagement. Hitchcock again reflects on the popular arts. As Gilbert preserves folk dances and music, he works with and performs an art. In the novel he was an engineer named Max Hare (those rabbits again) building a dam in the strange country. Hitchcock replaced the practical builder with an artist with social responsibility. On the other side, he changed the countess's banker to the magician, Doppo. Hitchcock clearly relates folk/popular art to political concerns. The arts encourage a sympathetic response to the strange old lady. Ultimately the artist (Gilbert), the playgirl (Iris), the traitor (the nun), two cricket-nuts, and an adulteress rededicate themselves to their community responsibilities. These themes save the film's political interest from topicality, but it does address its times.

Gavin Lambert describes the immediate context: "A few months after Chamberlain came to terms with Hitler at Munich, the British passengers still cling to an obstinate isolationism, reluctant to take the enemy seriously. . . . The conservative lawyer dies fluttering a white handkerchief."[8] Durgnat reads the political cast as internationalists (Gilbert and Froy) vying with the insularists (the clubmen and Todhunters) for the initially neutral Iris, while presumably the international threat lurks for the advantage (Hartz, the countess): "It certainly mirrors a British mood immediately after Munich, but that mood isn't one simple thought. It's probably fair to say that if the scenery has shifted from England in *Sabotage* to Mittel Europ it's because the fear of internal disorder has given place to the question of English intervention on behalf of Czechoslovakia and then Poland."[9]

But we shouldn't overstate the political context.[10] The film's unity, including the coincidence of what Hitchcock put in and what the audience takes out, lies in its integration of the motifs of family, music, sanity, and political and human commitment. The film exhorts us to human involvement, to recover an international fraternity, as personified by the protective Miss Froy.

Indeed Hitchcock's little old lady is far more active than in his source. Miss Froy is a committed secret agent and a strong presence even when she vanishes. The novel's innocent governess falls into danger when sees a political leader surprisingly at home, which could implicate him in an important man's death. Hitchcock's *The Lady Vanishes* is remarkably resonant and discreet for a political drama.

Jamaica Inn
1939

Hitchcock's British period formally ends with the release of *Jamaica Inn* on May 20, 1939. As a division point, the film seems an arbitrary choice, as *Rebecca,* his first film for David Selznick in America, is just as English in its cast, source, and setting. Hitchcock returned to England in 1944 to make two short films in French for the Ministry of Education, *Bon Voyage* and *Adventure Malgache,* then again in 1949–50 to make *Under Capricorn* and *Stage Fright.* In 1972 he returned to London for his adaptation of—paradoxically—Arthur La Bern's *Goodbye Picadilly, Farewell Leicester Square,* released as *Frenzy.* But *Jamaica Inn* does formally end the early period of Hitchcock's career.

Sadly, it is not a strong conclusion to his series of witty, thoughtful thrillers. Hitchcock found himself with some time before his American engagement, so he agreed to do *Jamaica Inn* for Erich Pommer and Charles Laughton,[1] their Mayflower Production Company needing a success after the failures of Somerset Maugham's *Vessel of Wrath* (a.k.a. *The Beachcomber*) and Clemence Dane's *St. Martin's Lane.*

Jamaica Inn from the beginning fared badly with the critics:

> The assaults, adventures, shipwrecks and clashes of characters
> in this film are invigorating rather than suspenseful. They are

striking in themselves, but have little value as part of accumulative suspense.

In other words, this is a penny dreadful, all frightfully shocking on the surface but lacking dramatic unity beneath the spate of action. (*Film Weekly,* May 20, 1939)

Devotees of Hitchcock will find little directional subtlety here, but rather straightforward treatment of meaty material, rousing storm sequences and a shadowy film of sinister corners and bleak coasts, finely photographed by Harry Stradling. (*New York Motion Picture Herald,* May 27, 1939)

But the juicy melodrama fared well at the box office and warranted rerelease in 1944 and 1948.

The orphaned Mary Yellen (Maureen O'Hara) comes to stay with her Aunt Patience (Marie Ney) and Uncle Joss Merlin (Leslie Banks) at an inn notorious for mysterious goings-on. Joss heads a ring of varlets who shipwreck vessels on the Cornwall coast, killing the survivors and plundering the wreckage. Lawman Jem Trehearne (Robert Newton, young and slender but already vixen-eyed) infiltrates the gang. Before his true identity is known, Mary saves Jem from being lynched by the gang.

The power behind the gang turns out to be the local magistrate, Sir Humphrey Pengallan (Charles Laughton). The gang shoots Joss when he saves Mary from them. Pengallan shoots Aunt Patience before she can name him as the ringleader. Pengallan tries to escape with Mary as his captive, but Jem and the military give chase and arrest his boat. Pengallan leaps from the mast to his death, leaving Mary to Jem.

Rare for a Hitchcock film, authorship problems arose from the power wielded by producer Pommer and star Laughton. Clemence Dane based the first screenplay on the popular Daphne du Maurier novel. It was reworked by Hitchcock and Sidney Gilliat. Laughton brought in J. B. Priestley for additional dialogue to plump up his part.

Hitchcock had problems with Laughton's slow pace in character development. Moreover, casting Laughton as the judge changed the film from a whodunit to a suspense film: "It was completely absurd, because logically the judge should have entered the scene only at the end of the adventure. He should have carefully avoided the place and made sure he was never seen in the tavern. Therefore it made no sense to cast Charles Laughton in the key role of the justice of the peace. Realising how incongruous it was, I was truly discouraged, but the contract had been signed."[2] The star's dominance over the director hurt the film.[3]

But the film remains a Hitchcock. Robber Harry Pedlar (Emlyn Williams), his dandy clothes a parallel to the criminal judge, is identified by his whistling. Both men project a larger presence by their style. The sailors' helplessness is imaged in the unmanned ship wheel's erratic spinning. Asides tweak both the torpid aristocracy and the petty lower class. The boy in the gang is eager to be handcuffed. When his wrists are too small for cuffs, he is fit to be tied. As his death nears, the lad dissolves from fright. Typical of a Hitchcock adaptation, he gives Mary a romantic undercover agent and the couple grows from bickering fugitives to lovers.

To accommodate Laughton, Hitchcock dropped the albino priest so the judge, a small, shadowy figure in the novel, becomes the spectacular embodiment of evil. Where the novel dramatized the infiltration of the spiritual domain by vanity, cynicism, and greed, the film more weakly shows the corruption of secular law. Hitchcock loses the intriguing image of the original pastor, a spectral aberration of nature, and his eerie home, for the more conventional decadence in which Laughton already had a well-known line.

To be fair, the film personifies religious corruption in the character of Salvation Watkins (Wylie Watson), whose relentless prophecies of doom, biblical quotations, and hypocritical moralizings echo du Maurier's priest. Watkins anticipates the drunk relishing the prospect of the apocalypse in *The Birds*. But in Watkins theological despair is reduced to the comedy of lower-class eccentrics. The film loses the macabre weight behind its opening Cornish prayer: "Lord, if there is to be a shipwreck let it be on Cornwall's coast." The pastor's vision of his congregation as sheep resurfaces in Uncle Charlie's self-justification in *Shadow of a Doubt*.[4]

Hitchcock omits the pastor's explanation for his crime: "Come, let us leave religion out of our discussion. When you know me better we will return to it, and I will tell you how I sought refuge from myself in

Christianity, and found it to be built upon hatred, and jealousy, and greed—all the man-made attributes of civilization, while the old pagan barbarism was naked and clean."[5] As in *Juno and the Paycock*, perhaps Hitchcock was not yet ready to deal with such a touchy issue, or he thought his audience wasn't. Du Maurier's villain could have been the center of a marvelous film by the Hitchcock, say, of *I Confess*.

To confirm Pengallan's monopoly on evil, his henchman Joss is stripped of the bestiality he has in the novel. Joss's evil and his frightening mix of strength and delicacy go to the squire. As a result Joss dwindles even beside his own gang, paling next to Harry's perversity. Similarly, Joss's black-sheep brother Jem loses his family connection, becoming just a lawman on assignment. This sentimentalizes Joss further, as *he* gets to be the reformed criminal, and Mary gets to improve nobody. Joss's reform heightens Pengallan's dignity as an uncompromising outlaw. He dies with panache:

> The Age of Chivalry is gone. . . . What are you waiting for, a spectacle? You shall have it. And tell your children how the great age ended. Make way for the great Pengallan.

From Moreau through Bligh, Laughton loved to play the great twisted man above the law. Hitchcock cast him as the lascivious judge in *The Paradine Case*. But even Pengallan's grandeur is a dilution of du Maurier's pastor:

> I live in the past, when men were not so humble as they are today. Oh, not your heroes of history in doublet and hose and narrow-pointed shoes—they were never my friends—but long ago in the beginning of time, when the rivers and the sea were one, and the old gods walked the hills.
>
> Yes, I am a freak in nature and a freak in time. I do not belong here, and I was born with a grudge against the age, and a grudge against mankind. Peace is very hard to find in the nineteenth century. The silence is gone, even on the hills. I thought to find it in the Christian Church, but the dogma sickened me, and the whole foundation is built upon a fairy-tale. Christ Himself is a figure-head, a puppet thing created by man himself. (244)

Beside this pastor's romantic despair, freakishness, and vanity, Pengallan is a shallow villain.

Essentially he is a sensualist. Our first word of him is the coachman's implicit warning to Mary: "You might try Squire Pengallan. They say he's partial to young women." In Pengallan's invitation to Mary—"Would you oblige me by taking off your coat, my dear?"—he requests an exposure but appears hospitable and assumes she will oblige his interest and power. Pengallan orders people around very courteously, when he wishes. Joss's admiration of Mary's hands is the only sign of his sexual threat (unlike in the novel).

Where the pastor had a creed, perversely obsolete, Pengallan's evil springs merely from his greed and his vanity:

> I know what to do with money, so I must have more of it. I must have more of it.

From the mast he taunts the lowly:

> I shall be down to you before you are up to me, Mr. Trehearne.

Reporting their unpaid bills, Pengallan's valet Chadwyck defends the butcher and baker's insistence: "They must live." "Must they?" asks the fat Pengallan, yawning. All this is juicy stuff. Laughton's villain is a rich and commanding image, but a retreat from du Maurier's evil.

Hitchcock chooses political statement over religious. He shifts the villain's disdain from the congregation to the constituency. Joss's softening, the comedy with the gang, Aunt Patience's duty to Joss, all serve a political purpose. The characters are polarized into a victimized lower class and a criminal, callous aristocracy. Pengallan dismisses Joss:

> You and your friends are just the carcass. The brains are here.

To confirm the audience's sympathy, the three gang members chasing the lovers pause to look forward to a good night's sleep when their job is done. Pengallan rewards the tenants who have served him long and faithfully, but denies the radical Berkin his rights, even a word of respect. Pengallan rewards only those who thrive on his condescension. Nature made him different from Berkin, Pengallan avers, and everything since has confirmed that difference. Du Maurier's freak of nature becomes a bad politician.

Pengallan's houseguests confirm the theme of an impotent, decaying aristocracy. But Pengallan's claims to Berkin are rebutted by Jem's style, energy, and class. Jem fills Lord George's suit more dashingly than Lord George (Basil Radford) does.

The film's political aspect may explain the final shot. Pengallan dead, the film ends not on the lovers, as we expect, but on the squire's faithful servant Chadwyck. He shakes his head regretfully as Pengallan's voice calls him. Chadwyck had suspected Pengallan of having inherited his grandfather's madness. Mary urged Jem and the soldiers not to shoot Pengallan because "He's mad. He doesn't know what he is doing. . . . It's not his fault. He can't help himself."

Jem's logic is more convincing than Chadwyck's sentimentality and Mary's delicacy, particularly when we recall the consequences of "Mrs. Ashenden's" intervention at the end of *Secret Agent*. Pengallan always knew what he was doing. He is not to be explained by the easy out of madness. Like Fry, Bates, and Uncle Charlie, Pengallan is a Hitchcock villain to whose "case" psychological explanations are shallow tangents. Hitchcock rejects the assumption that reason is superior to unreason, order more natural than chaos. So no science or rational system can explain his villains' evil. Pengallan has consciously adopted the energies, style, and morality normally considered evil. He lives it through, unrepentant to the end.

The madman is not Pengallan, whose spectacular death coheres with his style of life. The madman—if there is one—is little Chadwyck, who wasted his life in the unrewarded and humiliating service of the squire. Chadwyck is the sheep of the pastor's vision.

If we set aside the lost opportunities in the novel, Hitchcock's film makes a consistent statement. It enjoys Pengallan's spirit while rejecting him on moral terms. Chadwyck and Mary lack the strength of character to live like Pengallan. For this the values inculcated by their social system may be blamed. But they also lack the strength to judge Pengallan. For this they are to be blamed, as Berkin's and Jem's respective models of radical and conservative individualism alert us. If the squire took the pastor's evil, perhaps the pastor's moral vision is preserved in Berkin, Jem, and that last shot of Chadwyck.

But Hitchcock rarely addresses our moral sense directly. There is too much of the erotic, for example, Durgnat being as usual a sensitive guide:

> Pistol to hand, the smug and brutal Squire gags and binds the heroine . . . in a bondage which is more than physical, which is worthy of *The Story of O,* and which is by far the most romantically expressed emotion in the film. And in some ways not dissimilar submissiveness has become a socially ingrained second nature among Sir Humphrey's grateful tenants, and dominates, in religious terms, the wrecker who knows himself to be damned but retains just enough bizarrely hypocritical sincerity to offer religious consolation to the man he is about to kill.[6]

One can also admire Pengallan for sustaining old elegance, old manners. He justly jokes to his groom that Chadwyck is growing mad and he correctly evaluates Mary: "Stop crying. Be beautiful."

Jamaica Inn is a gothic thriller that roughly represents the best seller as which it posed. The film depicts the luxurious decadence that the stratified English society once suffered, demonstrating how evil can spring from a good system (religious in the novel, political in the film) that has calcified. The film's spirit is individualist, even radical, as the law's Jem feels weaker than either Berkin or Pengallan. The film and its political shift are what one might expect from a Hitchcock packed and on his way to the open society of America.

Conclusion

Hitchcock's Imagery and Art

Of the twenty-three feature films that Hitchcock directed in his first fifteen years, none is without some interest and some lively personal character. Hitchcock was Hitchcock from the outset—perceptive, progressive, and playful in his mischievous machinations against the simple securities of his audience, yet profound in the implications of his ironic stance. The early films show the same thematic concerns for which his later work is known, and the same expertise.

As in his later work, Hitchcock often paralleled characters of ostensible innocence and guilt to dramatize the thin line that undermines man's pretensions to purity. Thus Patsy Brand contrasts Jill Cheyne in *The Pleasure Garden*, the romantic policeman contrasts the lodger, and the two men of *The Manxman*. In *Easy Virtue, Rich and Strange, The Skin Game,* and *Jamaica Inn*, figures of simple innocence are seduced into criminal complicity. These foreshadow the drama of Bruno and Guy in *Strangers on a Train*.

Often the Hitchcock innocent is drawn into evil by boredom, a moral lassitude. Thus we have the passionless marriages of *The Pleasure Garden, The Manxman,* and *Sabotage;* the premature marriages in *The Ring, Easy Virtue,* and *The Skin Game;* and the boredom that prompts the girl to flirt with the artist in *Blackmail*. Hitchcock realizes how dull morality is and how exciting sin is. His delight is to make his moral points through exciting fictions, reminding his audiences of the difficulties of the moral life. These marriages foreshadow the cold, antiromantic situations that are developed in *Notorious, North by Northwest,* and *Topaz.*

Because innocence and guilt are so radically intertwined, a Hitchcock hero never enjoys a simple success. The innocent will die along with the guilty: the native girl in *The Pleasure Garden,* the pirate in *Rich and Strange,* Stevie Verloc in *Sabotage,* as later the children and Annie will in *The Birds* and Marion Crane will after she has resolved to surrender to police in *Psycho.* For man's laws fail in the allocation of justice.

In *Rope,* Jan asks playfully of a friend's description of her, "Did he do me justice?" Rupert replies sharply, "Do you deserve justice?" From the lovers of *The Pleasure Garden* through the murders of *Family Plot,* Hitchcock's heroes are of, at best, a dappled virtue and his villains of civilized elegance. Indeed, his villains are often extremely sympathetic people, as Verloc in *Sabotage* or Fane in *Murder!* Even the nasty Levet in *The Pleasure Garden* is allowed a death of charming civility.

Hitchcock's justice is tricky, poetic rather than legal. For his world is full of uncertainty. *Shadow of a Doubt* may seem to have a happy ending, but the killer is eulogized by the small town, and an innocent man was fed to an airplane propeller by mistake. In *Blackmail,* the murderers go free while a small-time blackmailer is killed in their stead. Even the happy endings, then, refuse the confidence of a secure order. No simple justice, no simple psychology, can be sustained in Hitchcock's world of quicksand insecurity. So almost all his films end on an uncertain image, from the new lovers in *The Pleasure Garden* to the mass of abiding doom at the end of *The Birds.* And in *Frenzy,* Blaney establishes his innocence by performing the crime for which he was wrongly sentenced; no matter that the woman he attacks in Rusk's bed is already dead.

Hitchcock often uses the X image to define man as a complex of innocence and evil. In *The Pleasure Garden* the two women's waves form an X to suggest their equivalence in their lover's mind. Having killed his mistress, the husband tries to kill his wife to complete the X. In *Blackmail* similar editing completes an X between the corpse's hand

and the policeman's, where the plot develops the illegality of the police's activities and the criminal parodies justice. The X imagery is developed most fully, of course, in *Strangers on a Train*.

Perhaps Hitchcock presents two different concepts of man's makeup. First, opposite tendencies unite to form a single, composite whole, as the ladies do in *The Pleasure Garden* and as those strangers do on a train. Here the X represents the unity of opposite motions and values in human nature. Similarly, in *I Confess* an X variant, the cross, unites Father Logan and killer Keller in a criminal sacrament that costs them Alma (the soul in its earthly existence). In the second image of human nature, opposite wholes are paralleled. Charlie and Uncle Charlie in *Shadow of a Doubt* are parallel opposites, albeit with such similarities as name, selfishness, vanity, and telepathic connection. They are not a unity. The good Charlie may have some flaws and the evil Uncle Charlie some elegant pretense to justice, but the characters diverge by their respective wills. In *Psycho*, Norman Bates pretends to be an X with his mother, but she is innocent, misrepresented even after she was murdered by her spoiled, jealous son. Norman and his mother are antitheses who only intersect in Norman's malevolent rationale. The bickering lovers in Hitchcock's romances (*Champagne, Mr. and Mrs. Smith*) and in his thrillers (*The 39 Steps, Saboteur, The Lady Vanishes*, and on through *Marnie*) are spirited strokes that are fulfilled as Xs.

The other quintessential Hitchcock image is the staircase. Whether upward or down, Hitchcock's stairs take his characters and his audience to the fears, dangers, and rewards of self-discovery. The most common staircase shot is downward though a seeming spiral, which leaves the impression of stairs within stairs. One finds this shot from *The Lodger* through *Vertigo*. As an emblem it recalls Peer Gynt's onion, concentric layerings around a void, with the addition of the danger that height always means in Hitchcock.

The occasional round staircase, as in *The Pleasure Garden* and *Secret Agent,* also suggests a plunge through layers of one's self. There are even three staircases in *Waltzes from Vienna*: the rickety ladder down which Schani's rival carries the heroine in the opening fire scene; its parallel, the ladder the girl climbs at the end to save Schani from the duel and to reclaim him romantically; and the palatial staircase down which the prince rolls his valet in a piano rift, an image of their difference in privilege and station. In *Juno and the Paycock* the stairs provide a straight dark descent from the family warmth to the cold public funeral and to their dispossession.

In *Shadow of a Doubt* Charlie's home has two parallel staircases, the clean public front and the dangerous, steep, private back, which Uncle Charles uses to escape and to threaten Charlie. The two-staired house works as an image of the human psyche and of a societal ideal, both of which project a front that is more attractive and safer than their hidden nature.

Stairs compel movement and with it, fear, as in Constance's ascent to Murchison's office in *Spellbound* and Arbogast's in *Psycho*. The camera (the maker) has a liberty over space and stairs that the character has not. Hence the open, expressionistic staircase in *The Lodger* and the brittle one in *Number Seventeen*. Hitchcock's stairs image both man's composition and the rigors and fears of his rise or plunge to awareness. The danger that always lurks around the stairs is the anxiety that undercuts all confidence (in the Hitchcock vision), all sense of secure footing and that provides both the central metaphor and title for *Downhill* and *Vertigo*. The source of the latter was a novel titled *Among the Dead*, but "vertigo" conveys Hitchcock's primary interest: man's fear to step between two moments of living.

Hitchcock's art is based on the dramatic appeal of the insecure. In the first place, his characters are typically secure people whose footing is swept out from under them. Thus Patsy loses her independence in *The Pleasure Garden* and the heroes lose their whole world in *Downhill* and *Champagne*. Sanders loses his station in *The Ring* and the fisherman his bliss, friend, and wife in *The Manxman*. Love provides only a false sense of security in *The Pleasure Garden*, *The Farmer's Wife*, *The Manxman*, and *Champagne*, where the reconciled lovers quarrel anew over their wedding arrangements. In *Mr. and Mrs. Smith* a marriage suddenly ceases to exist and, as in *Rich and Strange*, has to be rebuilt.

Nor is there security in the social contract. The processes of justice go awry in *Easy Virtue*, *Blackmail*, *Juno and the Paycock*, and *Murder!* In the thriller series from *The Man Who Knew Too Much* through *The Lady Vanishes*, the individual's private life is shattered by the social processes that supposedly protect him. Hitchcock's hero is often threatened by the police as much as by the enemy: *The Lodger, Blackmail, The 39 Steps, North by Northwest, Psycho, Frenzy*. Virtue and justice are endangered by the merely human law. Joe in *The Lodger* eventually subordinates his romantic interest to his public duty. But not until *Frenzy* will we have a Hitchcock policeman whose arrival at the truth is based on his sense of the criminal potential within himself.[1] For the others, the police are sheep (*The 39 Steps*) or careless shots (*Strangers on a Train*). In *The Trouble with Harry*, the springy villagers have but a single fear—discovery by the sheriff's deputy, the cold Calvin whose resurrections are confined to antique autos.

Hitchcock usually presents his theme of man's limited freedom in society as a conflict between love and duty. The tension is between love and friendship (a personal duty) in *Downhill, The Manxman*, and *The Farmer's Wife*. In the policeman drama the hero must choose between what his job requires and what his heart (and the lady) deserve: *The Lodger, Blackmail, Young and Innocent, Sabotage, Stage Fright, The Paradine Case*. The spy thrillers adjust the love versus duty debate to the tensions of war, where the hero must choose between his personal love and his international duty: *Foreign Correspondent, Notorious, North by Northwest, Torn Curtain, Topaz*.

Another form of this debate is the conflict between privacy and public involvement. Although the fullest presentation of this theme is in *Rear Window*, it is fully developed in both versions of *The Man Who Knew Too Much, Secret Agent, Sabotage*, and *The Lady Vanishes*. Possibly its earliest statement, however, is in the switchboard operator's scene in *Easy Virtue*.

If love and citizenship are two areas in which Hitchcock afflicts his characters with insecurity, the most dramatic is the family relationship. Richard Roud relates the motif of parental tyranny to the espionage plots: "Even his domestic dramas involve a kind of espionage in the sense that his characters, having discovered frightening realities buried beneath the surface, are obliged to turn spy themselves in order to discover the whole truth. Often it has something to do with the past, the past that comes back to confound the present, to compromise the future."[2] Thus we find so many tyrannical parents in Hitchcock's work, as we have noted in our discussion of *Downhill*. Cruel fathers crop up in *Downhill, Champagne, The Manxman*, and *Waltzes from Vienna* and treacherous father surrogates appear in *Sabotage, The Lady Vanishes,* and *Jamaica Inn* (particularly after Hitchcock's domestication of the villain in the latter). Even where the parent figures are not oppressive or negative, the parent must be abandoned at least temporarily, as in *Young and Innocent*. The family is presented as a fragile, sometimes false and always vulnerable, unit in all Hitchcock's thrillers of the late 1930s. In *Psycho* we have a pervasive feeling of parental oppression by Marion Crane's mother, Sam's father, and the happiness-buying Texas daddy; but in the main thrust of the film, it is the sick son that projects his guilt and inhibitions on his dead mother. In this respect, one of the key Hitchcock films is his comedy *The Trouble with Harry*. A little boy discovers a man dead in the forest; it's his stepfather, unknown to the boy. The dead Harry Warp harmonizes the entire community as each member assumes guilt for his death and they all combine to conceal him. In one shot the corpse is so arranged that his feet and legs seem to complete the body of the little boy (Jerry Mather), whom we see from the waist up. Later we see the captain (Edmund Gwenn) dozing in his rocker; we see all but the captain's feet, but on the wall behind him we see the shadows of the corpse's feet. These two shots prove Roud's point. The dead complete and shape the living, but the living can make their own use of the dead.

Thus we have the fatal "haunting" of Levet in *The Pleasure Garden;* the haunting of the women by their pasts in *Easy Virtue, The Skin Game,* and implicitly in *Blackmail;* and the community's haunting by the past in *Juno and the Paycock*. The individual can succumb to the pressure of his past—or blame it for his own weakness. But the haunting can work as regeneration, as in *The Trouble with Harry*. In *The Farmer's Wife,* too, the dead wife's message provides a new lease on life for her husband, as the lovers' exile will in *The Manxman*. As Roger Thornhill emerges chastened and solidified by his false death in *North by Northwest,* Richard Hannay assumes a responsibility from the death of the strange woman at the start of *The 39 Steps;* so do Ashenden and Elsa from Caypor's death in *Secret Agent*. Even in *Waltzes from Vienna,* Schani descends through the hell of the pastry cook, abandoned suitor, dueling rake, and disowned son, to emerge an Orphic hero. Hitchcock's hero can prove himself by surviving the tribulations that befall him (or that he claims to have inherited).

Conclusion

Even more than the insecurity of his characters, though, Hitchcock exploits the insecurity of his audience. Hence his penchant for subjective shooting angles. His early films abound with attempts to depict the character's mind through what he sees. Hence, too, Hitchcock's penchant for expressionistic devices. The camera and printing tricks of *The Lodger*, the hallucinations of *The Pleasure Garden, Downhill*, and *The Ring*, the swoop in *Young and Innocent*, all serve as unrealistic rhetoric to dramatize the character's state of mind. Hitchcock used images of the concrete to express the reality of the imagination. As Tom Ryall points out, "The openings from *The Lodger* (1926), *The Manxman* (1928), and *Blackmail* (1929) could be documentaries of the newspaper industry, the fishing industry and the police force respectively."[3] Hitchcock's delirium sequences use physical details and memories to document the hot currents of the character's mind. Durgnat's distinction between Hitchcock's "piercing realism" and his "vibrant irrealism" is a merely formal distinction, for Hitchcock's basic interest has always been in how our perceptions reshape our world. His realism constantly shades into the expressionistic imagery and extravagant technical devices by which he conveys emotional realism. His aquarium explosion of Picadilly Circus in *Sabotage* ranks with the best documentary poetics of Vertov.

Hitchcock continually violates his viewer's expectations. Thus we have the romantic deflations in *The Pleasure Garden, Champagne*, and the surprise of Drew's innocence in *The Lodger*. Where the genre requires a fight, Hitchcock will make it comic, as in *Downhill, Number Seventeen, Waltzes from Vienna*, and *The Lady Vanishes*, for there is no room in Hitchcock's vertiginous insecurities for a fight between efficient protagonists.

And from time to time Hitchcock allows his comic spirit, the vision of an anarchic principle at the heart of the universe, to run free. So we get the chaotic consequences of the courtships in *The Farmer's Wife*, the fumbling villains of *The Man Who Knew Too Much*, and old Ben in *Number Seventeen*. Of course, these comedies of chaos are only lighter versions of Hitchcock's essential vision that man's civilization is underpinned by chaos, as we have it in *The Pleasure Garden, Downhill, The Manxman, Champagne, Rich and Strange, Murder!, The 39 Steps*, and *Sabotage*. In his later work, Marion Crane must die because she is played by the star Janet Leigh. For Hitchcock's films are a relentless assault on the viewer's security, as well as his moral complacency.

The English films also prove that from the outset Hitchcock's technical innovations were close to the thematic center of his works. The experimental devices of *The Lodger* and *Blackmail* served those film's basic themes, the preoccupation of the former with the misleading power of perception, and of the latter with the obscurities of communication. Then, too, the scenes with off-camera orchestras in *Juno* and *Murder!* were the pivotal points in the psychological development of the narratives. This observation serves as well when we approach Hitchcock's later work.

For example, his massive orchestration of birds for *The Birds,* a staggering technical challenge, reasserts human enterprise in the face of the film's assault on man's pre-Copernican arrogance. The technical challenge in *Lifeboat* is analogous to its political theme, the fatal isolation of the Allies and their need for a selfless unity. The continuous shooting of *Rope,* which Hitchcock calls his "abandonment of pure cinema"[4] because it eschewed his normal dependence on dramatic editing, grows out of both the title image—something continuous that will tie one up—and the main theme of the film—the continuity of word into deed. A murderous reality is spun out of a musing that was considered safely theoretical. The restricted isolation of the camera in *Rear Window* relates to that film's central concern: the distinction between respecting one's brother's privacy and meeting his needs for a keeper. What Durgnat calls Hitchcock's "calmly hermetic aesthetic satisfaction"[5] might be better considered as his passionate synthesis of idea, irony, and technique. In his achievement of the emotional idea and the intellectual image he meets the aim of that other great film editor, Eisenstein. By so brilliantly uniting idea, image, and emotion, Hitchcock has come to make our nightmares for us with a clarity and thrust no other filmmaker has commanded.

Hitchcock's ironic detachment also explains those moments where we see the seams of his craft, where his technical work seems to be rough. One lesson the British films should teach us is that Hitchcock always knows what he is doing. His plots are carefully crafted. For example, he has Drexler rehearse the orchestra of Strauss Sr. so that their surprise performance of Schani's new waltz will not seem implausible. Where Hitchcock's technical work seems shoddy, what we really have is not a craftsman nodding but an artist extending his resources. Where Hitchcock's craft seems loose, we usually find his technique subserving his content, his literal realism shading into vibrant metaphor.

To put it another way, it is safe to assume that what seems to be a Hitchcock error is likely our failure to work out what he is doing. In *The Lady Vanishes,* for instance, the palpably false opening shot and the unreal proportions of the departing train are typical of how Hitchcock extends his realism into expressionism—only to be charged with poor technique. This liberty came from the German cinema. Thus Fritz Lang inserts a jarring interlude of false scenery into a key moment of *Rancho Notorious.*

William Johnson describes Hitchcock's "failure" in *Marnie:* "It so happens that there are certain departments in which Hitchcock has a patently blind eye. These include the phony backdrops that grate like TV commercials (especially in color), the bits of rapid montage that do not quite fit together, and the two-shots that are held so long that they almost ossify."[6] The false backdrops in *Marnie* are a concise image of the heroine's predicament: she lives in dislocation from her surroundings and from her own past. The false backgrounds provide a physical expression of the disjunction in her mind. Thus the first false back projection scene is her first scene riding Forio, when she is enjoying an artificial respite from her alienation. A rhetorical swell in the music coheres with the rhetoric of the false background. The second is the scene at her mother's home, where the ships' dock is flat and false behind the tenement. The painted ships loom larger than life and paler, imaging the phantom sailor unacknowledged from her past. The false register of both backgrounds move the shots from setting to active symbol. A false front stands behind the Rutland building, a building stripped of its back, or, a foreground unsupported by any integrated backing—like Marnie. Mark varies this motif by giving Marnie a 42,000-dollar ring instead of a family heirloom; he wants her to "have something that never belonged to anyone before." The line jocularly refers to her thefts, poignantly recalls her childhood, without a bed of her own, and provides another instance of an object without a past, a foreground without an integrated background.[7]

Similarly in *Torn Curtain* the palpable falseness of the garden path up which Newman leads Andrews (Hud leads Mary Poppins) undercuts the noble pretense of the hero's ambitious venture. And what Samuels finds to be the "contentless virtuosity" of *North by Northwest*[8] is the heart of the film: the film's central theme/effect is that total dislocation that the complacent hero and the typically injudicious cinema audience share. As the title implies, the film deliberately pursues a fantastical course.

It is similarly wrong to consider Hitchcock a craftsman first and only secondarily, accidentally, an artist. From his first feature on, even through that period of self-conscious "respectable" adaptation, Hitchcock's films had something to say, sometimes an obvious message (*Easy Virtue, Lifeboat*) but more often an integrated theme (*Pleasure Garden, Downhill*). Only because form is content can Hitchcock say, "I am interested not so much in the stories I tell as in the means of telling them."[9] Structure is theme in *Psycho, Vertigo, The Trouble with Harry,* but also as early as *The Pleasure Garden, Downhill,* and *The Ring.*

The early films are also notable for their ambitious conception. Though working in an unacknowledged medium, Hitchcock showed himself a serious artist even then. For Hitchcock, popular film is art. His art is the manipulation of the audience's emotions and fantasy through a variety of felt dangers and thrills, to send his viewers out at the end, calm of mind, all smugness spent, ready to brave the hairline moralities of real life. In his early films Hitchcock also dealt with the responsibilities of the artist. The dance-floor meat markets of *The Pleasure Garden, Downhill,* and *Champagne,* and the squared circle of *The Ring,* are fairly tawdry arenas of human enterprise. But even in those settings it is possible for an individual to achieve art, to fulfill his own creative and expressive impulses and to establish a community with the audience.

The laughing clown in *Blackmail* is Hitchcock's neatest statement about art. Coherent with the fertility of silent montage, the portrait gains new meaning from each juxtaposition, each context, yet it maintains the same detached, ironic stance. When all about are noisy, loud, ambiguous, Hitchcock's mute jester remains silent but eloquent in its accusatory stare, its moral probity, its shameless traditional garb. Beyond the inflections of that painting in the story itself, Hitchcock devotes himself to a career of critical irony independent of changes in mode and medium. The jester retains his acrid independence even when stored in the vaults of the most conventional (whether the police station or the commercial bastions of diversionary cinema).

From *Murder!* we can infer why Hitchcock was never to stray into the esoterica of Bergman, late Godard, or even the Penn of *Mickey One.* For *Murder!* is the drama of an artist who takes his artistic skills and interests into the prosaic business of real life. In *Murder!* some fulfill themselves through art (the theater folk), some conceal themselves in their art (the killer trapeze artist), but the noblest turns his art to the service of humanity (Sir John), to the discovery of truth and self-knowledge and the saving of lives—from prison or from boredom. The West End artist-aristocrat brings his style and sensitivity to serve the hurly-burly world.

For Hitchcock life is a matter of drawing art and reality together. In *Stage Fright,* Eve Gill comes from a separated family, a realistic but theatrical father and a whimsical but prosaic mother. Eve's salvation lies in ordinary Smith, a policeman who plays the piano, and in her own abilities at acting and setting scenes. The clues point to the guilt of the Marlene Dietrich figure, but as her song warns us, she is too lazy to be either criminal or moral. The real villain is the Richard Todd character. He is unable to distinguish pretense (art) from reality, so he kills for Dietrich and is ultimately prepared to kill Eve to prove his own insanity. As befits his unharmonized dichotomy, he is chopped in half by the safety curtain on the theater stage.

For Hitchcock, art comes from life (*Waltzes from Vienna*). But often life emulates art, as in the film parodies in *Sabotage, Saboteur,* and *North by Northwest.* Art at its best will cultivate, free, and invigorate the human spirit, both the emotion and the will, as the cartoon does for Sylvia in *Sabotage.* Sometimes art will deliver a narrow truth, as Mr. Memory does, or deliver one from bondage, as the child is freed by shot or by song in the two versions of *The Man Who Knew Too Much.* But its deeper function is to free the emotions. So Hitchcock often sets up a theatrical situation to expedite a character's physical escape: *The Pleasure Garden, Downhill, The Ring,* the fashion show in *The Lodger,* the auction in *The Skin Game,* Roger Thornhill's auction in *North by Northwest,* the ballet in *Torn Curtain.* In *Vertigo,* even more fully than in *Murder!* and *Stage Fright,* Hitchcock explores the corollary danger: losing one's self in the act of performance. Hence the penultimate image in *Psycho:* Norman Bates dissolves into the skull; the hidden reality overwhelms the muted, visible reality; the role overtakes the self. But like the Todd figure in *Stage Fright,* Norman Bates lost the sense of where life and art were to be distinguished. On this distinction and interplay, Hitchcock thrives for fifty years of splendid filmmaking.

Hitchcock's genius lies in his synthesis of mind, eye, and heart in the dynamic film experience. Some critics prefer the craft of the American period over the English, or the profundity of the later American films over the earlier diversions. William Pechter prefers Hitchcock's detailed realism of the English thrillers and bemoans his loss of contact with his audience in the American period. But even in 1931, C. A. Lejeune was to complain of Hitchcock's lack of "the warm humanity of a director like Griffith" and "Pabst's psychological insight": "His figures are photographic records of synthetic men, not men of flesh-and-blood translated into the medium of the motion picture. . . . The fault with Hitchcock's unreality lies in the fact that he has been essentially a director of realistic films; his subjects have been intimate, detailed and individual. He has dealt with one man, not with men."[10] Pechter harkens back to the golden age of the thrillers and Lejeune cavils at them, but both find Hitchcock naturalistically unsatisfying. Nor could anyone accuse the golden thrillers of realism!

Surely the realism of Hitchcock ranges from the physical settings of *The Lodger* to the imaginative inner worlds of *Downhill* and *The Ring,* and between those poles throughout his later career. Always he is a poet and always he is engaged with the moral and perceptual nature of man. The early films are full of emotionally charged scenes, it is true: the praying scene, the fevered kiss, the final killing in *The Pleasure Garden;* or the private reconciliation of old Strauss in *Waltzes from Vienna.* But there is a well of feeling in Lydia's scenes with the coffee cups in *The Birds* too. The films of Alfred Hitchcock are rich enough, varied enough, yet of a spiritual piece, to make their total enjoyment preferable to any arbitrary choice of preferences. One can watch Hitchcock's British films in order to come to a better understanding of the American ones. But also because they are so good in themselves, so moving, so thoughtful, and so much fun.

APPENDIX: HITCHCOCK'S APPEARANCES

One reason Alfred Hitchcock is the world's best-known film director is surely his signature appearance in many of his films. But there is more than just identification when Hitchcock steps into his frame. He is very careful about how and where he will appear. The manner of his appearance often provides a crucial approach to the meaning of the film.[1]

But not always. Often he appears just for fun, as in his jocular walk-ons in *Mr. and Mrs. Smith, Spellbound,* and *The Paradine Case.* When he appears in Micawberish garb in *Under Capricorn* there is a delightful incongruity about his costume that no one else in the scene has. For we expect actors to wear costumes. Hitchcock we don't take as an actor but as a man puckishly playing dress up.[2]

This is true of all the Hitchcock appearances. Their first effect is comedy, our chuckle of recognition as we spot the chubby elf and pride that we caught the in-joke.

More seriously, the Hitchcock appearances cause a ripple in the narrative flow, a disturbance in the film's surface.[3] The other people in the film are actors playing roles. Hitchcock is himself, not to be identified by his character within this film but known from his association in other films and (later) from the impudent persona of his television series. The intrusion of this real person into the fictional setting heightens the tension between *our* reality and the reality presumed by the fiction. It also provides a frisson, a jarring surprise of the sort that Hitchcock loves to mine his films with, say, by having a cigarette butted in a jar of cold cream or in a fried egg.

Hitchcock's appearances also remind us that we are watching a film, that we are being manipulated by a rhetorician who is so skillful and so confident that he can remind us that we are in his hands without fear of losing his hold. In this respect Hitchcock's appearances work like the frequent references to the idea of the play in Elizabethan drama.

These effects give a certain prominence, an emphasis, to the scenes in which Hitchcock appears. For example, Hitchcock's casual walk past the camera in *Murder!* occurs just after the landlady has threatened to send her son to jail for punishment. As Hitchcock was as a child once sent to the police for brief jailing, his appearance personalizes the anecdote in the film.

The remainder of Hitchcock's appearances are here discussed according to their two general functions. In the first group the appearances work in an emblematic way, encapsulating major themes from the film as a whole. Here Hitchcock gives a small scene or activity prominence by doing it himself. In the second group his appearances depend on our taking him as the creator of the world in the film, the maker, the god. In this latter category, Hitchcock's appearances anticipate—or inspire—Godard's functioning as informer in *A bout de souffle* and as questioner/reporter/prober in later films.

1. The Emblematic

In *Blackmail* we have a full frontal view of Hitchcock reading a book in the underground, while the heroes sit in profile on the right. The placement on the screen and the fullness of Hitchcock's face gives this bit player an emphasis denied the stars. The artist, the blackmailer, and the painted clown will be peripheral figures that again displace the heroes, giving us a wider worldview than they have.

More importantly: Hitchcock is trying to read a book but is disturbed by a noisy and pesky little boy. The reading is the important thing. Throughout the film Hitchcock systematically explores the limitations of aural communication, contrasting the new sound film with the venerable (and read) silent film. Hitchcock's reading relates to the classical culture represented by the British Museum, with its huge, silent gods, through which the final chase is run. The traditional—reading, culture, the silent film, a morality as rigorous and impersonal as Scotland Yard—is tested by the more flexible and pragmatic modes and morality of the modern. Hitchcock in the underground lends his weight to the traditional—and finds the new rather needlessly noisy.[4]

As Hitchcock walks by in *The 39 Steps* he tosses away a paper wrapper. In the background Hannay and the mysterious lady mount a bus, which happens to advertise an insurance company called "Cooperative Permanent." Hannay's relation to the lady will prove cooperative if not permanent. The paradox of brief permanence Hitchcock catches in his own function of careless disposal. Further, Hannay figures out the mystery later when he realizes Mr. Memory's usefulness as a spy. Able to commit everything to his memory, he can dispose of the need for paper. Hitchcock's appearance replays two elements in the plot.

The Lady Vanishes is about a girl's growth from self-centered apathy to commitment, social and political. Hitchcock appears in the train station, smoking, lunch pail in hand, giving a prominent shrug of unconcern. He embodies the apathy Iris has overcome to save Miss Froy and must overcome again to leave her stodgy fiancé and marry Gilbert.

In *Rebecca* Hitchcock is outside the phone booth while George Sanders chatters on inside and a bobby eyes Hitchcock suspiciously. The phone booth is Hitchcock's Manderley; he has the heroine's paranoia and sense of exclusion from Sanders's world. "In a sense the picture is the story of a house," Hitchcock tells Truffaut. "The house was one of the three key characters of the picture."[5] His phone booth is a comic miniature of the house, and Hitchcock a parody of the heroine.

In *Foreign Correspondent* we have two shots of Hitchcock approaching the camera, reading a paper, while hero Joel MacRae hears someone call Van Meer, the man he wants to interview. We are held on the image of an insignificant character while the important figure is introduced off camera. Our first reaction might be to mistake Hitchcock for Van Meer. This prepares us for the deceptive impressions we are later to have of the Van Meer impersonator, the Herbert Marshall character, and MacRae's mistaking of Laraine Day's identity—a pattern of mistaken judgment and identification. As well, Hitchcock appears as one of the common people, the "little people" over whom Van Meer sentimentalizes, and MacRae later with Ben Hecht's propaganda message, the "well-meaning amateurs" that the Day figure seeks to mobilize into political power. Hitchcock's citizen reads the newspaper that apathetic newspapermen like the Robert Benchley character are wasting, and that politically involved, selfless newspapermen like the hero will exploit to win the war.

In *Shadow of a Doubt* Hitchcock is a bridge player on the train that is bringing Uncle Charlie to Charlie, in miraculous answer to her prayer. Hitchcock holds a hand of thirteen spades, another miracle! Like Uncle Charlie, Hitchcock has a hand full of the images of death, a completely self-contained hand, that seems to need no help to complete it, and his total power over the two matrons against whom he is playing is diagnosed by his partner as sickness! One of the film's themes is the illusion of self-sufficiency. The minor characters babble along in their own worlds. The father's friend remarks that one can't club oneself to death. Self-containment is impossible. Charlie can win a debate single-handedly but needs Uncle Charlie's opposite pole to awaken her moral sense. The hand of thirteen spades needs a partner to pass on the bid of seven spades and a team to play against for its power to be fulfilled. No hand is an island.

In *Lifeboat* Hitchcock appears in before and after pictures in a reducing ad in a newspaper that William Bendix picks out of the sea. The product, Reduco, is an "obesity slayer"—a nice touch that only the still reveals. One of the film's basic themes is a reduction of the characters to their human essence, stripped of their pretensions and their social props. So Smith/Schmidt is stripped of his simple Americanism, his carefree social life, and his leg; he finally removes his own weight from the boat. The Tallulah Bankhead figure loses all her supports and remarks when the sail dumps her typewriter, "Little by little I'm being stripped of all my earthly possessions." The stripping brings her the love of the John Hodiak Marxist. In their final reduction the civilized allies turn on the German navigator. Their naked viciousness surprises us but is what the second German survivor expects.

Further, we see Hitchcock while Bendix reads a news story about a similar case of naval survivors. The fictional character reads what purports to be a factual story; the "factual" image of Hitchcock that backs the story lends credence to the fiction of the film itself. As an inveterate reader of "the other stuff" on filmed newspaper pages, I can report that the Reduco page also advertizes two kinds of coats (Hodiak cloth and Bankhead fur) and a shampoo, Dawn Glory. It also features two headlines, one of loss ("Fire destroys state arsenal") and one of cooperative benefit ("Prominent citizens together with civic bodies combine to make city park a success").

In *Strangers on a Train* Hitchcock puts a bass fiddle on the train, then mounts himself. (He carries one off in *The Paradine Case.*) This parodies the base fiddle that Bruno will put to Guy on the train. There is a visual pun as well as this verbal one: the bass is large and round, a double to Hitchcock's build, as the angle of the shot emphasizes. The man and his instrument parallel the complex of X shapes in the film, by which Bruno and Guy, killer and instrument, evil and innocent, madness and civilized, are defined as the inevitable halves of the human unity.

"What a murderous thug I look," remarks Swan at his Cambridge reunion photo in *Dial M for Murder*. But so does Hitchcock, seated in the same photograph. Here Hitchcock aligns himself against the husband and with the adulterer, in another of his playful forays into the uncertainties of innocence. And he accepts association with the criminal, albeit the Cambridge crowd of criminals. That he chooses a flat image for himself in his 3-D movie recalls his *Blackmail* association with the conservative tradition in his art.

In *To Catch a Thief* Hitchcock is on the bus with the fleeing Cary Grant, here an innocent suspected wrongly of crime. In *North by Northwest* the elements of Grant, bus, and Hitchcock work differently. After the credits Hitchcock tries to get on the bus but the doors slam in his face. The Grant figure is more culpable here than in *To Catch a Thief*, playing a man whose initials are ROT, the O signifying nothing, a hollow core. Hitchcock is the ordinary victim, the norm, in his defeat by the bus, in contrast to Grant's Thornhill, who steals other people's cabs. The opposition of simple Hitchcock to smoothie Thornhill is confirmed with a vengeance when the bus leaves Thornhill on the open plain. Where Hitchcock stood left of the bus in the opening, here the doors that close on Grant leave him standing on the right, oppressed by the weight of the bus and then by its—dangerous—vacated space.[6]

In the second *The Man Who Knew Too Much* Hitchcock stands with his stars to watch the Arab acrobats perform. The doer watches. Later the Doris Day figure, a retired singer, will revive her act to recover her son.

Appendix

In *Psycho* Hitchcock is another big-hatted Texan with his back to Marion Crane and the real estate office. He appears in the middle of the dissolve from Loomis despondent in their hotel room to the office, Marion rushing back to work. Hitchcock bridges two of the character's worlds, as he does in *Shadow of a Doubt* and *Vertigo*. Given the pattern of oppressive parents in *Psycho*, Hitchcock here might seem an insensitive father figure. Conversely, his disinterestedness stands out nobly in a landscape that teems with voyeurs, snoops, and spies.

In *The Birds* Hitchcock leaves the pet shop with two white dogs on a leash, the personification of complacent man whose dominance over the animal world is about to be upset.

In these last three films Hitchcock is not just a character emblematic of the film as a whole. Already his meaning depends on our taking him as the maker of the film. The uncaring Texan in *Psycho* and the man with a petty power over animals in *The Birds* assume a chilling dimension when they are taken as maker, not man. The black vision of both films require they be.

2. The Maker

Hitchcock's first appearance was in a role analogous to his function as director. In *The Lodger* Hitchcock is a newspaperman dispatching reporters to cover the murders. He later appears in the mob out to kill the hero. There he moves from peripheral figure to standing front and center. Initially he feeds the public frenzy over the Avenger, but in his last appearance the madness subsides. The Christ-image of the hero impaled on the fence supports our sense of the maker witnessing his hero's trial.

In *Young and Innocent* Hitchcock is a clumsy still photographer futilely trying to motion people out of the way, while the hero escapes custody. This maker seems out of control of his characters and his craft. Colonel Burgoyne is in a similar situation, as the maker and director of the titular heroine. Colonel Burgoyne at the end finds his remaining power over his daughter is light, not forced. But the filmmaker reasserts his power at the end with that bravado swoop in on the drummer's eye.

In *Notorious* Hitchcock is nonchalantly drinking champagne, but each glass hastens the moment when the waiter, to get more champagne, will go for the key that the heroine has stolen. By his famous appetite, then, the maker hastens his heroes' moment of truth.

When Hitchcock passes Jane Wyman in the street in *Stage Fright,* he turns to give her a second look because she is talking to herself. "I'm Doris Tinsdale," says Eve Gill (Jane Wyman), going to spy on Charlotte Inwood (Marlene Dietrich) as her maid. The director catches his character as she shifts into a role-within-a-role. His appearance heightens the theatricality of her action. As citizen, Hitchcock spies on the spy. As maker, he watches as his creature seems to assume a role and a falseness for which she was not intended. But only seems: it is all necessary for his larger design to be fulfilled.

In *Rear Window* Hitchcock fixes the clock on the composer's mantle. He is helping the character find his right time, his rhythm, necessary both as composer and as actor. So Hitchcock is there again as director. And as citizen, he is the first character in that tenement to help another.

In *Vertigo* Hitchcock walks across the screen between the scene where James Stewart totters off the kitchen chair and the scene where Stewart is high in an office building, where his old friend asks him to follow Kim Novak. The maker enjoys an easy, level walk and a confidence denied his characters, with their various uncertainties of footing, ambitions, and vertigos.

In *Marnie* Hitchcock is the heroine's maker and uncoverer. He steps out into the hallway behind her like a rather plump skeleton from her closet. Throughout the film, her threats and reminders loom up from the left.[7]

Hitchcock's appearance in a hotel lobby in *Torn Curtain,* changing an obviously wet baby from one knee to the other, has excited some wags to comment that the master has been embarrassed by his offspring. But there is an alternative. The citizen shifting a child parallels the hero's theft of the old East German scientist's brainchild. But again this citizen is the god of this film, the maker of everyone and everything there. So he registers embarrassment, even befoulment, by the doings of his creatures, most notably as the romantic heroes sneak their selfish and costly quest past our sentimental sympathy. Hitchcock's god in the lobby reminds us that even deeds of amoral derring-do in the cold war

Appendix

may be witnessed by a higher judge. As someone may be watching us watch James Stewart watch Miss Lonely-Hearts swallowing her pills and Miss Torso entertaining hers.

In *Topaz* Hitchcock obviously replies to his critics. He has himself wheeled into a lobby by a nurse, the image of the helpless old man that the reviewers considered him. Then he blithely rises and walks off on his own.

In *Frenzy* Hitchcock is the only skeptic in the crowd listening to the English politician's promise that the poisons in man and in the environment can be eliminated. Hitchcock knows—and his ensuing story demonstrates—otherwise. His Inspector Oxford solves the case by recognizing in himself the force and the limits of the convicted man's furious emotion.

In *Family Plot* Hitchcock is a shadow behind the pebbled glass door of the Registry of Births and Deaths. Behind the Deaths, Hitchcock admonishes the figure behind the Births. Where one character works with clear gems and the other with a crystal ball, the maker is to be perceived only through a glass, darkly.

Of course, Hitchcock's most straightforward appearance as himself was at the beginning of *The Wrong Man,* where he appeared in a prologue to introduce his uniquely factual story of Manny Balestrero.

Hitchcock is most clearly God the Maker in his most theological film, *I Confess.* This film opens with Hitchcock walking across the high city horizon, right to left, sharply silhouetted against the cloudy night sky. The one-way traffic signs in the opening sequence all point left to right, but Hitchcock strides imperiously against the flow, against the mortal grain, sublimely aloof from the worries, regulations, ambivalences, and rigidities by which man—particularly when he tries to find his God—is plagued.[8]

There is even a telling example of a nonappearance by Hitchcock. At the tea party in *Rope,* Mrs. Atwater enthuses about Cary Grant:

> He was thrilling in that new thing with Bergman. What was it called now? "The Something of Something." No, no, that was the other one. This was just plain "Something."

The "Something" is likely *Notorious*. Here Hitchcock establishes his presence by citing his other work. The maker is known by his work, not by his appearance, his self. Of course, one of the film's most important themes is the distinction between the morality of a word and the morality of a deed. Rupert is horrified to find his words turned to deed:

> You've thrown my own words right back in my face, Brandon. You were right too. If nothing else a man should stand by his word. But you've given my words a meaning that I never dreamed of.

Rupert's consolation is that he never acted on the ideas he espoused in debate, so he can still act as society's agent in the murderers' arrest and prosecution. As Rupert is judged by his deeds, not by his words, Hitchcock appears here only by his work.

Hitchcock's appearances in his films, however casually he may seem to slip in, serve a variety of dramatic, emblematic or thematic purposes. For that matter, so do almost all the other details in his carefully preplotted films. Hitchcock's appearances remind us that he is an irrepressible ironist, playfully proffering an image of himself in his work that is not necessarily a direct reflection of himself. He is also the cocky Cockney whom movies gave the opportunity to become a creative god, to stand apart from the fictions and the follies of his successful, complacent characters, and point—like the clown in *Black-mail*—in silent, eloquent accusation.

NOTES

Introduction

1. Eric Rohmer and Claude Chabrol, *Hitchcock,* Classiques du cinema, vol. 6 (Paris, 1957), 42.

2. Robin Wood, *Hitchcock's Films* (London, 1965).

3. Kirk Bond, "The Other Alfred Hitchcock," *Film Culture* 5, no. 41 (1966): 30–35; John M. Smith, "Conservative Individualism: A Selection of English Hitchcock," *Screen* (Autumn 1972): 51, 70.

4. Rachael Low, *The History of the British Film: 1918–1929* (London, 1971), 307–8.

5. E.g., John Russell Taylor, "Hitchcock's Fifty Years in Film," *Times* (London), July 19, 1975, 7; Carol Wakarska, "Hitch at the Helm," *Village Voice,* September 8, 1975, 109–11, 144; Andrew Meyer, "The 'Plot' Thickens," *Film Comment* (September–October 1975): 21, 23.

6. Louis Levy, *Music for the Movies* (London, 1948), 147.

7. Alfred Hitchcock, *Henley,* June 1919; reprinted in *Sight and Sound* (Autumn 1970): 186–87.

8. Raymond Durgnat, *The Strange Case of Alfred Hitchcock* (London, 1974).

The Pleasure Garden

1. Francois Truffaut, *Hitchcock* (1967; London, 1969), 31.

2. Hitchcock, interview by Herb Lightman, "Hitchcock Talks about Lights, Camera, Action," *American Cinematographer* (May 1967): 333.

3. "Sheer Stroheim," observes Bond. He has a point.

4. Durgnat, *Strange Case of Alfred Hitchcock,* 67.

5. The denial of the X in *Shadow of a Doubt* is also imaged forth in an early overhead shot of the streets, as Uncle Charlie eludes the detectives. The shot presents two parallel sidewalks with complementary sections in gray and white, i.e., the gray section of one side is matched by a white section across on

the other side. The emblem is of white and gray, innocence and shadow, running in a parallel order but not intersecting. The two Charlies are parallel, one innocent and one guilty, without the kind of intersection that Bruno and Guy make in *Strangers on a Train,* where Bruno acts out Guy's wish. There is even little physical touch between the Charlies, rather the telepathic contact of parallel but detached sensibilities. The Charlies form a parallel continuum, not a cross. For a harsher view of Charlie, see Charles T. Samuels, *Encountering Directors* (New York, 1972), 238.

      6. Patricia Highsmith, *Strangers on a Train* (1950; New York, 1974), 189. Ronald Christ is simply wrong to claim that "the emphasis of the movie [is] in contrast to the book, where the word 'crisscross' occurs only incidentally in the description of a fence" ("*Strangers on a Train:* The Pattern of Encounter," in *Focus on Hitchcock,* ed. Albert LaValley [Englewood Cliffs, NJ, 1972], 107).

      7. Similarly, Hitchcock places crossed swords over the Burgoyne hearth in *Young and Innocent,* where again an innocent and a guilty cross, two men intersecting at the woman who supports them. As a verbal equivalent, Hitchcock has the hero Tisdall confuse his pseudonym Beachcroft Manningtree as Beachtree Manningcroft, in chatting with the aunt at the birthday party.

      The X is a more important emblem in Hitchcock's *Mr. and Mrs. Smith* (1941), where the heroine's skis are crossed into an X for the last shot of the film. The X image of the skis works as a miniature of the heroes' marriage. The film opens with the Smiths together but estranged, having set the habit of staying together in their bedroom until any disagreement between them is settled. Their marriage found nullified, they go through separate courtships before Mrs. Smith accepts Mr. Smith again, at a remote ski resort. There the skis are an image of connection of transport to the main inn, but also of remoteness from it, as marriage connects the partners by detaching them from others. Mrs. Smith uses her captivity in the skis as her way of succumbing to Mr. Smith's finally forceful courtship.

      8. Bond, "The Other Alfred Hitchcock," 32. Smith also gives the film a full reading ("Conservative Individualism," 53, 54). George Pearson refers to "Hitchcock's *The Lodger* with Ivor Novello, and his *Pleasure Garden* which revealed even more his sure sense of screen values" (*Flashback* [London, 1957], 144). Low admits the film has "a banal story, but Hitchcock's pace and technique were already evident and he was considered promising" (*The History of the British Film,* 167). Hitchcock calls the film "Melodramatic. But there were several interesting scenes in it" (Truffaut, *Hitchcock, 36*). He goes on to detail the financial problems he had in the filming, the same stories (except for the periodic swim anecdote) that he unloaded in "My Screen Memories" for John K. Newnham (*Film Weekly,* May 2, 1936, 16–18). For

Durgnat it is a "rather impersonal film, too steeped in period uncharm to be very bearable now" (*Strange Case of Alfred Hitchcock,* 67). Somehow Rohmer and Chabrol have the native mistress kill herself and the husband die in an earthquake (*Hitchcock,* 14)! Peter Noble produces the following review from *Bioscope* (March 25, 1926): "A powerful and interesting story, this has been well adapted to the screen, and admirable acting and masterly production all combine to make this a film of outstanding merit. The story is clearly and logically constructed, the subtitling is concise and to the point, and the dramatic interest is held to the last minute. The scenes during Patsy's honeymoon on Lake Como, photographed by Baron Ventigmilia, present enchanting pictures and assist the dramatic appeal of the story. As Alfred Hitchcock's first production, this promises well for future efforts" ("Index to the Work of Alfred Hitchcock," *Sight and Sound,* suppl. no. 18 [May 1949]: 6).

    9. Peter Bogdanovich, *The Cinema of Alfred Hitchcock* (New York, 1963), 4.

The Mountain Eagle

    1. Noble, "Index to the Work of Alfred Hitchcock," 7.

The Lodger

    1. "*The Lodger* was the first true 'Hitchcock movie,'" Hitchcock tells Truffaut (*Hitchcock,* 48).

    2. The film follows the novel rather closely. It omits the domestic entanglement (Daisy is Mr. Bunting's daughter from a previous marriage in the novel) and the family trip to the Yard horror chamber. Its main divagation is the ending, where in the novel the lodger is clearly the killer. The same story was remade in 1933 by Maurice Elvey again with Ivor Novello, by John Brahm in 1944 with Laird Cregar, and by Hugo Fregonese in 1954 with Jack Palance as the man in the attic.

    3. Liam O'Leary repeats the frequent error that the film reveals Hitchcock's "early inclination towards the psychological thriller" (*The Silent Cinema* [New York, 1963], 109). Lindsay Anderson, in his famous *Sequence* article on Hitchcock, finds *The Lodger* "again a melodrama, but biased this time towards violence rather than romance. . . . This improbable development of the plot is partially disguised by the conscientious realism of its locales and characters" ("Hitchcock," in LaValley, *Focus on Hitchcock,* 49). My edition of the novel—the Four Square Paperback from 1966—makes the same mistake on its jacket blurb: "This spine-chiller is a psychological study of a mass murderer which concerns itself with the burning question 'Why?'"

It does nothing of the sort. But on the film, Alan Casty makes the same irrelevant claim: "*The Lodger,* dealing with the sexual psychopathy of Jack the Ripper, is clothed in the moodiness of German Expressionism but concerns itself very little with inner tensions" (*Development of the Film* [New York, 1973], 218). Somewhat closer is Roger Manvell's speculation on the "very whimsical air about *The Lodger,*" though he attributes it to the "fancy world" that silent films were expected to provide ("Revaluations 8: *The Lodger,*" *Sight and Sound* [January 1951]: 377–78).

4. Hitchcock tells Samuels, "All such touches were substitutes for sound. I wanted to show, by means of that shot, that the woman downstairs was probably hearing a creaking noise" (*Encountering Directors,* 239); "Today we would substitute sound for that. Although I think that the handrail shot would be worthy of today in addition to sound" (Bogdanovich, *Cinema of Alfred Hitchcock,* 11).

5. Marie Belloc Lowndes, *The Lodger* (1913; London, 1966), 11, 34, 84.

6. Ivor Montagu, *Film World: A Guide to Cinema* (Harmondsworth, UK, 1964), 127–28.

7. As Hitchcock told his listeners at the American Film Institute, "I'm a believer in the subjective, that is, playing a scene from the point of view of an individual. But if you do your master, and then you go in close up that's like the theatre to me. That's like sitting in the orchestra looking at a play—purely objectively. Whereas we have the power in film to get right into the mind of a character" (*Dialogue on Film* 2, no. 1:11). Similarly in *Marnie* Hitchcock films Marnie's fall from her horse from different angles, repeating the fragment of the incident on the screen.

8. On the lit hair, see Truffaut, *Hitchcock,* 49. The illuminated milk in *Suspicion* has a source in the novel, where Johnny brings Lina "a glass of milk-and-soda on a little tray," with tears in his eyes and the untraceable poison alkali in the milk (Francis Iles, *Before the Fact* [New York, 1932]).

9. On the star casting problems in *The Lodger,* see Truffaut, *Hitchcock,* 48–49. In *Suspicion,* the body of the novel grows out of its second sentence: "Lina Aysgarth had lived with her husband for nearly eight years before she realized that she was married to a murderer." The film develops out of the third sentence: "Suspicion is a tenuous thing, so impalpable that the exact moment of its birth is not so easy to determine" (Iles, *Before the Fact,* 1). In both *Suspicion* and *The Lodger* Hitchcock enjoys a doubling of the suspense by retaining the possibility of the suspect's innocence: Is he? Will he? By centering on the victim's mind instead of on the murderer's, he amplifies the fright and identification of the audience, doubling the suspense.

10. Taylor typifies the modern impatience with the film: "Allowances have to be made; to enjoy it fully requires an exercise of deliberate

'thinking back,' to see it in the context of the British cinema of the time (not to mention a willingness even in this context to disregard the hamminess of Ivor Novello's performance) . . . it is all rather too self-conscious, too determined to impress" (*Cinema Eye, Cinema Ear* [London, 1964], 172–73); Manvell's sense of the film's "whimsy" is picked up by Bond's, "I cannot escape the thought that this film at any rate is a burlesque" ("The Other Alfred Hitchcock," 34). Cf. Rohmer and Chabrol, *Hitchcock,* 16–17. For a full discussion of the film, see Charles Higham, "Hitchcock's World," *Film Quarterly* (Winter 1962–63): 3–16.

11. "For the film's theme is panic as a social network—the angry crowd is its final, climactic crystallisation" (Durgnat, *Strange Case of Alfred Hitchcock,* 70).

12. Samuels, *Encountering Directors,* 239. Of course, Hitchcock can never be taken at face value. He tells Catherine de la Roche, "It's just possible that I made some passing reference to the effect that this figure (Drew) resembled Christ's when being taken down from the cross. But the scene was not intended to suggest this. . . . No—what interested me was the drama of being handcuffed" ("Conversation with Hitchcock," *Sight and Sound* [Winter 1955–56]: 158). When Truffaut raises the Christian possibilities of the same scene, Hitchcock goes along: "Naturally, that thought did occur to me" (*Hitchcock,* 54).

Downhill

1. This joke about the bun in the oven must have lurked in Hitchcock's mind. Similarly much of the casual imagery in *Psycho* and the interjected sexuality of the central figure may well derive from the traditional joke about the lively Bates family: Mr. Bates, Mrs. Bates, and their little son Master Bates.

The waitress's accusation of Roddy includes the possibility that she is charging him with theft from the cash register. This seems the excuse provided for the family audience. Her reference to his father suggests a paternity suit.

2. The line was apparently risible even on its first run. As his biographer, Peter Noble, reports, "Ivor told me that this became a catch phrase at Islington Studios for years afterwards" (*Ivor Novello,* 3rd ed. [London, 1951], 131).

3. Rohmer and Chabrol go further: "La déchéance du heros suit une direction: du Nord au Sud. Littéralement, il descend. Cette idée est exprimée très clairement par la mise en scène dans la séquence subjective du délire à Marseille, et qui n' est qu' escaliers et passerelles descendues: illustration, par

Notes

la virtuosité technique, d'une idée psychologique et morale, exemple excellent de l'interdépendance de la forme et du fond. . . . Notons seulement que dans *Down Hill*, le collège est traité en travelling-avant horizontal, la boîte de nuit en une série de panoramiques exprimant une stagnation, et le port de Marseille en travelling vertical dehaut en bas" (*Hitchcock*, 19).

4. Hitchcock has a rosy memory of the poetess. "I showed a woman seducing a younger man," he tells Truffaut (*Hitchcock*, 57). Roddy is immediately repelled by her, but in Hitchcock's memory, "She is a lady of a certain age, but quite elegant, and he finds her very attractive until daybreak." Rohmer and Chabrol suggest the cabaret scene, with its avid, terrifying woman, anticipates the monstrous females seen and cited in *Shadow of a Doubt*: "Nous verrons pourtant que cette misogynie n'est qu'apparente et tire son origine d'une tres haute conception de la femme" (*Hitchcock*, 18).

5. Montagu, *Film World*, 141; cf. Alan Lovell, "Interview: Ivor Montagu," *Screen* (Autumn 1972): 80.

6. On the "lie" in *Stage Fright*, see Durgnat, *Strange Case of Alfred Hitchcock*, 215–16.

7. Siegfried Kracauer, *Theory of Film: The Redemption of Physical Reality* (1960; London, 1965), 276.

8. Hitchcock, interview by Charles Higham and Joel Greenberg, *The Celluloid Muse: Hollywood Directors Speak* (New York, 1969), 103. Hitchcock describes the *Downhill* delirium to Truffaut: "No dissolve, just straight cutting. . . . In those days dreams were always dissolves and they were always blurred. Though it was difficult, I tried to embody the dream in the reality, in solid, unblurred images" (*Hitchcock*, 57).

9. Jack Foley reflects on "the relationship between Hitchcock's 'innocent criminals' and his many Oedipal, mother-dominated characters. . . . One is guilty of sexuality but the guilt may be taken upon oneself (in which case the hero is a criminal) or projected onto others (in which case the hero is falsely accused). In a film like *Shadow of a Doubt* desire for the mother gets transmuted into desire for the father (or father figure: Uncle Charlie, the girl's real father being hopelessly sexless)" ("Notes on *Hans Christian Anderson* and the Oedipus Complex," *Journal of Popular Film* 4, no. 2:123). Cf. Charles Baxter, "*Cherchez la mere*: Hitchcock's Troubled Children," *Ethos* (University at Buffalo, SUNY), February 27, 1975, 13–17.

10. Durgnat, *Strange Case of Alfred Hitchcock*, 169.

11. Andre Bazin, "Hitchcock vs. Hitchcock," *Cahiers du cinéma* (English), no. 2:65.

12. Hitchcock tells the story in Charles Davy, ed., *Footnotes to the Film* (London, 1938), 14–15.

13. Low, *The History of the British Film*, 258–59.

14. Robert Mundy parallels *Downhill* to *I Confess,* arguing that "it was not the Catholic element of the scenario which appealed to Hitchcock. . . . The view of Hitchcock as a Catholic moralist is untenable when *I Confess* is compared to *Downhill:* public school morality is assigned the same significance as Catholic dogma. The situation where guilt is transferred is what appeals to Hitchcock, and this situation is not *necessarily* charged with any religious significance" ("Another Look at Hitchcock," *Cinema* [August 1970]: 11).

Easy Virtue

1. Durgnat, *Strange Case of Alfred Hitchcock,* 77.

2. William K. Everson's "Rediscovery: *Easy Virtue*" is the only discussion of the film I have found. It appears in *Films in Review* (May 1975): 293–97.

3. Noble, "Index to the Work of Alfred Hitchcock," 9–10; Rohmer and Chabrol, *Hitchcock,* 19, 20.

4. The play *Easy Virtue* appears in *Curtain Calls* (New York, 1940), 377–473.

5. Hitchcock confesses his abhorrence of the line in Truffaut, *Hitchcock,* 57–58.

The Ring

1. On its release, *The Ring* was given the following notice in *Bioscope:* "Hitchcock has directed one of the finest films that has ever been presented to the public—a film that would satisfy the most critical tastes. We have a truthful and unglamorised picture of hard-working fairground folk, and also of the boxing ring, presented with a richness of essential detail and the skilful use of every artistic and technical device that makes a picture of outstanding merit. Jack Cox's photography is admirable. This is the most magnificent British film ever made" (October 6, 1927). Taylor considers *The Ring* "arguably Hitchcock's best silent film, since there at least the technique is all properly functional and the aim unpretentious" (*Cinema Eye, Cinema Ear,* 173). Bond finds it "a beautiful and complex story of human nature" ("The Other Alfred Hitchcock," 32).

2. Anthony Asquith adapted the device of superimposed titles to suggest speed in *Shooting Stars* (1928).

3. Hitchcock made capital of the wedding ring in *Rear Window* as well. See Durgnat, *Strange Case of Alfred Hitchcock,* 238–39; Truffaut, *Hitchcock,* 274–76. In *Shadow of a Doubt,* as Charlie hums the Merry Widow Waltz

in her room, Uncle Charlie blows smoke rings (!) in his. She feels her wrists, sore from Uncle Charlie's grip, as she homes in on the detective's suspicions: "Are you trying to tell me I shouldn't think so highly of my Uncle Charlie?"

4. Hitchcock claims that his starting point in *The Ring* was the formality of the English spectators at boxing matches and the pouring of champagne on the fighters before the last round (Bogdanovich, *Cinema of Alfred Hitchcock,* 12). Hitchcock usually mentions the fresh round card, the posters, and the flattening champagne at his best "touches" in the film (see, e.g., Truffaut, *Hitchcock,* 59–61; Davy, *Footnotes to the Film,* 10, 11). *Close-Up* found the poster device laborious and pretentious (qtd. in Low, *The History of the British Film,* 236).

The Farmer's Wife

1. Truffaut, *Hitchcock,* 61; Eden Phillpotts, *Widecombe Fair* (London, n.d.), 8.

2. Bond, "The Other Alfred Hitchcock," 32–33; Smith, "Conservative Individualism," 57–58; Durgnat, *Strange Case of Alfred Hitchcock,* 82–83. At its original release the film received the following review in *Bioscope:* "Hitchcock's artistic and skilful production of Eden Phillpotts' play gives an excellent picture of rural life thirty or forty years ago. It is delightful entertainment" (March 8, 1928).

As usual, Hitchcock's own remarks must be taken with a pound of salt. He accepts Truffaut's compliments on the unstaginess of the film: "What you mean is that the camera is inside the action" (*Hitchcock,* 62–63). But in his interview with Bogdanovich, Hitchcock calls the film "merely a photograph of a stage play with lots of titles instead of dialogue. It was just a routine job" (*Cinema of Alfred Hitchcock,* 12).

3. Eden Phillpotts, *The Farmers Wife* (London, 1929), 6.

4. Ibid., 9, 19, 39.

Champagne

1. Truffaut, *Hitchcock,* 63.

2. Bogdanovich, *Cinema of Alfred Hitchcock,* 12

3. Truffaut, *Hitchcock,* 63–64.

4. Bogdanovich, *Cinema of Alfred Hitchcock,* 12

5. Hitchcock often emphasizes his naivete. See particularly his interview with Oriana Fallaci, "Mr. Chastity," in *Limelighters* (London, 1968), 83–99.

6. Truffaut, *Hitchcock,* 64.

7. In Samuels, *Encountering Directors*, 233. The drugged milk further anticipates the illuminated milk Cary Grant brings Joan Fontaine in *Suspicion*, with its archetypal associations with innocence, nourishment, security, etc.

The Manxman

1. Hall Caine, *The Manxman* (London, n.d.). All quotations from this novel will hereafter be cited in the text. The novel was published in August 1894, and had been reprinted thirty-six times by 1924 and translated into German, Danish, and Swedish. The moral—"What shall it profit . . ."—appears on the title page of the novel but not in the body.

2. Taylor, *Cinema Eye, Cinema Ear*, 172.

3. Rohmer and Chabrol, *Hitchcock*, 20, 25, 26–27.

4. Truffaut, *Hitchcock*, 66.

5. Bogdanovich, *Cinema of Alfred Hitchcock*, 12.

6. Noble, "Index to the Work of Alfred Hitchcock," 12.

7. Bond, "The Other Alfred Hitchcock," 33.

8. In a talk on the BBC Home Service, *The Time of My Life*, recorded on July 30, 1966, Hitchcock commented on the fact that all but five of his first forty-five leading ladies were blondes: "I really think it's . . . it's not my attraction to them. I think it's traditional. You see, it seems to me that—er—ever since the beginning of movies the leading lady, I suppose starting with Mary Pickford, was the blonde and the leading man has always been a brunette. The only difference is that in many cases—er—my leading ladies are a little more svelte. They don't have their sex hanging around them like baubles. In other words the obvious blonde, even the Marilyn Monroe type—er—wouldn't appeal to me at all because there is no mystery in the sex. The sex is so obvious and I would rather have the sex discovered. I suppose the first was Madeleine Carroll in *39 Steps*. . . . As I used to call Grace [Kelly] afterwards, the snowcovered volcano." A transcript of the program is available in the library of the British Film Institute. There is a sensitive discussion of Hitchcock's blondes and brunettes in Molly Haskell, *From Reverence to Rape* (New York, 1974), 349–54.

9. In *Saboteur* the mother of Barry's dead friend has a lampshade that is decorated with an eagle-and-star design, a rather vulgar expression of the family's virtue and patriotism in contrast to the "class" of the villains. Hitchcock's details are always significant.

10. For a fuller comparison between Hitchcock and Antonioni, see Durgnat, *Strange Case of Alfred Hitchcock*, 316–17.

11. Hitchcock evades Samuels's speculation that he might have developed into a different kind of artist had his thrillers not proved his most popular work (*Encountering Directors*, 240).

Blackmail

1. One of the more enjoyable but essentially pointless methods of Raymond Durgnat's study of Hitchcock, *The Strange Case of Alfred Hitchcock,* is to compare the film to a variation of Durgnat's own invention. Hitchcock's version usually proves the inferior. To wit: *Suspicion* (179), *Shadow of a Doubt* (187), *North by Northwest* (305), *Rope* (206), *Under Capricorn* (210), for a sample. The only cases where the film should benefit from approach via an alternative projection is in *The Paradine Case,* where Hitchcock himself has declared the unsatisfactoriness of his casting and named the cast-types he had in mind.

2. See, e.g., Bogdanovich, *Cinema of Alfred Hitchcock,* 13; Truffaut, *Hitchcock,* 70–71.

3. Unless otherwise stated, the quotations are from the dialogue sheets, available in the British Film Institute library. Citations will hereafter be given in the text.

4. Lady Smith, writing in the *Bystander,* was "pleased to say that this is the English film for which we have all been waiting for some years," with some reservations about Hitchcock's "immoderate mania for staircases," of course (August 14, 1929). "By this masterly production Alfred Hitchcock amply fulfils the promise shown in his earlier efforts. He has given us a story of vital interest, played and directed in a manner which is convincing proof that the talking film affords opportunities to British producers which cannot be equalled in any other country" (*Bioscope,* June 26, 1929).

Kenneth MacPherson worked through a detailed praise of the film to conclude, "Some of us are beginning to say that talkies are an art" (qtd. in Low, *The History of the British Film,* 212).

5. E.g., Taylor, *Cinema Eye, Cinema Ear,* 173; cf. Anderson, "Hitchcock," in LaValley, *Focus on Hitchcock,* 50–51.

6. See Low, *The History of the British Film,* 203–6. The crew on *Blackmail* blossomed. Hubert Bath and Henry Stafford, who did the music, went on to distinguished careers, as did art directors Norman Arnold and Wilfred Arnold. Derick Williams was a camera assistant, Ronald Neame clapper-boy, and Michael Powell still cameraman. The dialogue director (or director of elocution, as he was more roundly called) was R. E. Jeffrey, later famous as the commentator on the Universal Talking News.

7. Hitchcock to Newnham, "My Screen Memories," *Film Weekly,* May 9, 1936, 7; cf. Truffaut, *Hitchcock,* 70–71.

8. The track is analyzed in Roger Manvell and John Huntley, *The Technique of Film Music* (1957; London, 1971), 27–28.

9. Durgnat, *Strange Case of Alfred Hitchcock,* 85–105, 375; Marsha Kinder and Beverle Houston, *Close Up* (New York, 1972), 52–58. Cf. Smith,

"Conservative Individualism," 59–60; and Jonathan Rosenbaum's review of the film in *Monthly Film Bulletin,* October 1974, 234.

10. Durgnat, *Strange Case of Alfred Hitchcock,* 100; cf. Anderson, "Hitchcock," in LaValley, *Focus on Hitchcock,* 50.

11. Hitchcock, in Davy, *Footnotes to the Film,* 3.

12. There is even something bathetic about Hitchcock's first line of heard dialogue, as if turning from silent to sound was just another day's work: "Well, we finished earlier tonight than I expected." A "You ain't heard nothin' yet," that isn't. Cf. Rohmer and Chabrol: "Le jeu, tel que le concevait Hitchcock, exigeait la parole. A cet égard, la différence est frappante entre les deux versions: malgré la médiocrité de la déclamation, la parlante parait mieux jouée que la muette. La stylisation qu'Hitchcock imposait, plus ou moins consciemment, à ses interprètes, trouvait avec le son sa vraie raison d'être" (*Hitchcock,* 31).

13. On the famous "knife" sequence, see Kracauer, *Theory of Film,* 122–23. Technically, the obtrusive "knife" is only an aural variation on the familiar device of visual emphasis, as for example the unnaturally gleaming knife that the killer spies over the girl's shoulder in Pabst's *Pandora's Box,* or Hitchcock's poisoned coffee shown large in *Notorious* and the drugged drinks in *The Lady Vanishes.*

14. Kinder and Houston see the mustache as a spider (*Close Up,* 54); see Hitchcock's remarks on it in Truffaut, *Hitchcock,* 74; Bogdanovich, *Cinema of Alfred Hitchcock,* 13. The noose shadow has not to my knowledge been remarked on.

15. Cf. Rohmer and Chabrol: "Tout le film est axe sur les rapports des personnages entre eux. Borreaux et victimes se relaient de sequence en sequence: le bourreau devient victime, la victime bourreau. Dans une meme scene, parfois dans un meme plan, les positions morales des protagonistes basculent" (*Hitchcock,* 29).

By the shadow play both the artist and the lady, the two seducers and victims, are also victimized by their shadows, their projections. In *Blackmail* as in *The Lodger,* then, Hitchcock plays on the trickery of the senses. Even in *The Wrong Man,* one might reflect, Manny Balestrero's identification as the robber is made despite his obstruction by a cash wicket, his hat, and the microphone over the police lineup. At the end of Manny's tribulation, when he turns against the real robber, he is himself falsely accusing the man, i.e., accusing him of something he did not do, plot, or even cause.

16. Durgnat, *Strange Case of Alfred Hitchcock,* 93.

17. Cf. Henry Ringel, "*Blackmail:* The Opening of Hitchcock's Surrealistic Eye," *Film Heritage* (Winter 1973–74): 17–25.

18. Samuels is wrong to accuse Hitchcock of having "posed moral problems only to evade them" ("Hitchcock," *American Scholar* [Spring 1970]: 295). Hitchcock poses problems of considerable profundity. His "evasion" is nothing more than the preference for the ironist's stance over the didactic's.

This play with the clown portrait is better than the example of Stewart's face in *Rear Window*, which Hitchcock usually cites in homage to Kuleshov's experiments. Cf. Rohmer and Chabrol, *Hitchcock*, 29–30.

19. To Smith, the British Museum represents "age and stability in concrete form" ("Conservative Individualism," 60). So too should Scotland Yard, but its sign here quavers and distorts. The museum has the primary character of culture. In *Saboteur* Hitchcock uses the Statue of Liberty and in *North by Northwest* the American presidents on Mount Rushmore in a similar way to his use of the British Museum here: traditionally warm symbols become cold, indifferent obstacle courses.

Elstree Calling

1. Bogdanovich, *Cinema of Alfred Hitchcock*, 13.
2. Truffaut, *Hitchcock*, 66.

Juno and the Paycock

1. James Agate, *Around Cinemas* (London, 1946), 59–61.
2. Ibid., 59.
3. Bogdanovich, *Cinema of Alfred Hitchcock*, 15.
4. Truffaut, *Hitchcock*, 74.
5. Ibid., 74–75. Hitchcock confesses his shame again in Andrew Sarris, *Interviewing Film Directors* (New York, 1967), 203; and in *Dialogue on Film* for the American Film Institute, 8.
6. London, 1933.
7. Agate, *Around Cinemas*, 61.
8. Clemence Dane and Helen Simpson, *Enter Sir John* (1929; New York, 1971), 107. Cf. Rohmer and Chabrol: "*The Ring, The Manxman* et *Blackmail* sont des films d'inspiration catholique. Les rapports entre les êtres, la notion de couple, de famille, d'adultère, tout concorde à designer Hitchcock comme un auteur catholique. Mais il se refuse et se refusera toujours au sermon, au prosélytisme. . . . On comprend ce qui choqua Hitchcock dans l'oeuvre de Sean O'Casey. De prosélytisme, *Juno and the Paycock* n'etait pas exempt, tant s'en faut. Hitchcock aime l'ambiguïté, la subtilité, le mystère. Il n'y a rien de tout cela dans Sean O'Casey" (*Hitchcock*, 33).
9. Hitchcock discusses this and the phonograph scene in his BBC program *The Time of My Life*.

Murder!

1. For example, Fane is referred to as the "fiancé" by Truffaut, *Hitchcock*, 80; by Taylor, *Cinema Eye, Cinema Ear*, 147; and by Rene Predal, "La peur et les multiples visages du destin," *Etudes cinematographiques*, no. 84–87 (1971): 108.

2. Durgnat, *Strange Case of Alfred Hitchcock*, 110–11. Durgnat also allots to Sir John Doucie's lunch of cheese and Guinness, violating Hitchcock's parallel. Durgnat seems to regard Diana Baring as the center of the film, not Sir John. He misses the clear motive given for her sheltering of Fane: she is certain he had nothing to do with the case (cf. ibid., 113). "Find out what time Fane is on tonight" is as close as I can find in the film to Durgnat's claim of "all sorts of circumstantial detail as to train times" (ibid., 111). In his discussion of *Marnie*, Durgnat again blurs the plot, transferring Strutt to Mark Rutland's office.

3. Bond, "The Other Alfred Hitchcock," 30–35. To omit the "!" from *Murder!* is surely as serious a mistake as to omit the "?" from Hawks's *Man's Favorite Sport?*

4. Durgnat redeems himself. Regarding *The Lodger* and *Blackmail*, "The murders in the former aren't solved, and the emphasis doesn't lie on who-done-it, only on who-never-done-it. In the latter we know who-done-it, it's only Scotland Yard what don't know who done it" (*Strange Case of Alfred Hitchcock*, 109). The murders in *The Lodger* are solved, though we don't see the killer.

5. For Hitchcock's typical reflections on suspense and mystery, see Truffaut, *Hitchcock*, 79–81.

6. Hitchcock replies to Truffaut's direction of the discussion toward the homosexuality motif in the film: "The whole film was about theatre" (*Hitchcock*, 83). Hitchcock puts the point more elaborately in Samuels's *Encountering Directors*: "*Murder* was an interesting film, though, because I intended it as a satire on the theatre. In those days, the actor-manager was king: Sir Henry Irving, Sir Herbert Beerbohm-Tree, Sir Gerald du Maurier. Du Maurier used to have an office over His Majesty's Theatre, called the Dome, where he conducted his business. That's why I dressed Herbert Marshall, who plays the hero, in black coat and striped pants, like a cabinet minister. They never went into the provinces. So, when my actor-manager does, he finds himself experiencing conditions which, up to then, he had disdained. When he starts investigating the murder there, he feels he's suffering the indignity of a lower order of actor" (241).

The finished film, however, has lost its satire against Sir John or theater. Indeed with Truffaut Hitchcock slips into a du Maurier pose: "Anyway, to get back to *Murder*, it was an interesting film and was quite successful in London. But it was too sophisticated for the provinces" (*Hitchcock*, 84).

When Hitchcock starred du Maurier in his production of *Lord Camber's Ladies* in 1932, du Maurier was "the leading actor in London at the time, and in my opinion, the best actor anywhere" (ibid., 89).

7. Agate, *Around Cinemas*, 60. The review appeared originally in the *Tatler* on March 5, 1930. The word appears in the shooting script of *Enter Sir John*, dated March 5, 1930, as well, on page 57. The line is typed as "It's ridiculous, I tell you. Absolutely ridiculous." Each "ridiculous" is crossed out and "absurd" written above it.

OED examples cohere with Agate's usage. In *The Lady Vanishes* Iris says to the waiters (of another bit of staging), "The whole thing's too absurd."

8. Another piece of Hitchcock's framing, this time by overlapping sound, parallels the stage as Diana's play begins with her first night in jail. From the curtain rising at the theater Hitchcock cuts to a white masking lifting up off Diana in her cell. The camera pulls back through the spyhole on her door to reveal that it is the cell. We hear the theater applause and someone say, "That's Mrs. Baring's understudy going on now." In jail, of course, Baring is Fane's "understudy," playing his role of "guilty" for him.

9. According to the shooting script of the film, when it was still carrying the title *Enter Sir John*, after the play and novel by Helen Simpson and Clemence Dane, there was to be a lengthier preamble to the trial involving a newsboy's placard advertising the trial, two fanfares for the judge's arrival, and individual introduction of jurors, all of which Hitchcock dropped. The shooting script is on deposit at the library of the British Film Institute in London.

The novel focused on Diana through the trial, not Sir John. In the novel, Sir John was not on the jury but an interested bystander, struck by the character of the actress charged. Quotations from the novel are from the 1971 reissue by Tom Stacey.

10. Shackleton's entire speech is as follows:

> I think the whole business is hateful. There's too much responsibility put on our shoulders. Either we have got to let her go free and that's not fair to the rest of the world if she's guilty. Or we have got to hang her—and that's barbarous.
>
> Mercy—is that what you call it? Twenty years out of her life, the best years—and to spend them in hell. Have you ever been inside a prison? It takes a civilized community to think out a punishment like that.
>
> No, but that's what we try to do, run the world on sentiment. Save the unfit. Get more babies and make glorious wars to be rid of them. The world's a reeking pit of sentiment. (38–39)

In the shooting script one lady wants to reach an early verdict to get home for her husband's supper. I think this was cut from the film, but it resurfaced in the first *The Man Who Knew Too Much*.

11. As Rusk in *Frenzy* puts it, the police usually "have the whole thing ass about face," which explains the erroneous judgment by the juries in *Murder!* and in *Frenzy* and the poor judgment of the judge and the mob in *I Confess*. Erring judges and juries are an extension of Hitchcock's fumbling policemen, as only in *Sabotage, Shadow of a Doubt, Stage Fright, Dial M For Murder,* and *Frenzy* do we get from Hitchcock responsible, sober, and humane police. The undercover Newton in *Jamaica Inn* is close to a police figure.

In any case, *Murder!* precisely parallels Hitchcock's trick in *Frenzy*, where a thick plate glass keeps us from hearing the verdict on the hero. Hitchcock then gives us a shot of Inspector Oxford's pensive view of the emptied courtroom. In *Frenzy* the motif is not the framing of *Murder!* but of Oxford revisiting the scene of the trial as later he will return to the scene of a crime.

The most profound parallel between *Murder!* and *Frenzy* is that both Sir John and Inspector Oxford continue the case after the trial and verdict by placing themselves in the psychological position of the accused. From his own domestic, mainly culinary, tensions Oxford senses what Blaney had told his girl, that he had no motive or spirit to kill the woman to whom he had been married so long, and from whom he was divorced. See Leland A. Poague, "The Detective in Hitchcock's *Frenzy*," *Journal of Popular Film* 2, no. 1 (1973): 47–59.

12. According to the shooting script, the farce at the beginning was a loose parody of the main plot. During the interrogation in the wings Fane was to be heard from stage in falsetto: "Reginald, darling, hasn't that cat gone yet? (Laughter) Oh, it's you, constable, is it? Don't you try and run away from me. Come here when I speak to you. No, no you don't that's the bathroom. Come here! Are you afraid of a poor weak woman!" (21).

Then Fane in uniform arrests Druce, the dead woman's husband, who played the drunk that in the novel he actually was. When Sir John passes the theater later, "It is to be noticed that the current play is advertised by a poster outside the stage door with the words 'Nothing But The Truth' on it" (100).

13. Hitchcock discusses the technical delights of the orchestra and the interior monologue in Truffaut, *Hitchcock*, 81–82; Bogdanovich, *Cinema of Alfred Hitchcock*, 15; and way back in "My Screen Memories," *Film Weekly*, May 9, 1936: 7.

14. O. B. Hardison, "The Rhetoric of Hitchcock's Thrillers," in *Man and the Movies*, ed. W. R. Robinson (1967; Harmondsworth, UK, 1969), 147.

15. Durgnat, *Strange Case of Alfred Hitchcock*, 112.

Notes

16. In Forsyth Hardy, ed., *Grierson on Documentary* (London, 1966), 71–74. One cannot fairly say that Hitchcock ridicules the poor here. His culpable jury at the Baring trial is a cross-section that well represents the upper middle class. Had he cared to make fun of the lower classes he would have kept the juror Mr. Ludovici from the novel, whose verdict is "let her go. . . . Guilty, yes, only not for hang . . . let her go. Not guilty. A woman, what is that? It is not like a man. She mean no harm. Yes?" (104).

17. Ernest Betts, *The Film Business: A History of British Cinema, 1896–1972* (London, 1973), 122.

18. Durgnat, *Strange Case Of Alfred Hitchcock*, 112–13.

19. Truffaut, *Hitchcock*, 82; cf. Rohmer and Chabrol, *Hitchcock*, 35–36.

The Skin Game

1. The film is usually dismissed as a straightforward adaptation of the play: "I didn't alter the Galsworthy play very much. It opened up a bit more than *Juno*. Not too much, though. Photographed theatre, really" (Bogdanovich, *Cinema of Alfred Hitchcock*, 15). And "I didn't make it by choice, and there isn't much to be said about it" (Truffaut, *Hitchcock*, 85). Noble compares to *The Farmer's Wife* the charm of Jack Cox's pastoral photography, and quotes the October 17, 1931, issue of *Picturegoer*: "This extremely powerful and dramatic picturisation of Galsworthy's play proves that Hitchcock is one of England's most brilliant directors" ("Index to the Work of Alfred Hitchcock," 16–17). For the historian's attack on the play (and film), see Hardy, *Grierson on Documentary*, 107–9.

2. Durgnat, *Strange Case of Alfred Hitchcock*, 116. He made the same mistake in his first draft of the discussion of the film, which appeared in *Films and Filming* (July 1970): 52.

3. At the auction Hitchcock keeps Galsworthy's directions, with their political suggestiveness: Hornblower bids on the left, Dawker (for the Hillcrists) on the right. The winning, subverting bid comes from behind. The placing of the Hornblower family on the left wing and the Hillcrist family on the right wing is loosely adhered to throughout the film.

Rich and Strange

1. Hardy, *Grierson on Documentary*, 75–76.

2. Taylor, *Cinema Eye, Cinema Ear*, 175.

3. Hitchcock gives Samuels an unsatisfactory explanation of his use of place name titles: "Oh, you had to. You've got to remember that some people in the audience won't be able to identify a remote place just by seeing it"

(*Encountering Directors,* 241). A wider explanation is needed, for Hitchcock's use of titles goes beyond place names. Rohmer and Chabrol offer another: "Mieux encore, le metteur en scène le plus en vue de Grande-Bretagne se paie le luxe et l'audace de réaliser un film dans les conditions d'un amateur" (*Hitchcock,* 41).

4. "La séquence dans la cabine est certainement l'une des plus significatives de toute l'oeuvre d'Hitchcock. *L'absurdité* de cette surface liquide et inexorable depeint, mieux que les mots, l'abîme inattendu que les futilites de la croisière ont dressé au coeur de ce couple mesquin. Le tres beau thème de l'Unité de toute chose, qui est l'une des clés principales de toutes les grandes oeuvres d'Hitchcock" (Rohmer and Chabrol, *Hitchcock,* 40). "Cette parabole a la limite de l'absurde, Hitchcock l'a conçue avec une sereine franchise, et n'y a introduit aucune roublardise" (ibid., 41).

5. See Truffaut, *Hitchcock,* 85–86, where Hitchcock describes his naive blundering into a brothel with his wife. Two scenes that Hitchcock describes from the film do not appear in the print in the British film archives:

> (1) a young boy trying to swim between a girl's legs is locked between them (Truffaut, *Hitchcock,* 86)
>
> (2) "my most devastating appearance in a picture": after the rescue the Hills meet Hitchcock in a lounge. They tell him their story, "and I say, 'No, I don't think it'll make a movie.' And it didn't." (Bogdanovich, *Cinema of Alfred Hitchcock,* 15) In the print that is available the characters do not meet their maker.

6. Richard Combs suggests perceptive parallels between *Rich and Strange* and *Torn Curtain* in *Monthly Film Bulletin,* August 1975, 187. In casting Julie Andrews and Paul Newman (Mary Poppins and Hud) in *Torn Curtain* Hitchcock averted the error he claims to have made in *Rich and Strange:* "The actors were all right, but we should have had a stronger cast—in the box office sense, I mean. I liked the picture; it should have been more successful" (Truffaut, *Hitchcock,* 87). "My mistake with *Rich and Strange* was my failure to make sure that the two leading players would be attractive to the critics and audience alike. With a story that good, I should not have allowed indifferent casting" (ibid., 91).

When a National Film Theatre audience questioned the lead casting in *Torn Curtain,* Hitchcock (as is his wont) readily agreed. The film was "totally miscast. I should have had a singing scientist."

Number Seventeen

1. Bogdanovich, *Cinema of Alfred Hitchcock,* 16. Benn Levy was one of Hitchcock's scenarists on *Blackmail.*

2. Ibid.

3. Truffaut, *Hitchcock,* 91.

4. Durgnat, *Strange Case of Alfred Hitchcock,* 119; cf. Rohmer and Chabrol, *Hitchcock,* 43.

5. J. J. Farjeon, *No. 17* (London, 1926). All quotations from this novel will hereafter be cited in the text.

6. Rodney Ackland and Elspeth Grant, *The Celluloid Mistress* (London, 1954), 36–37.

Waltzes from Vienna

1. The play is still in print, published in London by Josef Weinberger.

2. Durgnat, *Strange Case of Alfred Hitchcock,* 120–21. Noble retreats to the sources of *The Man Who Knew Too Much* when it comes time to discuss *Waltzes from Vienna* ("Index to the Work of Alfred Hitchcock," 19).

3. Esmond Knight, *Seeking the Bubble* (London, n.d.), 78; cf. Michael Thornton, *Jessie Matthews* (1974; London, 1975), 125–27.

4. On Hitchcock's care in the musical aspects of the production, see his interview with Stephen Watts, "Alfred Hitchcock on Music in Films," *Cinema Quarterly* (Edinburgh) 2, no. 2 (1933): 80–83. There is a short quotation in Manvell and Huntley, *The Technique of Film Music,* 45–46.

5. In his autobiography, Hitchcock's musical director, Louis Levy, quotes Sigmund Romberg: "Strauss used to work the same way. He would go out for a walk and put his impressions into a waltz. After all, if music is the expression of human emotions, why should not human emotions suggest expression in music just as in words?" (*Music for the Movies,* 96). Levy also explains that a two and a half hour stage show can have nine to twelve musical numbers but a film of one hundred minutes cannot have more than five. Hitchcock severely reduced the number of songs in his adaptation.

6. In *Notorious* Grant's head is audacious, as he has himself crashed the party. His hidden face anticipates his concealment of his own emotions later and his covert activities, at the same time registering on us the enigmatic and unsettling effect that the front of his head is clearly having on the Ingrid Bergman character at the time. As he breaks off a kiss to take the important phone call the camera circles them to show only the back of his head again, this time giving the character an instant of privacy.

Taken with the wigged judge of *Easy Virtue,* the three examples illustrate Hitchcock's ingenuity in discovering a striking device and then variously exploiting it by inflections and different contexts over the years. The famous kiss in *Notorious* can similarly be compared to the breathtaking fatal kiss of the revolutionary in *Topaz.*

The Man Who Knew Too Much

1. Qtd. in Noble, "Index to the Work of Alfred Hitchcock," 20.

2. Qtd. in Charles Oakley, *Where We Came In* (London, 1964), 118. For an anecdote about the film's difficulty with distributors, see Montagu, *Film World*, 239.

3. Peter John Dyer, "Young and Innocent," *Sight and Sound* (Spring 1961): 81.

4. David Castell, *Films Illustrated* (July 1972): 22.

5. Bogdanovich, *Cinema of Alfred Hitchcock*, 16.

6. Truffaut, *Hitchcock*, 102. Penelope Houston prefers the first version (see "A Hitchcock Double," *Sight and Sound* [Summer 1956]: 31; and "The Figure in the Carpet," *Sight and Sound* [Autumn 1963]: 163).

7. The screenplay (in the British Film Institute library) has a closing scene in police court, where Uncle Clive is sentenced to twenty shillings or a week for disturbing the peace. The last shot is Clive's indignant face. Charles Bennett—a Hitchcock scribe since *Blackmail*—adapted the Bulldog Drummond story by "Sapper" with D. B. Wyndham-Lewis writing the dialogue. The idea of terrorist kidnappers came from John Buchan's *The Three Hostages*. "Abbott" was based on a real-life character named Peter the Painter. The siege scene was based on the famous Sydney Street siege of a Communist cell around 1910 and upset the censors, who did not want British police depicted with guns. See Leslie Perkoff, "The Censor and Sydney Street," *World Film News* 2, no. 12 (1938): 4–5; Truffaut, *Hitchcock*, 94–95; and Bogdanovich, *Cinema of Alfred Hitchcock*, 17.

8. All quotations from the screenplay are from the copy in the British Film Institute Library and will hereafter be cited in the text. In the screenplay, Ramon is named Levine. The change was likely made so as not to offend Jewish people.

9. "While her husband's inner conflict is represented in his being face to face with Abbott's corrupt narcissism (the extreme version of the father's own insistence on his individuality) her related conflict is portrayed as the loss of an inadequate self-control (she swoons; she is seen in tight, insistent profile close-up; her vision blurs). The emotional stress is hers, and Hitchcock emphasises the interiorness of her struggle, as opposed to her husband's which is enacted in character-confrontations. While the director gives convention its due (for instance, in the death of Louis Bernard) he portrays individualism and its personal emphases as the centre of a true order" (Smith, "Conservative Individualism," 65).

10. In *Mr. and Mrs. Smith* the shaving scenes are moments of particular intimacy between the couple.

Notes

11. Cf. the James Stewart character in *Vertigo*, rounding on Kim Novak with a gratified but bitter "You shouldn't keep souvenirs of a killing. You shouldn't be so (choke) sentimental."

12. Durgnat, *Strange Case of Alfred Hitchcock*, 123–24. Taylor makes a good defense of the film as "just" a thriller (*Cinema Eye, Cinema Ear,* 175–77).

13. Bogdanovich, *Cinema of Alfred Hitchcock,* 17.

14. Samuels, *Encountering Directors,* 241. In the screenplay Hitchcock has the wool running up one man's leg, brushing another's hair so that he thinks it is a pretty girl's advances, and so on. Later an Englishman asks who was shot. "Oh, a Frenchman." "'The death of a mere foreigner is of subsidiary importance for him." This notion, dropped here, resurfaces in *The Lady Vanishes.*

15. On Hitchcock's use of the brooch, see V. F. Perkins, *Film as Film* (Harmondsworth, UK, 1972), 55–56.

The 39 Steps

1. Taylor, *Cinema Eye, Cinema Ear,* 179. The film won rave reviews, of which Sydney Carroll's in the *Sunday Times* for June 9, 1936, can be taken as an example: "In *The Thirty-Nine Steps* the identity and mind of Alfred Hitchcock are continually discernible, in fact supreme. There is no doubt that Hitchcock is a genius. He is the real star of the film." Rohmer and Chabrol spurn its commercialism (*Hitchcock,* 49).

2. On "pip," see Eric Partridge, *A Dictionary of Slang and Unconventional English* (New York, 1961), 633. Mr. Memory is based on a famous variety act, Datas, who would answer any question and conclude with the catchphrase, "Am I right, sir?"

3. Hitchcock often uses signs ironically. Manny Balestrero is entangled in a robbery of "Associated Life of New York." One of the basic paradoxes of the film *The Wrong Man* involves the web of associations that city life brings, the contrast between the intense web of tangling associations (with strangers and nearalikes) versus the response of Rose to it all, detachment, withdrawal, alienation.

Marnie is recognized by a man who waits to peer at her again in front of a "Mutual Window." Both characters are revealed by the terms in which he identifies her. When a place-sign opens *Psycho* with the note that it is Phoenix, we are prepared for the resurrection of the rare Bates bird from its bisexual ashes.

4. Smith's claims for Hannay here would be better suited for Sir John in *Murder!* or for the Jane Wyman character in *Stage Fright:* "He is constantly taking on, assuming, using aspects of the people and places in

which he finds himself: the milkman's clothes, the train, the girder on the bridge, the crofter's jacket and prayer-book, the sheep, the waterfall, rather than merely to hide or disguise himself with: they are those parts of his being which he can draw upon in his need, the concretisation of his adequacy, in the face of his own impulse to evil" ("Conservative Individualism," 66).

5. In *Dial M for Murder* the story that writer Bob Cummings makes up for husband Ray Milland to tell the police to clear the wife happens to be the truth, so of course it is not believed. In *Stage Fright* Alistair Sim's wife doesn't believe him when he tells her the truth about Todd, nor does she believe "Smith" is really a detective. When the truth is spoken sincerely, it can hurt: Sim's calling to Wyman that Todd is the killer increases her danger, as it prompts Todd to kill her so he can plead insanity. In *Murder!* Sir John's play was intended to elicit the truth by dramatizing it.

6. Hannay's speech scene is alluded to in Greene, Reed, and Welles's *The Third Man,* where Joseph Cotten finds himself bustled into a similar situation and for a brief moment, with the arrogance of the American writer abroad, thinks he can achieve Hannay's success. Of course, he cannot, as the European culture as well as practical worldliness are far beyond him. George Perry calls Hannay's effort a "nonsense speech" (*The Films of Alfred Hitchcock* [1965; London, 1970], 50).

7. The speech scene is Hitchcock's substitute for Buchan's, where Hannay visits a political radical candidate. Buchan's visit becomes Hitchcock's activity. The bullet-stopping Bible is Hitchcock's substitute for Buchan's help from "The Literary Innkeeper." For an explanation of his other changes, see Hitchcock, "Making 'The 39 Steps,'" *Film Weekly,* May 23, 1936, 28–29. Cf. Stuart Y. McDougall, "Mirth, Sexuality and Suspense: Alfred Hitchcock's adaptation of *The Thirty-Nine Steps,*" *Literature/Film Quarterly* (Summer 1975): 232–39. Jordan in the novel "could hood his eyes like a hawk." The missing finger is far more cinematic. So is the obligatory addition of a romantic accomplice in the pursuit.

8. Similarly in *North by Northwest* the policeman turns on the drunk Roger Thornhill: "What am I, a telephone operator?" Hitchcock's police do have an identity problem, it would seem, a descant to their debate between love and duty, perhaps.

9. Less liberal was the British Board of Film Censors. Two persons of opposite sex could not be shown on a bed together unless one foot was on the floor. Even if handcuffed, one presumes. So according to Montagu, *Film World,* 264.

10. For an alternative ending, see Samuels, *Encountering Directors,* 242–43.

Notes

Secret Agent

1. Bogdanovich, *Cinema of Alfred Hitchcock*, 18; cf. Truffaut: "Because it's a negative purpose, the film is static" (*Hitchcock*, 114).

2. The film was John Gielgud's first important role on-screen but he had had earlier exposure. He made his debut in 1924 in *Who is the Man?* in the lead role that Sarah Bernhardt had created for her from Louis Verneuil's *Daniel*. Gielgud played the Prologue in *Michael Strogoff* in 1926, and in Edgar Wallace's *The Clue of the New Pin* in 1929, *Insult* and *The Good Companions* in 1932, then *Secret Agent*. Mrs. Caypor was played by Florence Kahn, Max Beerbohm's wife, who claimed never to have even seen a movie. The cabby was the famous French actor Michel St. Denis, who dropped by the set to visit Gielgud and stayed on to play the role. See John Gielgud, *Early Stages* (London, 1938), 228–30, for his feelings about working on films and with Hitchcock at the time.

3. Somerset Maugham, *Ashenden* (1927; London, 1951). All quotations from this novel will hereafter be cited in the text. The quote here is on page 67.

4. Truffaut, *Hitchcock*, 114–15.

5. Durgnat, *Strange Case of Alfred Hitchcock*, 133.

6. In Hitchcock's original ending, Robert Young is supposed to cry out from the wreckage for water. Lorre brings him his flask of brandy. The camera holds on Young's face as he starts to drink the brandy and is shot by Lorre, who is then shown smiling. Presumably the censors found the ending sadistic. In the present film Lorre is killed by Young while bringing him water.

7. On the theme of neutrality in *Torn Curtain*, cf. Durgnat, *Strange Case of Alfred Hitchcock*, 376–77.

8. Since *The Manxman* Hitchcock's scripts have shown remarkable verbal wit and consistency. Here the credit must be shared by a number of contributors: Charles Bennett on screenplay, Ian Hay on dialogue, Alma Reville on continuity, and Jesse Lasky Jr. on additional dialogue. Of course Hitchcock had his influence on the writing team as well. This list of writing credits is extraordinary for a film, and more so for a film where there is such clear emphasis on the visual statement.

9. On Hitchcock's use of familiar settings, see Truffaut, *Hitchcock*, 115–16; and Higham and Greenberg, *The Celluloid Muse*, 99. Otis Ferguson's review is rich in its attention to the fine sound effects in the film (in *Garbo and the Night Watchman*, ed. Alistair Cooke [London, 1971], 209–12).

10. Montagu, *Film World*, 124.

11. "It is all done within the thriller mould, of course, and quite successfully, though the rupture of tone is disturbing" (Taylor, *Cinema Eye, Cinema Ear*, 180). Cf. Taylor, ed., *Graham Greene on Film* (New York, 1972), 74–75.

12. Dyer's respective complaints are in "Young and Innocent," 83, and in "The Murderers Among Us," *Films and Filming* (December 1958): 15.

13. Hitchcock, "My Spies," *Film Weekly,* May 30, 1936, 27. Hitchcock tells Samuels, "I only read the book once. We go to all sources for material, don't we?" (*Encountering Directors,* 243). As Gielgud describes Hitchcock's adaptation, "He more or less threw the story away, starting again with various locations that had caught his fancy, and then concentrating on getting his characters from one to another of them as quickly as possible, with minimum concern for probability" (*Sight and Sound* [Autumn 1968]: 210).

Sabotage

1. Mark Van Doren reviewed the film in *The Nation,* March 13, 1937. The review can be found in S. Kauffmann and B. Henstell, *American Film Criticism* (New York, 1972), 356. Script credits include Charles Bennett, Ian Hay, Helen Simpson, Alma Reville, and E. V. H. Emmett.

2. Taylor, *Graham Greene on Film,* 122. On *Secret Agent,* see ibid., 74–75.

3. Truffaut, *Hitchcock,* 127.

4. Durgnat, *Strange Case of Alfred Hitchcock,* 137.

5. "The boy was involved in a situation that got him too much sympathy from the audience, so that when the bomb exploded and he was killed, the public was resentful . . . it was a grave error on my part" (Truffaut, *Hitchcock,* 118–19). But Hitchcock makes a contradictory claim to Bogdanovich: "The bomb should never have gone off. . . . If you build an audience up to that point, the explosion becomes strangely anticlimactic. You work the audience up to such a degree that they need the relief" (Bogdanovich, *Cinema of Alfred Hitchcock,* 118).

6. Montagu reports that Sylvia Sidney broke into tears from the frustrations of not being able to act through such an intense scene (*Film World,* 120). Hitchcock explains his technique in the scene in Davy, *Footnotes to the Film,* 6–9; "Director's Problems," *Listener,* February 2, 1938, 241; Truffaut, *Hitchcock,* 120–26.

7. Rohmer and Chabrol, *Hitchcock,* 54.

8. Joseph Conrad, *The Secret Agent* (1907; New York, 1953), 68, 85. The fidelity of the film to the novel is well established by Michael A. Anderegg, "Conrad and Hitchcock: *The Secret Agent* Inspires *Sabotage,*" *Literature/Film Quarterly* (Summer 1975): 215–26.

9. Conrad, *The Secret Agent,* 82.

10. The shooting script is available in the library of the British Film Institute. The quotation is from shot 163.

11. Similarly in *Saboteur* the villain Fry ducks into a movie house where a comedy suddenly turns into a shooting match and real bullets from behind the screen kill members of the audience. The cinema situation is repeated when Barry Kane rides off from the Tobin ranch, pursued by a posse, and at the charity ball where Barry, dressed as if from another movie altogether, tries to "act" his way out. The first close-up of the Statue of Liberty shows the unseeing eyes of the statue, with a gawking horde of people at the windows on her crown. Ironic scenes in cinemas go back to Asquith's *A Cottage in Dartmoor* (for sound effects) and Keaton's brilliant *Sherlock Jr.* (for visuals).

12. In the novel the eye is twice presented as a scorching, intruding presence (Conrad, *The Secret Agent*, 23, 28). In the film Ted has an apposite pun: "I think it's a blinking shame, robbing people like that." The "blink" came when the cinema show was stopped by darkness. There are two worse puns in the vendor's dismissal of the boy with the bomb: "Buzz off you little basket."

13. Hitchcock tells Truffaut that Verloc's death had to appear accidental "to maintain the public's sympathy for Sylvia Sidney" (Truffaut, *Hitchcock,* 120). Dyer goes too far: "Her desperation increases relatively to Verloc's own anxiety that she should get it over with by plunging the bread-knife in his back, and so grant him final peace from his conscience" ("The Murderers Among Us," 15). Verloc shows virtually no remorse. He moves against Sylvia to silence her (shot 454–59).

Young and Innocent

1. Durgnat, *Strange Case of Alfred Hitchcock,* 141, 174. Taylor applauds its freedom from "even this touch of pretentiousness; it is entirely an entertainment" (*Cinema Eye, Cinema Ear,* 180). When Alexander Walker chose the film in a National Film Theatre Critic's Choice series in the spring of 1964, it was "partly the child and partly the critic" that did, for "its gentleness as well as its gentlemanliness. . . . I like the film with affection and if all this tells you more about me than about it, I am sorry but really see no need to defend myself. Or it."

2. Hitchcock again seems to contradict himself. He tells Bogdanovich, a propos of this film, "When you are dealing with melodrama, you mustn't let the characters take themselves where they want to go. They must come where *you* want to go. . . . You lay out your story and you put the characters in afterwards. That's why you don't get really good characterizations" (*Cinema of Alfred Hitchcock,* 19). But Perry quotes him from a contemporary newspaper article as follows: "We went into a huddle and slowly from discussions, arguments, random suggestions, casual, desultory talk and furious intellectual quarrels as to what such and such a character in such

a situation would or would not do, the scenario began to take shape. The difficulty of writing a motion-picture story is to make things not only logical but visual" (*The Films of Alfred Hitchcock,* 59). Perhaps there is a touch of sarcasm to Hitchcock's description of his story conference.

3. Truffaut, *Hitchcock,* 127; Hitchcock's BBC talk. In his autobiography, Louis Levy discusses at length the importance of a good film title, particularly in the case of this movie. Confused, he claims the confusion was over whether to name this film *The Girl Was Young* ("very apt for Nova" and "mysterious, but not puzzling") or stick to the original title of the source, Josephine Tey's *A Shilling for Candles.* Levy says the latter was abandoned because "many people found it very difficult to remember—including the critics." Actually the original title had to be dropped because the subplot involving shillings and candles was dropped in the adaptation. Perhaps it was the collocation of youth and innocence that the critics had trouble remembering.

4. Hitchcock was impressed by Nova Pilbeam's performance in *The Man Who Knew Too Much:* "What struck me most about her was her common sense. There was no question of directing a child. Even at that time she had the intelligence of a fully grown woman. She had plenty of confidence and ideas of her own" (Hitchcock, "My Strangest Year," *Film Weekly,* May 16, 1936, 29).

In several ways the film is paralleled by *Foreign Correspondent.* Again the young man leads a girl to a break with her father, later in a more dramatic situation. The later heroine could speak for Erica in her assertion that "Well-meaning professionals" have messed things up, so that it is time that "well-meaning amateurs" should be given a chance. There is even a similar situation of the man and woman hiding from the father, using an aunt. Again, Hitchcock blithely inflects old inventions.

5. Josephine Tey, *A Shilling for Candles,* reprinted in *Four, Five and Six by Tey* (New York, 1959). Quotations from this novel will hereafter be cited in the text. The description here is from page 35. Rohmer and Chabrol overstate the degree of Hitchcock's alterations (*Hitchcock,* 55).

6. There are similar sinkings in *Number Seventeen* and *Psycho.* Clothes are burned for similar effect in *Stage Fright.*

7. Pope's *Rape of the Lock* is full of examples of bottles crying for their corks, etc.

8. Smith misreads the film completely to claim: "There would be no difficulty in demonstrating the film's social conservatism (it invites us to do so); the lower classes and the socially deprived are used to represent violence, disorder and the general disturbance in the nature of things" ("Conservative Individualism," 67). To the contrary, the lower classes have tight and trustworthy bonds, the hoboes in one community, the truckers in another, which are

disturbed only by the catalytic intrusion of Erica and the fugitive. But then so are the police, the aunt's party, and the father's life. In the novel Old Will is a vicious, greedy, even sexual threat to Erica. Hitchcock presents him in a different light altogether, as a genial, warm, friendly, humorous outsider. Few characters in the upper classes here are more attractive, virtuous, or helpful than Will.

9. Cf. the Merry Widow Waltz that plays behind the credits in *Shadow of a Doubt*. Often Hitchcock's opening visuals will set up a pattern in anticipation of the action of the film, e.g., the splits in the units of the lettering in *Psycho*, making each letter an image of a split or layered self; the angles in the credits of *North by Northwest* giving the film a second reference to *Hamlet*, where by indirections direction is found out; the brown splattering droppings that announce *The Birds*.

10. For their discussion of the most beautiful dolly shot in the history of cinema, see Rohmer and Chabrol, *Hitchcock*, 56–57. Preston Sturges pays Hitchcock homage in *Unfaithfully Yours* when his camera tracks across a concert hall onto one of Rex Harrison's eyes.

11. Peter Wollen, "Hitchcock's Vision," *Cinema* (UK), no. 3 (1969): 2–4.

The Lady Vanishes

1. For reviews of the film, see Noble, "Index to the Work of Alfred Hitchcock," 25, 26; Alan Stanbrook, "The Lady Vanishes," *Films and Filming* (July 1963): 45–47; J. G. Boyum and A. Scott, *Film as Film* (Boston, 1971), 219–28. But for Rohmer and Chabrol, *"The Lady Vanishes* a des allures de dictionnaire. C'est tres exactement la somme de la serie Gaumont-British"* (*Hitchcock*, 59).

2. "They show it very often in Paris; sometimes I see it twice in one week" (Truffaut, *Hitchcock*, 171).

3. Redgrave tells his story in Richard Findlater, *Michael Redgrave: Actor* (London, 1956), 42. "I simply didn't care a damn," Redgrave confesses. "I was nearly half-way through the picture before I started to try."

4. Ethel Lina White, *The Wheel Spins* (London, 1936). All quotations from this novel will hereafter be cited in the text.

5. In the novel the younger of two maiden sisters remarks that "If we didn't dress in evening wear for dinner we should feel we were letting England down" (36). Durgnat is particularly perceptive in his comments on Caldicott and Charters (*Strange Case of Alfred Hitchcock*, 146–47, 154). Hitchcock discussed the two with Pete Martin, who considers them thoroughly British: " 'No,' Hitchcock said. 'The British knew it was merely a humorous exaggeration. Such things have been called the Hitchcock touch, but they're

really examples of English humor based on carrying understatement to an absurd extreme'" (in Harry Geduld, ed., *Film Makers on Film Making* [Harmondsworth, UK, 1967], 127). In the summer of 1975, the friends of George Davis attacked the English society again where they felt it would hurt symbolically the most: the test match!

6. The release script—in the British Film Institute Library—opens with the following statement: "The Bandriekan spoken throughout the film is a fictitious language. The English translations are put down to convey the meaning of the sequence. The language sounds Russian. In the script Blanche says off-camera that "Bandrieka may have a dictator but tonight we're painting it red."

7. Durgnat, *Strange Case of Alfred Hitchcock*, 157–58. The obvious models of the opening shots give the whole film a fairy-tale aura.

8. Gavin Lambert, *The Naked Edge* (London, 1975), 242.

9. Durgnat, *Strange Case of Alfred Hitchcock*, 153.

10. Perhaps Leif Furhammar and Folke Isaksson overstate the case: "Alfred Hitchcock had brought with him from England a clever and well-tested thriller formula which worked well for the purposes of propaganda. In his British picture, *The Lady Vanishes* (1938), he had already warned about the danger of Hitler, and he continued this anti-Nazi line using the same thematic pattern in *Foreign Correspondent* and *Saboteur*. But in his next film, *Lifeboat*, he chose a semi-allegorical theme with which to express an uncompromising view of the German question" (*Politics and Film* [London, 1971], 68).

Jamaica Inn

1. Pommer produced *The Blackguard* in 1924 on which Hitchcock worked as writer and art director.

2. Truffaut, *Hitchcock*, 138–39. The *New Statesman* reviewer made his own case: "The criterion of this sort of film is simply, does one wriggle? And I, for one, wriggled insufficiently" (May 13, 1939).

Hitchcock told Bogdanovich: "The root problem was that there was no mystery. This is the story of the parson who preaches in the pulpit. . . . And in *Jamaica Inn* you have Charles Laughton playing the parson. Who's the wrecker? Who's the wrecker? What are you going to do—have a little bit-player turn out to be the central figure? Doesn't make sense. It's very difficult to make a who-done-it. You see, this was like doing a who-done-it and making Charles Laughton the butler" (*Cinema of Alfred Hitchcock*, 20).

3. On the problems between Laughton and Hitchcock, see William Brown, *Charles Laughton* (New York, 1970), 101, 106–7. On his BBC talk Hitchcock remarked: "Charles, well he was mercurial. Charles was difficult at times.

He was a very simple man in his way but he was a very difficult man. I remember on the film I made—*Jamaica Inn*, which I didn't care for, in fact I tried to duck the picture two weeks before we started shooting. . . . I felt that it was going to be troublesome and—er—it wasn't Charles' fault. That was the way he was made, you know. He had to—em—feel it or not feel it and there was one scene in *Jamaica Inn*, one close-up I wanted to get and—er—he couldn't get it." Finally Laughton got it and later confessed he'd gotten it by imagining himself a ten-year-old boy who had just wet his knickers.

    4. "But they're human beings, aren't they?" Charlie asks, referring to the merry widows that had been executed. "Are they?" replies Uncle Charles. "Or are they fat, wheezing animals?" Later he finds swine beneath the social veneer. In *Suspicion* when Johnny pulls up to lie to Lina about why he was fired there are two sheep on the hillside behind, an image of Johnny's view of Lina. Hitchcock consistently has his villains regard ordinary people as foolish animals, the flock of detectives in *The 39 Steps* being the notable exception.

    5. Daphne du Maurier, *Jamaica Inn* (1936; London, 1965). All quotations from this novel will hereafter be cited in the text. The quote here is from page 246.

    For the record, here is du Maurier's remark on the film: "I was in Egypt at the time it was made, and I saw it in London on my return. I was disappointed. It was made at a time when British films were not very good, and exterior shots would have helped—particularly if they had been taken on Bodmin Moor. I thought that the opening scenes captured the flavour of the story but the elimination of the albino parson and the disproportionate role of the squire proved to the detriment of the film as a whole. . . . I thought that Leslie Banks (Joss) was good, and the rest of the cast adequate" (qtd. in Michael Burrows, *Charles Laughton and Fredric March*, Formative Film Series [Cornwall, 1969], 14).

    If du Maurier seems to slight Laughton's performance ("adequate" seems hardly the word, one way or the other), it might be remembered that Hitchcock was for many years a friend of the du Maurier family, back to Gerald.

    6. Durgnat, *Strange Case of Alfred Hitchcock*, 165. Graham Greene was less kind: "This passionate, full-blooded yarn could only have been conceived by a young authoress of considerable refinement" (Taylor, *Graham Greene on Film*, 222).

Conclusion

    1. See Leland Poague, "The Detective in Frenzy," *Journal of Popular Film* (Winter 1973): 47–59.

2. Richard Roud, "In Broad Daylight," *Film Comment* (July–August 1974): 36.

3. Tom Ryall, "Durgnat on Hitchcock," *Screen* (Summer 1975): 123. Hitchcock told Leslie Perkoff: "I would like to make documentary films, because here you have states of action or movement which can be easily treated by photography and cutting. But a cataclysm in any film, for example, is akin to documentary material. It begins with the camera and goes directly to the cutting room" ("The Censor and Sydney Street," *World Film News* [March 1938]: 4). Hitchcock here yearns for the fantastical opportunities provided by documentary! He exploited them most obviously in the plotline and settings of *Rich and Strange,* and in the opening scenes of *Champagne, Blackmail, The Manxman, The Wrong Man,* etc.

4. Bogdanovich, *Cinema of Alfred Hitchcock,* 28.

5. Durgnat, *Strange Case of Alfred Hitchcock,* 367.

6. William Johnson, "*Marnie,*" *Film Quarterly* 18, no. 1:38–42.

7. David Thomson provides a more general interpretation of the device in *Movie Man* (London, 1971), 72.

8. Samuels, "Hitchcock," 301. Of course, Hitchcock is famous for the painstaking attention he gives his work before going on the set. See the following articles from *American Cinematographer* as evidence: Hilda Black, "The Photography Is Important to Hitchcock: *I Confess*" (December 1952): 524–25, 546–7, 549; Frederick Foster, "Hitchcock Didn't Want It Arty" (February 1957): 84–85, 112–14; Charles Loring, "Filming *Torn Curtain* by Reflected Light" (October 1966): 680–83, 706–7; and Lightman, "Hitchcock Talks about Lights, Camera, Action," 332–35, 350–51.

Hitchcock's famous preplanning and subsequent appearance of casualness about the actual shooting may have contributed to the ready disdain for his technical "sloppiness." It certainly alienated Andre Bazin (see his "Hitchcock vs. Hitchcock," *Cahiers du cinéma* [English], no. 2:51–60).

9. Bazin, "Hitchcock vs. Hitchcock," 55.

10. William Pechter, *Twenty-four Times a Second* (New York, 1971), 175–94; C. A. Lejeune, *Cinema* (London, 1931), 11–12.

Appendix

1. For a selection of Hitchcock's appearances, see *Film Comment* (July–August 1974): 34–35.

2. George Angell questioned Hitchcock about his appearances, on a BBC interview transmitted August 28, 1966. Angell rejected the notion of exhibitionism: "I think this is more your sense of fun, isn't it?" "Oh yes of

course, yes. Sure," replied Hitchcock, ever eager to agree with his interviewers; cf. Bogdanovich, *Cinema of Alfred Hitchcock*, 14; Truffaut, *Hitchcock*, 187.

3. For a full discussion of similar variations in the narrative in drama, see Francis Berry, *The Shakespeare Inset* (London, 1965).

4. See the discussion of *Blackmail* in Kinder and Houston, *Close Up*, 52–57.

5. Truffaut, *Hitchcock*, 150.

6. Samuels makes a rare comment on Hitchcock's appearance, regarding *North by Northwest*: "Like his creator, the hero of this film is a man with less than expected control over his environment" ("Hitchcock," 300).

7. The entire pattern of doors and Marnie's compulsions with regard to doors is mentioned in Roy Huss and Norman Silverstein, *The Film Experience* (New York, 1968), 42.

8. For a fuller discussion of the theological parody, see my "Hitchcock's *I Confess*," *Film Heritage* 8, no. 2:19–24.

INDEX

Index

Index

Index